The Tangled Chain

RUTH A. FOX

The Tangled Chain

The Structure of Disorder in the *Anatomy of Melancholy*

University of California Press

Berkeley, Los Angeles, London

University of California Press
Berkeley and Los Angeles, California
University of California Press, Ltd.
London, England
Copyright © 1976, by
The Regents of the University of California
ISBN 0-520-03085-0
Library of Congress Catalog Card Number: 75-17296
Printed in the United States of America

For my family

His speech was like a tangled chain;
   nothing impaired, but all disordered.
                              —SHAKESPEARE,
                        A Midsummer-Night's Dream

And this is that Homer's golden chain,
   which reacheth down from heaven to earth,
   by which every creature is annexed, and
   depends on his Creator.
                                    —BURTON,
                        The Anatomy of Melancholy

Contents

Preface

To begin with apology in order not to end with it: my reading of the *Anatomy of Melancholy* is a formal one, which is aimed at inducing from the *Anatomy* itself Burton's structural and thematic problems and their solutions. It may thus prove disappointing to those readers who wish to see Burton's book always placed in larger contexts of anatomies and books on melancholy. To such readers I can suggest the writings of William Mueller and more especially the standard works by Lawrence Babb, *The Elizabethan Malady* (1951) and *Sanity in Bedlam* (1959), and the more recent book by Bridget Gellert Lyons, *Voices of Melancholy* (1971). I have not attempted to rework these readings of the *Anatomy*'s connections with contemporary writing, since to do so would not only be supererogatory, but would undoubtedly make impossible my own job of handling Burton's structure within reasonable limits of space and time. I should perhaps suggest here, as in the notes to Chapter I, that Richard Nochimson's unpublished doctoral dissertation does a creditable job of tracing through the mid-1960s most of the important Burton criticism, much of which has been concerned with matters of contemporary contexts for the *Anatomy*.

More pleasant than saying what kind of book this is
not is the job of thanking those who have helped me
make it what it is. I could not have started, much less
written this book, without the example and advice of
Joan Webber. I could not have completed it without the
critical insights of the following, none of whom merits
blame for its shortcomings: Janet Adelman, Stanley
Fish, Donald Friedman, John Gabel, Robert C. Jones,
Mark Morford, Richard Rodriguez, Jonathan Tuck. The
readers for the University of California Press aided me
greatly with their comments and demands. Dean
Wheatcraft helped with typing and encouragement. I
wish also to thank the Committee on Research of the
University of California for aid with typing and photo-
copying funds; the Regents of the University of California for a Summer Faculty Fellowship which enabled
me to revise the book; Simon and Schuster, Inc. for the
right to quote from René Dubos' *The Torch of Life*; and
the Huntington Library, San Marino, California, for
permission to reproduce Burton's title page.

A note on the citation: I have used the Everyman edition of the *Anatomy of Melancholy*, edited by Holbrook
Jackson (New York, 1932), three volumes. This is an
edition of the 1651 *Anatomy* corrected by the fifth (1638)
edition. I have given full reference in my text as follows:
(I.2.1.6;215) means partition and volume I, section 2,
member 1, subsection 6, page 215. References closely
following on a full citation from the same subsection, or
in an extended argument concerning one subsection,
are given as page numbers only. Citations to the Preface
in volume I are noted: (Preface, 97), except in Chapter IV, where after the first reference only the page
number is given.

When quoting from Burton I have tried where possible to exclude interpolated material so that Jackson's translations of Burton's Latin have been regularly and silently expunged; on the other hand, I have sometimes attempted to work paraphrases into my text when Burton himself did not translate and where clarification seemed advisable, and here Jackson's translations served as guide. In a few places I have thought it best to leave the editor's renderings of the Latin *in situ,* and they appear bracketed as in his text; or I have cited them instead of the Latin, in which case the fact is noted in the parenthetical documentation. In sum, ellipses in quoted passages indicate only matter excised from Burton's text.

Abbreviated List of
Secondary Sources

BABB Lawrence Babb. *Sanity in Bedlam: A Study of Robert Burton's "Anatomy of Melancholy."* East Lansing : Michigan State University Press, 1959.

COLIE Rosalie Colie. *Paradoxia Epidemica: The Renaissance Tradition of Paradox.* Princeton University Press, 1966.

FINLAY Daniel Henry Finlay. "A Study of Form in the *Anatomy of Melancholy.*" Ph.D. diss., University of Virginia, 1966.

FISH Stanley E. Fish. *Self-Consuming Artifacts: The Experience of Seventeenth-Century Literature.* Berkeley, Los Angeles, London: University of California Press, 1972.

HALLWACHS Robert G. Hallwachs. "Additions and Revisions in the Second Edition of Burton's *Anatomy of Melancholy.*" Ph.D. diss., Princeton, 1934.

KING James Roy King. *Studies in Six 17th Century Writers.* Athens: University of Ohio Press, 1966.

LYONS Bridget Gellert Lyons. *Voices of Melancholy: Studies in Literary Treatments of Melancholy in Renaissance England.* London: Routledge and Kegan Paul, 1971.

MUELLER William Mueller. *The Anatomy of Robert Burton's England.* Berkeley and Los Angeles: University of California Press, 1952.

NOCHIMSON Richard L. Nochimson. "Robert Burton: A Study of the Man, His Work, and His Critics." Ph.D. diss., Columbia, 1967.

OSLER Sir William Osler, Edward Bensly, and others. "Robert Burton and the *Anatomy of Melancholy.*" Ed. F. Madan. *Oxford Bibliographical Society Proceedings and Papers,* 1 (1927).

SIMON Jean Robert Simon. *Robert Burton (1577-1640) et L'Anatomie de la Mélancolie.* Paris: Didier, 1964.

WEBBER Joan Webber. *The Eloquent 'I': Style and Self in Seventeenth-Century Prose.* Madison: University of Wisconsin Press, 1968.

I. The Cutter's Art

Ten distinct squares here seen apart,
Are joined in one by cutter's art.
                              —BURTON,
          "The Argument of the Frontispiece"

The *Anatomy of Melancholy*, a book more often read in part than as a whole, criticized as art yet only with some discomfort approached as an artifact, less easily comprehended than it is dissected, this medical treatise written by an Anglican divine holds a peculiar place in the canon of seventeenth-century English prose literature. Robert Burton forged the *Anatomy* out of his Renaissance scholar's familiarity with the literature of Western civilization, working centuries of authors into a compendium of science, philosophy, poetry, history, and divinity which contains examples of numerous literary genres yet remains *sui generis*, the singular expression of its author's humane knowledge. Unlike other Renaissance "anatomies" generally accounted to be primarily artistic creations—*Euphues*, for example—the *Anatomy of Melancholy* contains a scientific discourse treating a medical subject by means of traditional methodology in a traditional schema. And unlike other Renaissance studies of melancholy—Timothy Bright's, for example—the *Anatomy* has always been accepted

1

less for what it says about a particular disease than for what it is, a pleasing and useful encyclopedia of human ideas. It is a book which, when its debts to other authors and its connections with various genres have been acknowledged, still demands to be confronted on its own terms as a unique artistic creation, and the reading of the *Anatomy* presented in the following study will attempt to meet that demand.

To read the *Anatomy* on its own terms is to deal with structure—to assess, that is, the relationship between the matter of the book and the shape which informs that matter with meaning. Among the premises with which this study necessarily starts is the idea that the art of a literary work like the *Anatomy* may be described as a conjunction of its themes and its structure and that such a description will reveal the artist's design in the work and allow for our estimation of his artistry. Formal analysis is not, of course, the only method criticism may employ, and it may not even be universally the best method. But the Renaissance had a great respect for the capability of the artificial construct and the artificial mode of expression to say what the merely natural cannot—a respect evidenced, in Burton's own century, in the conceits, even the shapes of metaphysical poetry as in the design of *Paradise Lost*—and Burton's book is a paradigm among artistic works that declare their meaning through structure which is patently artificial, self-consciously planned. Renaissance art more often than not exhibits the artist's control through formal structure. Even a Lazarillo or a Jack Wilton does not drift aimlessly down a stream of consciousness toward accidental self-revelation. And more normally, Renaissance literature is presented in fourteen lines of iambic pentameter, or in five acts of prose and blank verse rounded off with rhymed couplets, or in twelve books of verse paragraphs, or in *carpe diem* love poems constructed around syllogistic logic. Simply, the artifact tends to say what it says while calling attention to the rational force behind its making, even when irrationality—or melancholy—is the subject matter.

Structure—the fact that the book is made up of parts that make up larger parts that make up still larger parts that make up the whole—is the first, and though he sometimes does not realize it, the most important thing a reader sees of Burton's book. When he opens the *Anatomy* and finds an apparatus of synoptic tables, carefully plotted title page, explanatory and exhortative poems to book and reader, and alphabetized index, when he turns the pages and discovers the author laying his matter out in sections and subsections, the reader is being shown the nature of this literary work as a consciously assembled artifact. And yet, he soon perceives, explicit denotation of artifice is not an affirmation of perfect artistic control. At one end of the book, rational scientific comprehensiveness declares itself:

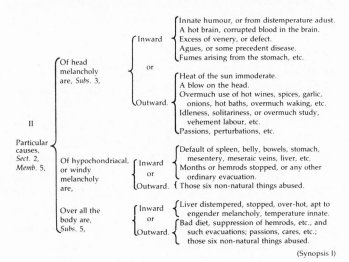

(Synopsis I)

At the other end of the book is seen comprehensiveness of a different sort, the coincidental alphabetical listing in the "Table" which affirms that the *Anatomy* includes everything in the world, whether or not scientific rationality defines the "everything":

Heavens penetrable, . . . Infinitely swift
Hearing what
Heat immoderate cause of mel.
Health a pretious thing
Hell where
Help from friends against melanch.
Hellebor white and black purgers of mel.

(*Anatomy*, London, 1651)

The synopses and the Table, as we shall see in a more extensive discussion shortly, are two ways Burton has of showing us what his book is about and how it goes about doing what it does. Rational system and illogical circumstance coexist as truth in the *Anatomy*, and their combinations in differing amounts at different moments express the fact that form and resistance to form are both essential to the book's meaning. Burton's subject matter is implicitly and explicitly opposed to definition: it is chaos, the post-lapsarian state of man. He cannot finally rule that subject matter by logic, but he can and he does rule it by art, by imposing on it a structure which binds chaos into form. The structure is "artificial" in two senses: it orders and shapes the book's contents by art, and it serves as artifice to disguise the contents' resistance to order, leaving the book's form a complicated pattern of logical organization modified by the tendency of the subject matter to defy logical control. The *Anatomy* is thus a creation which declares to its readers at every turn the clarifying art and the concealing artifice of its form.

A word about form: we are accustomed to looking, as Daniel Henry Finlay's work points out, for qualities of clarity, coherence, and unity in works of art, but the Renaissance, he argues, did not have our particular critical biases and worked with traditions of composition which allowed for a loose, encyclopedic rather than an "organic" approach to the treatment of subjects.[1] Yet the *Anatomy*, with its complex series of partitions and sections, insists upon its structure to the point of having an exoskeleton—its synoptic tables—so that either to recognize as we must that Burton's art is not directed toward fulfilling modern ideals of artistic unity, or to recognize the undisputedly encyclopedic qualities of his book, does not allow us to ignore the book's highly artificial structure, but compels us to question seriously whether Burton did not use that structure as the primary means of artistic statement in the *Anatomy*. Finlay's answer is negative; he decides that the methods of organization, the definition and division evidenced in the partitions, sections, members, and subsections of the book, provide a framework for the material of the *Anatomy* without functioning as the means whereby Burton discovers his meaning to himself and his readers (see Finlay, Ch. ii). Though I do not disagree with some of his argument, my own answer, as will appear, is positive.

Besides formal structure, I believe, another of the terms on which one must meet the *Anatomy* is its whole-

1. "A Study of Form in the *Anatomy of Melancholy*" (Ph.D. diss., University of Virginia, 1966), pp. 11-12 and passim. David Renaker argues more briefly than Finlay that Burton's methodology exhibited in the synopses is useful *in that* it is subsequently overpowered by total illogicality in the book: "Robert Burton and Ramist Method," *Renaissance Quarterly*, 24, No. 2 (1971), 210-220.

ness. (For the moment I leave aside the notion of
"unity," and especially of "organic unity": the rest of
this study will show the peculiar kinds of unity I see the
book claiming for itself.) The *Anatomy* must be seen as
whole, as a work which embraces diverse matter and
diverse times in a single form. Indeed, the salient
feature of the book's structure is its ability to comprehend an extreme diversity of statement. From the pharmacopoeia of a medical treatise to a consolation of philosophy, from satirical denunciations of human folly to
sermons on charity and despair, from analyses of man's
physiology to descriptions of the cosmos or of the
workings of good and evil spirits, the *Anatomy* is by its
very nature a comprehensive work on a grand scale.
Furthermore, the book is not just an instance, but the
entire expression of Robert Burton's literary art, incor-
porating into a single structure all that he cared to
publish of himself (except for some minor academic
poems) through the course of a lifetime.[2] Published first
in 1621, then reissued, "corrected and augmented by
the author," in 1624, 1628, 1632, and 1638, and finally
given its last authoritative form in the posthumous sixth
edition of 1651, the *Anatomy* at first expanded significantly but later underwent more minor changes and
corrections.[3] Yet the form of the *Anatomy* never chang-

2. Burton did not publish his academic play, *Philosophaster*. It and
the poems were collected by Paul Jordan-Smith in *Philosophaster with
an English Translation of the Same* (Stanford University Press, 1931).

3. For accounts of the changes in the *Anatomy* see Lawrence Babb,
Sanity in Bedlam: A Study of Robert Burton's "Anatomy of Melancholy"
(East Lansing: Michigan State University Press, 1959), ch. ii, "Genesis
and Development"; and Robert G. Hallwachs, "Additions and Re-
visions in the Second Edition of Burton's *Anatomy of Melancholy*"
(Ph.D. diss., Princeton, 1934).

ed, and in a large sense the book of 1651 is the same as the book of 1621, for it grew within the structure of anatomy which Burton describes in the title and in the synoptic or analytic tables of the first edition.

Only one unit of the structure was ever deleted, the "Conclusion of the Author to the Reader" which appeared at the end of the first edition, in which Burton "unmasked" his pseudonymous character Democritus Junior and disclosed his own name to his readers. The dropping of this Conclusion in 1624, however, did not much affect the material of the book, for Burton used most of its comments elsewhere (mainly in the Preface—see below, Chapter IV).

Some major accretions occurred within the *Anatomy*, notably that of the sermon against despair in the partition of Love-melancholy (see below, Chapter III); and other treatments of the non-technical portions of the book were gradually expanded, particularly the Preface, the sections of Love-melancholy, and the digressive material within the First and Second Partitions.[4] The only actual addition to the matter outlined in the synopses was the inclusion in the third edition of a subsection on the "Symptoms of Maids', Nuns', and Widows' Melancholy," and the significance of such an addition, as we shall see in the discussion of the synoptic tables, lies in the fact that it could occur without changing the basic structure of the whole work. Other minor additions, also to be discussed, were those various pieces of front and back matter which accrued to the book over the years: the "Table" or index (1624); the

4. Hallwachs' study, with respect to the second edition, documents these general obserations on the revisions.

"Argument of the Frontispiece" with the engraved title page and the poems "Democritus Junior ad Librum Suum" and "The Author's Abstract of Melancholy" (1628); and the lines "Heraclite, fleas" added (1632) after the note "Lectori Male Feriato" which had, from the first, followed the Preface. Yet despite these changes, the "skeleton" of the book, the shape of the whole, remains the same; the *Anatomy*'s definition of itself is constant throughout the editions.

The *Anatomy* brings together different kinds of writing, then, into its single structure, and it brings together several decades of its author's literary work. Further, it must be seen as one encompassing entity because, as Robert Burton's "cento out of divers writers" (Preface, 25), it unites in the space of a single book his expansive reading in classical authors, Church Fathers, medical authorities, Scripture, ancient and modern poets, and all the other kinds of fictional, scientific, historical, philosophical, and theological writers who filled the library and the mind of a solitary Oxford scholar. In all of these ways the book declares itself to be a single artifact made out of the diversity of human knowledge itself, a compilation of a man's understanding of mankind under the general topic, melancholy. The wholeness of the book is the wholeness of anatomy, of numerous distinct parts brought together and seen as a single object.

To a great degree this study of the book will have achieved its purpose if it can show the student of the *Anatomy* that Burton was not talking only about the art of the engraver who made the title page when he wrote the lines which stand at the beginning of this chapter. For an anatomist is a "cutter" too, and the art of the

Anatomy of Melancholy is that of an artist who joins in one by cutting apart. The cutter's art which anatomizes melancholy's causes, symptoms, prognostics, and cures into partitions, sections, members, and subsections, comprehends through all of the division and definition a single explication of mankind. The form of the *Anatomy*, like the form of the title page, is complicated but ordered. The structure itself is the statement of Burton's chief concern in the book, the reassertion of order in the world through the assertion of order in art. And the "tangled chain" which is disordered but not finally impaired is both the world of creation whose confused state the artist anatomizes and the book which represents in its structure the reclamation of order in the midst of disorder. For "structure" in the *Anatomy* takes two coexisting forms, the scholastic one of three partitions and another of Preface, Partitions I and II, and Partition III, and the tension between these structures gives the book both an artificial (or "gothic") unity and an "organic" unity inherent in the person of Democritus Junior, who as scholar-artist makes a study of disease into an artifact and gives the disorder of human life the form and order of art.

To see the wholeness of Burton's book, to see its diversity through the unity imposed upon multiplicity by the structure of anatomy, is essential to our understanding of the cutter's art. And it is the more necessary since the prevalent views of the book are those which have not recognized or have not dealt with the *Anatomy* as an ordered whole. Some criticism has now begun to try to account for the relationships of the parts of the book to the whole, but the predominant critical attitude with regard to the form of the book has been one which tends to attribute to the whole the meaning of one or more of its parts.[5] A brief glance at some of the older representative notions regarding the *Anatomy* might serve as useful background to my discussion of the book's substance and structure, since I shall be arguing that to read the *Anatomy* without constant awareness of context is not to read the book which Burton created by joining the distinct components of his treatise into one construct. Leaving aside the appreciators and depreciators who through the nineteenth century tended to enjoy or disparage Burton as an encyclopedist with a quaint style but not much sense of form (the *Anatomy* seen as "a sweeping of the miscellaneous literature from the Bodleian Library"[6]), we find that more judicious criticism may yet overlook the comprehensive forest of the book for one or more of the trees that stand in it.

Sir William Osler, who was responsible in our century for reconstituting the *Anatomy* with a serious purpose, saw the book with the eyes of a physician and admired it as a medical treatise,[7] but in doing so he had to ignore the great bulk of the book which is not concerned with the disease of melancholy. The critic William Mueller, on the other hand, made the book into a sociologist's study of England's political, social, and religious ills by drawing most of his evidence from the Preface.[8] Other

5. The reader may wish to consult Richard L. Nochimson's fuller review of the major Burton criticism up to 1967, "Robert Burton: A Study of the Man, His Work, and His Critics" (Ph.D. diss., Columbia, 1967).

6. Quoted by Holbrook Jackson in his introduction to the Everyman *Anatomy*, (New York: Dutton, 1964), I, xiv.

7. Sir William Osler, Edward Bensly, and others, "Robert Burton and the *Anatomy of Melancholy*," in *Oxford Bibliographical Society Proceedings and Papers*, ed. F. Madan, 1 (1927), 175-176.

8. See especially William Mueller, *The Anatomy of Robert Burton's England* (Berkeley and Los Angeles: University of California Press, 1952).

critics recognize the *Anatomy*'s multiple topics and diverse generic models, but their acknowledgment of the great amounts of material which stray from Burton's apparent subject of the humoral disease of melancholy leads them into difficulties in accounting for his structure. Lawrence Babb calls the *Anatomy* a "compound book, not one work but several," having "lesser discourses imbedded in the text of the greater," and he sees a duality between the sections on humoral psychology and the commentary on the figurative madness of the world which indicates a "purpose superimposed upon a purpose" in the book. Thus he is led to question the basic design of the *Anatomy*, its very definition of partitions and sections, causes and cures, which makes it an anatomy of melancholy; and while he acknowledges that it would have been against Burton's nature to have done so, he nevertheless suggests that perhaps the author "should have redesigned his work so as to subordinate the psychiatric material to the critical comment" (Babb, pp. 8, 28). James Roy King goes further; he decides that Burton "experienced some confusion about his purpose" and that his skill "lay obviously in the smaller forms, which could be embedded in larger, unshaped masses of material," and he admires the "degree of finish and coherence" exhibited in the sermons and essays of the book.[9]

But the *Anatomy* is not just the medical treatise of melancholy, nor is it just the Preface with its Utopia or the partition of Love-melancholy, nor is it primarily "critical comment" in detachable sermons and essays or digressive expatiation on topics ancillary to melancholic

9. "The Genesis of Burton's *Anatomy of Melancholy*," in *Studies in Six 17th Century Writers* (Athens: University of Ohio Press, 1966), pp. 66, 75.

disorders. It is all of these things joined in one *Anatomy of Melancholy*, and repeatedly, through six editions, so joined and so titled. Despite the "compound character" of the book, it might not "suitably be entitled *Opera Burtoni*" (Babb, p. 9), though it might well be subtitled *Opus Burtoni*.

I have warned the reader who examines the book with me that he will be asked to see simultaneous dissection and unification, cutting and joining, as the essential artistic act of the *Anatomy*'s author. In some sense, this means that my own analysis can become a kind of rhetorical imitation of Burton's method, as it takes apart and puts together the *Anatomy*, giving an apparently new order to the book in the hope of elucidating Burton's own cutter's art. Several recent, often brilliant, studies of the book have seen Burton's purposes, recognized his tone, dealt with his method or style or character, and usually have managed to confine their observations to the space of a single chapter.[10] My reading will not content itself with that scope (a fact which might threaten to tire out if not madden those who try to follow me over Burton's terrain), but I am forced by my conception of Burton's art to see, and to say, that the meaning of the book lies in all its parts fully

10. I am thinking especially of the chapters on Burton in the following books: Rosalie Colie, *Paradoxia Epidemica: The Renaissance Tradition of Paradox* (Princeton University Press, 1966); Joan Webber, *The Eloquent 'I': Style and Self in Seventeenth-Century Prose* (Madison: University of Wisconsin Press, 1968); Bridget Gellert Lyons, *Voices of Melancholy: Studies in Literary Treatments of Melancholy in Renaissance England* (London: Routledge and Kegan Paul, 1971); and Stanley E. Fish, *Self-Consuming Artifacts: The Experience of Seventeenth-Century Literature* (Berkeley, Los Angeles, London: University of California Press, 1972).

considered. Stanley Fish, with whose analysis I often agree and disagree (as will be especially evident in Chapter IV on the Preface), might unwillingly justify my more exhaustive if less compelling treatment of the *Anatomy*; toward the close of his discussion of the book he says of Burton's intent: "By busily reading of melancholy, we may avoid it too. If Burton cannot give us a better mind, he can perhaps give us a mind not much involved with its own pain. The *Anatomy of Melancholy*, in all of its distracting confusion, is finally something of a mercy, and it is the only mercy to be found within its confines" (Fish, p. 349). I have to contend that if this statement began rather than ended Fish's chapter, his reading would start to suggest what I hope to be able to prove, that the *Anatomy* is not, *after all*, a "self-consuming artifact" in which Burton "unbuilds the superstructure of his great work until finally it stands for a failure to effect a declared intention" (Fish, p. 350), but a tangled chain instead, an artifact whose disordered order and ultimate meaning is indeed "mercy," the mercy that comes to melancholy man through the civilizing force of art itself.

Art gives life form, and the form which Burton uses to contain universal confusion is that of his single, always expandable but always unaltered *Anatomy of Melancholy*.

The stated topic of the book is not, of course, the chaotic world of mankind, but a disease of men. Yet the topic of melancholy "philosophically, medicinally, and historically" treated is by tradition one which encompasses man himself. The *Anatomy of Melancholy* is an encyclopedia of human ideas because to treat melancholy is to deal with the whole nature of man. For melancholy is that peculiar disease which affects man's material and spiritual essences together, a "common infirmity of body and soul, and such a one that hath as much need of a spiritual as a corporal cure" (Preface, 37). Timothy Bright's *Treatise of Melancholy* (1586), Thomas Wright's *Passions of the Minde* (1601), and Thomas Adams' *Diseases of the Soule: A Discourse Divine, Moral, and Physicall* (1616) all testified in Burton's time to melancholy's affliction of man's body and mind and, with varying emphases on physical and mental aspects, offered explanation of the complicated disease and advice in overcoming it.[11] The whole man is thus the matter of any treatise pretending to cure melancholy, a fact which Burton acknowledges not only by declaring himself to be both a physician and a divine in writing his book (Preface, 37), but also by making his ancestor in the effort the philosopher Democritus. For the ancient Democritus sat in his garden cutting up carcasses to discover the material seat of melancholy, but with the ultimate hope, he told Hippocrates, of finding a cure for man's mental and spiritual aberrations, his folly and lack of understanding: "I do anatomize and cut up these poor beasts, to see these distempers, vanities, and follies, yet such proof were better made on man's body, if my kind nature would endure it" (Preface, 51). So Burton's *Anatomy of Melancholy* necessarily concerns

11. For an account of these documents, see Mueller, pp. 13-19, and Lyons' introductory chapter, "The Expository Books and Their Background." Lyons places Burton's *Anatomy* in the context of melancholy "sourcebooks," but goes further than Mueller can in estimating the *Anatomy*'s place among literary expressions of Renaissance preoccupation with the "universal disease" (ch. v: "The *Anatomy of Melancholy* as Literature").

itself with body, mind, and soul as these portions of his being are afflicted with their common disease. He treats the whole man by treating man the rational animal in Partitions I and II and man the passionate animal in Partition III. And in the Preface, which conduces to both these views of human nature, he discloses the infirmities and the possibilities for cure of man the civilized creature.

Man is seen, then, "under the aspect of melancholy" (Webber, p. 113), which means that he is seen in this world, a world of confusion. The introduction to the *Anatomy*, which is not the Preface (see below, Chapter IV) but the first member of Partition I, section 1, leads into Burton's anatomy of melancholy by showing what man is—a diseased creature in a disordered world—in the light of what he was—God's perfect creature in an ordered universe. The member begins with the most breathtaking sentence in all the *Anatomy*, which expresses by its order the work of creation, molding words and phrases into a progression that reaches out toward an exuberant definition of all the beauty of God's own created image. Man, says Burton, was at first perfect.

Man, the most excellent and noble creature of the world, "the principal and mighty work of God, wonder of Nature," as Zoroaster calls him; *audacis naturae miraculum*, "the marvel of marvels," as Plato; "the abridgment and epitome of the world," as Pliny; *Microcosmus*, a little world, a model of the world, sovereign lord of the earth, viceroy of the world, sole commander and governor of all the creatures in it; to whose empire they are subject in particular, and yield obedience; far surpassing all the rest, not in body only, but in soul; *Imaginis imago*, created to God's own image, to that immortal and incorporeal substance, with all the faculties and powers belonging unto it; was at first pure, divine, perfect, happy, "created after God in true holiness and righteousness": *Deo congruens*, free from all manner of infirmities, and put in Paradise, to know God, to praise and glorify Him, to do His will, *Ut dis consimiles parturiat deos* (as an old poet saith) to propagate the Church.   (I.1.1.1;130)

But from the order of God's creation, "this most noble creature" has derived confusion: man "is fallen from that he was, and forfeited his estate, become *miserabilis humuncio*, a castaway, a caitiff, one of the most miserable creatures of the world, if he be considered in his own nature, an unregenerate man, and so much obscured by his fall that (some few relics excepted) he is inferior to a beast." By the second sentence of the treatise of melancholy, the chain is tangled, order is overturned; and the remainder of the member leads into the treatise by defining all disease as the disorder of body and mind visited upon man through the "sin of our first parent Adam" (p. 131). The wars of the world are in and through man; all nature attacks him, and he is his own greatest enemy. From man comes chaos, the misrule of sin and the tyranny of disease. We are introduced to melancholy by being led through definitions of disease: Burton divides all diseases into those of body and those of mind, then treats those of "the head and mind," and singles out "such as properly belong to the phantasy, or imagination, or reason itself" (I.1.1.3;139), whereby he arrives at the "equivocations of melancholy" and, finally, at "this melancholy of which we are to treat" (I.1.1.5;146). But all of the preparation for explication of the disease is made in the light of its causes, which arise not from his original nature, but from the revised human nature man has given himself.

Our intemperance it is that pulls so many several incurable diseases upon our heads, that hastens old age, perverts our temperature, and brings upon us sudden death. And last of all, that which crucifies us most, is our own folly, madness, . . . weakness, want of government, our facility and proneness in yielding to several lusts, in giving way to every passion and perturbation of the mind: by which means we metamorphose ourselves and degenerate into beasts. (I.1.1.2;136)

Regardless of whether he is treating the "definite" humoral disease of melancholy or the "indefinite" disease of Love-melancholy, throughout the book Burton's chief concern is never simply *a* disease, but is always this "most general of all diseases" which is mortal man's "mark of living" in a world after the Fall (Colie, p. 434). To be human is to be melancholy in some sense or other, for adversity is the human condition, and melancholy epitomizes this essential fact of life: "All fears, griefs, suspicions, discontents, imbonities, insuavities, are swallowed up and drowned in this Euripus, this Irish Sea, this ocean of misery, as so many small brooks. . . . I say of our melancholy man, he is the cream of human adversity, the quintessence, and upshot; all other diseases whatsoever are but flea-bitings to melancholy in extent: 'tis the pith of them all" (I.4.1;434).

From the beginning of the book, then, the disease of melancholy is set in the context of the disorder—morally, physically, theologically considered—of the universe. What was once good, like man, is now, through man's corruption rather than by its own nature, "pernicious unto us": "the earth accursed, the influence of stars altered, the four elements, beasts, birds, plants,

are now ready to offend us" (I.1.1.1;133). In "opening
and cutting up" melancholy, Burton is opening and
cutting up the body of the disordered world of man,
seeking to explore man's knowledge of himself—body,
mind, and soul—by exploring his quintessential disorder. Knowledge of melancholy turns out to demand
knowledge of all areas of human endeavor, and
Burton's references in the book have been calculated to
include citations from some twelve hundred fifty authors (excluding Scripture and anonymous works)
representing the fields of medicine, science, philosophy, occult studies, history, geography, belles-lettres,
and theology.[12]

Thus, since the matter is universal, and the universe
is chaotic, the book which would explore the matter of
melancholy should tend to be chaotic as well. And so it
is: chaos tries to rule the book. The reader is constantly
made aware of Burton's struggles with his subject
matter as he attempts to do the seemingly impossible
job of ordering, defining, untangling confusion: "If you
will describe melancholy, describe a phantastical conceit, a corrupt imagination, vain thoughts and different,
which who can do?" (I.3.1.4;408). And Burton is not
only trying to order the material of chaos, but to order
the knowledge of that material which appears in his
authorities: he has, that is, not only to follow, but to
contend with all the "best writers" who give him
different directions concerning how to define his topics.

When the matter is diverse and confused, how should it
otherwise be but that the species should be diverse and

12. Jean Robert Simon, *Robert Burton (1577-1640) et L'Anatomie de la
Mélancolie* (Paris: Didier, 1964), p. 429.

confused? Many new and old writers have spoken confusedly of it, confounding melancholy and madness, as Heurnius, Guianerius, Gordonius, Sallustius Salvianus, Jason Pratensis, Savonarola. . . . Some make two distinct species, as Ruffus Ephesius, an old writer, Constantinus Africanus, Aretaeus, Aurelianus, Paulus Aegineta: others acknowledge a multitude of kinds, and leave them indefinite.   (I.1.3.4;174-175)

But even as he puts before us his difficulties in arranging his subjects, Burton always affirms his own determination not to "leave them indefinite." Complaint leads almost inevitably to a *"yet nevertheless."*

In such obscurity, therefore, variety and confused mixture of symptoms, causes, how difficult a thing it is to treat of several kinds apart; to make any certainty or distinction among so many casualties, distractions, when seldom two men shall be like affected *per omnia*! 'Tis hard, I confess, yet nevertheless I will adventure through the midst of these perplexities, and led by the clue or thread of the best writers, extricate myself out of a labyrinth of doubts and errors, and so proceed to the causes.   (I.1.3.4;177)

Burton's constant effort in the *Anatomy* is to distinguish and define the components of the confused state of things, especially when they seem least liable to definition.

As we read the book, then, and turn from one partition to another, from one subsection to the next, from cause to symptom to cure, from "definite" to "indefinite" melancholy, we are following Burton in following traditional methodology, which is to organize first by defining his subject matter, then by dividing topics into subtopics, redefining and redividing as occasion demands (see Finlay, pp. 55-60). Burton's methodology is the same methodology of his book's most hoary ancestor, Galen's *De melancholia, sive atrae bilia morbo,* the organization of definition, symptoms, kinds, causes, cures.[13] But we are following Burton also as he deals with the tradition, for he is constantly allowing us to watch his difficulties and constantly calling attention—" 'Tis hard, I confess, yet nevertheless"—to his own determination that chaos will *not* rule the book. Method, as we shall discover in studying the Preface, is not merely a means in the *Anatomy*, but is in a very real sense the end toward which Burton makes the book tend; for when he weaves the new cloth of the *Anatomy* out of the "divers fleeces" of all his books and authors, he attests to his own function as the one who gives form to diverse matter: "the composition and method is ours only, and shows a scholar" (Preface, 25). The single issue of the *Anatomy* is melancholy, which is the disordered condition of man, while the book insistently aims to order confusion. From the title through each partition, section, member, and subsection, the *Anatomy* makes its structure felt, so that we are always aware of Burton's hand setting out units and separating ideas—arraying, not just writing, his book. And outside of the book he shows us in its accompanying apparatus both the formal attempt to order this matter of melancholy and the matter's continuous resistance to definition.

I have suggested, and in the following arguments will hope to maintain, the importance of the *Anatomy*'s structural edifice to the reader's comprehension of its total meaning. About ten years before Burton first published his book, John Donne's *Pseudo-Martyr* appeared,

13. Timothy Bright, *A Treatise of Melancholie*, ed. Hardin Craig (New York: The Facsimile Text Society, 1940), p. ix.

prefaced by an "Advertisement to the Reader" in which
Donne told his audience why he had not written the last
two chapters noted in the table of contents, begged
them not to prejudge him for underestimating the value
of true martyrdom until they had finished the book, and
suggested various practical steps they should follow in
reading it. Donne's "Advertisement" is worth noting
here because of this explicit recognition by an author of
his reader's need to have read the whole book before he
can actually be a *reader* of any part of it.

> Though I purposed not to speake any thing to the Reader,
> otherwise than by way of Epilogue in the end of the Booke,
> both because I esteemed that to be the fittest place, to give my
> Reasons, why I respited the handling of the two last Chap-
> ters, till another time, and also, because *I thought not that any*
> *man might well and properly be called a Reader, till he were come to*
> *the end of the Booke*: yet, because both he, and I, may suffer
> some disadvantages, if he should not be fore-possessed, and
> warned in some things, I have changed my purpose in that
> point.[14]

The *Anatomy* is an even more involved and complex
work than the *Pseudo-Martyr*, and Burton felt his contemporary's need to "fore-possess" his reader not just
of "some things" but of the whole book—to make him,
in effect, a Reader in Donne's terms, before he starts to
read. The parts of the apparatus precede the book and
disclose it beforehand, just as the Preface precedes it
and discloses it in a wholly different way. For the
Anatomy demands not only the browser who will wander pleasantly in its confines, but the reader who will
attend to Burton's own careful construct and who will

14. John Donne, *Selected Prose*, ed. Helen Gardner and Timothy
Healy (Oxford: The Clarendon Press, 1967), p. 45 (my italics).

read the parts with knowledge of the whole, in order that he "might well and properly be called a Reader."

The synopses of the partitions[15] present the overall pattern of the discourse, describing the *Anatomy*'s logical order. These graphic representations of the book's structure have been seen as evidence of Burton's comic sense, for they testify to a tautness of logical control which the book, with its subject matter of confusion, folly, disease, and disorder, seems to belie. They have appeared, that is, to be detached and ironic comments on the "architecture globale" of a work whose traditional order they define: they reveal, according to this view, "une ingéniosité analytique à la fois prodigieuse et dérisoire, comme un étalage d'inutile virtuosité" (Simon, p. 422). The synopses are undoubtedly imitations of the forms of scholastic treatises, and no seventeenth-century Anglican was more amused by the medieval schoolmen's ceaseless disputation and endless rationalizing on insane questions than was Burton. Nevertheless, the synopses do reflect the methodology of the book, their "ingéniosité analytique" belongs to it too, and, as an admirer of the *Anatomy* once said, if the tables are humorous imitations of the schoolmen's treatises, then "the joke is on Burton, for he followed the outline."[16] What is in the synoptic tables is in the book, and what is in the book is abstracted in the synoptic tables. Although they do not contain all the "wealth of material" that the book holds, it is not quite

15. The first two are called "synopses," whereas that of the Third Partition is regularly titled "Analysis," though it does not appear that any substantive distinction is being made.

16. Henry William Taeusch, *Democritus Junior Anatomizes Melancholy* (Cleveland: The Rowfant Club, 1937), p. 14. See also David Renaker's article mentioned above.

accurate to say that they are "a superficial guide" to the matter of the *Anatomy* (Finlay, p. 52), for they define the "wealth of material" from the general causes to the digressions to the corollaries and questions, even though they cannot, being synopses, fully express it. The analysis of the tables is that of the whole book, and so in presenting such a diagrammatic image of his book's structure to his readers, Burton was being more than humorous. He was suggesting by this explicit statement of form that to understand the book as we read it, we must recognize first the workings of its structure and comprehend the whole before we begin to investigate the parts.

The art historian Erwin Panofsky has described scholasticism's basic tenet of *manifestatio* or elucidation, by which the schematic "system of logical subordination" which organized arguments into *partes, membra, quaestiones,* and *articuli* became, in effect, a goal in itself: the adherence to a dialectical scheme, he says, means that the scholastics "felt compelled to make the orderliness and logic of their thought palpably explicit—that the principle of *manifestatio* which determined the direction and scope of their thinking also controlled its exposition and subjected this exposition to what may be termed the POSTULATE OF CLARIFICATION FOR CLARIFICATION'S SAKE."[17] Burton's synoptic tables are a very

17. Erwin Panofsky, *Gothic Architecture and Scholasticism* (Cleveland: The World Publishing Co., 1957), pp. 34-35. In describing Burton's "scholastic" structure and by using Panofsky's comparison between medieval scholastic works and Gothic architecture, I am attempting to illustrate the *Anatomy*'s structural complexity, but I am not ignoring later influences on Burton. Ramistic structure is surely in Burton's mind when he devises the synoptic tables, as David Renaker has effectively argued. The reader interested in Ramistic method and Burton's use or misuse of that method should consult Renaker.

explicit *manifestatio* of the *Anatomy*'s "obsession with systematic division and subdivision" (Panofsky, p. 36), and as such they require our attention. For the tables would seem to claim for the book, by their very solid appearance of logical control, the marks of a *summa*: "(1) totality (sufficient enumeration), (2) arrangement according to a system of homologous parts and parts of parts (sufficient articulation), and (3) distinctness and deductive cogency (sufficient interrelation)" (Panofsky, p. 31). The synopses are thus a direct answer to the appearance of Renaissance "looseness" of method which Finlay finds predominant in the *Anatomy*, and they negate his contention that Burton does not claim he has written a *summa*, a complete collection of man's knowledge of melancholy (Finlay, p. 53). The synoptic tables make the claim of totality for Burton; their very medieval, very scholastic insistence on the form of the argument suggests that he wished us to look at his structure not only as the correct one for a treatise of melancholy, but as a way of controlling and presenting a total vision of truth about the human condition: the synopses explicate the title's "*all* the kinds, causes, symptoms, prognostics, and cures." I shall return to this question of the synopses' claims for the book, for Burton is not a Thomas Aquinas, and I am not arguing that the tables actually represent the perfection of logical definition and exposition in the book. The *Anatomy*, as we have seen, is about disorder, and it, like the world, is a tangled chain.

But before turning to the matter of how Burton modifies his *manifestatio* of logical order, I want to borrow Panofsky's ideas of the analogies between scholastic treatise and Gothic cathedral in order to explain further the function of the synopses. These not only define the *Anatomy* by telling, like a table of contents, what it contains; they also contain the book, for each synopsis gives the overview of the partition simultaneously with its dissected parts. They represent the sort of "visual articulation of the [printed] page" which Panofsky (pp. 38-39) sees translated from the scholastic treatise into all the arts of the time as a clarification "of narrative contexts in the representational arts, and of functional contexts in architecture." In doing so they are to the *Anatomy* what the facade of a cathedral is to the Gothic structure beyond. Like the facade which reflects in its tripartite, three- or four-storied form the logic of the tripartite nave and the elevation of the interior walls, the synoptic tables express graphically the relationships within the partitions and disclose the logic which controls the presentation of material. To look at the synopses is thus to see the *Anatomy* more clearly, though in less detail, than when one is within it, as one can stand back from the cathedral and see the idea of the whole in the elucidation and articulation of the facade.

Indeed, some closer examination of the synopses than critics have been wont to engage in would reveal a tighter control of logic, a less haphazard adherence to equivalences and subordination than Burton has ordinarily been granted. That there are three kinds of Love-melancholy is immediately apparent from the synopsis of Partition III, as are the logical relationships of these types (see below, Chapter III). That the digressions are not scattered throughout the book, but are formal units within Partitions I and II only, is as clear from those synoptic tables (see below, Chapter II). The book's organization is complex, and one can lose sight of its

logical subordination, as, in a small way, did the critic who cites "two quite different integral consolations of philosophy," one "classical *consolatio*" and another "Christian consolation, in the form of a sermon, [Burton's] 'Consolatory Digression'" (Colie, pp. 437-438). The argument differentiating the two kinds of consolation is valid, but might have gained force and a different perspective if the consolation "Against Sorrow for Death of Friends or otherwise" had been recognized as one of eight consolations, including the "General" or Christian one, which together make up the single Consolatory Digression. The second synopsis presents the matter clearly:

Memb.

Sect. 3.
A consolatory digression, containing remedies to all discontents and passions of the mind.

1. General discontents and grievances satisfied.
2. Particular discontents, as deformity of body, sickness, baseness of birth, etc.
3. Poverty and want, such calamities and adversities.
4. Against servitude, loss of liberty, imprisonment, banishment, etc.
5. Against vain fears, sorrows for death of friends, or otherwise.
6. Against envy, livor, hatred, malice, emulation, ambition, and self-love, etc.
7. Against repulses, abuses, injuries, contempts, disgraces, contumelies, slanders, and scoffs, etc.
8. Against all other grievous and ordinary symptoms of this disease of melancholy.

The manifestation through the synoptic tables of the *Anatomy*'s contextual relationships (seen here in a very simple example) testifies to Burton's care for his book's sufficient enumeration, articulation, and interrelation and suggests that to get his meaning right, we should take equal care to read his structure as we read his book.

The *Anatomy* may be seen, then, as a kind of "Gothic" construct, a formulation of logical contexts which describes a single vision or "totality" of truth. Its divisions and subdivisions are, technically, "rooms" of the scholastic treatise. And the synoptic tables clarify the expression of the whole by calling attention to context and by insisting that the reader be aware of the relationships of any part to the idea of the whole. The synopses also claim the reader's attention by announcing through their very complexity the structural difficulties inherent in Burton's anatomy. The reader who examines them will find the book clarified in them, but not simplified, for it is not their function to make the book easier by restating it in simpler terms than its own; rather, they make starkly apparent the involutions, the logical balances and imbalances, the far-flung relationships of ideas which characterize the *Anatomy*. It is an exercise to follow the synoptic tables through their analysis of an idea, to find the logical equivalents Burton sets out, to trace the full articulation of a given topic by tracking down the appropriate astrological symbols assigned to it or by finding the analysis in a subsequent table and reconstructing, sometimes by means of mental gymnastics, an imaginary plan which allows a fuller topical elucidation than the printed page—even a folio page—will admit. What the synoptic tables do, then, is demand that the reader recognize the kind of intellectual exercise the book itself will require of him if he is to see it and grasp its meaning rather than simply to wander in it.

Of course, the *Anatomy* is not a cathedral; the synoptic tables are not even joined together to present a single "facade," but they do make some of the same kinds of statements about the functional contexts and logical relationships in the book that the facade makes for a Gothic building. Indeed, though the synopses are always printed as three separate "maps" (to use Renaker's term), the job of being a Donnean Reader of the *Anatomy* requires that one mentally assimilate Synopses II and III into their appropriate places within Synopsis I. Even the digressions in Partitions I and II are outlined in the synopses, and the Third Partition, which I shall argue is the last and major digression, is to be seen at the outset as part of the *Anatomy*'s single organization. Both "[melancholy's] cures; the subject of the second Partition," and "Indefinite [melancholy]; as love-melancholy, the subject of the third Partition" are found within the framework laid out in the "Synopsis of the First Partition," so that the whole book is ultimately a single, if infinitely varied statement.

Furthermore, the very form of the synoptic tables clarifies how it is that Burton's book can admit internal change without undermining the external fabric, for the structure of partitions, sections, and so on allows him to expand or even add portions at one level without destroying the contextual relationships of the other parts and parts of parts. Thus, a new subsection 4 is inserted (1628) into the structure of Partition I, section 3, member 2, when Burton decides to write about nuns' and widows' melancholy. The partition grows; a new "room" is added within; but the exterior walls of the book do not have to be torn down.

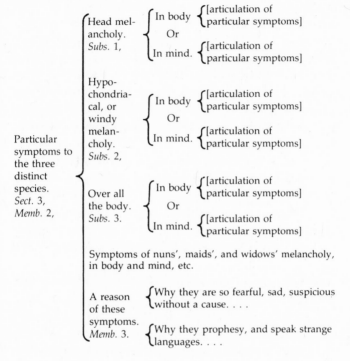

Particular symptoms to the three distinct species. *Sect.* 3, *Memb.* 2,

Head melancholy. *Subs.* 1,
- In body { [articulation of particular symptoms]
- Or
- In mind. { [articulation of particular symptoms]

Hypo-chondria-cal, or windy melan-choly. *Subs.* 2,
- In body { [articulation of particular symptoms]
- Or
- In mind. { [articulation of particular symptoms]

Over all the body. *Subs.* 3.
- In body { [articulation of particular symptoms]
- Or
- In mind. { [articulation of particular symptoms]

Symptoms of nuns', maids', and widows' melancholy, in body and mind, etc.

A reason of these symptoms. *Memb.* 3.
- { Why they are so fearful, sad, suspicious without a cause. . . .
- { Why they prophesy, and speak strange languages. . . .

The *Anatomy*, like a cathedral, is almost infinitely open to renovation. Addition or revision may modify the statement made by the construct, but it does not change the structure and therefore does not change the overall meaning either of the argument or of the building.

Burton added to the explicit clarification of his facade in succeeding editions. The synoptic tables made the declaration in 1621, and they continue as the basic components of what I have called the book's exoskele-

ton, its introductory statement of overall form and
meaning. The additions of the verses, of the concluding
"Table," or index, and particularly of the engraved title
page, then emphasized and reemphasized, as the book
was republished, the importance Burton evidently
attached to our "fore-possessing" the definition of the
whole given us by the traditional form of the book.

The first in the series of additions to the book's "clarification" of its contents was the Table, appended in
1624. An index, of course, is a very pragmatic piece of
scholarly business, and I do not at all discount the idea
that Burton may simply have decided to render his
readers a service by giving them this alphabetical table
of topics. Yet the Table, unlike the synopses, is by no
means exhaustive, and its purpose appears to be more
to suggest a different viewpoint on the material of the
Anatomy than to index fully its contents. In fact, the
Table represents a kind of foil to the synoptic tables by
giving the reader another entrance, as it were a back
door, into the structure, and by thus indicating that the
synopses' statement of the book's contextual relationships is not the only possible one.

To page through the Table is to see a different clarification, though not a different definition, of the book's
meaning. One can approach the encyclopedic content of
the *Anatomy* by way of the front door, progressing from
causes and symptoms to prognostics and cures, from
Partition I through Partition II to Partition III. That way
lies logic and recognition of the meaning that context
gives to statements. And the Table does admit that
method.

Religious mel. a distinct species, his object 633. causes of it
642. symptomes 658. Prognosticks 678. cure 680. religion,
policy, by whom 646.

                                                    (*Anatomy*, London, 1651)

But the Table recognizes the method which answers to the reader's interest as well as that which answers to logic, and "religion, policy, by whom" is beside the order of the logical discourse. The index gives the reader ways of seeing subject matter that the analytical structure obfuscates: poor men exemplify various facts about melancholy in the treatise, while the index reveals them to be one of its concerns—"Poor mens miseries 157. their happiness 337. they are dear to God 343." The book defines man by discoursing on melancholy; and the Table, as I suggested earlier, supplies a wholly illogical way of looking at the *Anatomy of Melancholy* which reaffirms, under consideration, that to study melancholy is in fact to study man and the universe: the space from Heaven to Hell is inclusive of Hearing, Heat, and Health, and the Help of friends is as relevant a purgative for melancholy as Hellebore, white or black. Furthermore, the Table provides a vantage point for recognizing that the essential matter of the treatise is a blend of the technical and necessary with the unnecessary but pleasing and human, that its subject is men in particular as well as particular causes of melancholy. God and the devil are the only persons who make their ways into the synoptic tables, though many specific *things* appear there. In the index, it is a different story:

Antimony a purger of melancholy
Anthony inveigled by Cleopatra
Apology of love melancholy
Appetite

or again:

Pork a melancholy meat
Pope *Leo Decimus* his scoffing.

The scholastic definitions of the *Anatomy,* as we have

noted, are never unified into a single massive synopsis
affirming the perfection of the book's logic. Instead,
Burton uses the synopses to call attention to the idea of
logical control and then modifies their impact by admitting the Table into the book's external declaration of
form and content. The other parts of the apparatus add
to this process of reclarification, abstracting the *Anatomy*'s meaning in various ways through various authorial poses. Both poems, "Democritus Junior ad
Librum Suum" and "The Author's Abstract of Melancholy" present the book as a totality made of diversity.
"Ad Librum Suum" introduces the *Anatomy* to a world
of readers who will find different ways of accepting it
and admonishes it to speak to them variously as they
will, with universal tolerance which yet claims always
the right to deny any too narrow interpretation (the
poem is thus another way of saying, like the Table, that
there are numerous entrances into the book's meaning).
The "Abstract," or "dialogue" (its subtitle), presents the
heart of melancholy man's condition, the extreme
sweetness and sadness with which melancholy alter-
nately fills him. Another abstract may be seen in the
note, "Lectori Male Feriato" (present in the first edition)
and in the lines, "Heraclite, fleas," for the former
focuses on the world of fools who laugh at the satirist
without recognizing his wisdom and their own folly,
and the added verses strike the *Anatomy*'s insistent
chord—shall I weep with Heraclitus or laugh with
Democritus?—in opposing "Heraclite, fleas" to "Demo-
crite, ride." The apparatus as a whole thus "abstracts"
not only the essential form of the book, but its central
moral and psychological paradoxes as well: that melancholy afflicts man, but he cannot live without it; that it is

both his joy and sorrow, his folly and wisdom, his comedy and tragedy.

On the "outside" of his discourse on melancholy, then, Burton has built a kind of facade which shows us that method, context, the meaning derived from apprehending the relationships of ideas—all are centrally important to our understanding of his endeavor as an artist; but a facade, too, which reveals the fact that logical definition does not entirely explain, cannot completely rationalize, the matter which lies within. To look closely at the synopses is to see that they do not quite work. Members or sections are not always logically equivalent, as a glance back at the scheme reproduced on page 29 will verify: member 3 of that section, a structural equivalent of member 2, appears to be logically subordinate to the preceding member; and we shall examine this same kind of logical imbalance on a grand scale when we study the Third Partition. The apparatus of the *Anatomy* insists on form, but if the book thus borrows the methodology and the principles of scholastic disputation, if it is "Gothic" in some sense, it is not finally a *High* Scholastic *Summa* nor is it like a *High* Gothic cathedral, each of which "tended to approximate, by synthesis as well as elimination, one perfect and final solution" (Panofsky, p. 44). The index hints by its own clarification that the *manifestatio* of the synoptic tables is not the only elucidation of the book, that there are illogical but true relationships within it which the exterior form of the book also must express. And the engraved title page (1628 and thereafter) with its accompanying "Argument" affirms that the solution of the *Anatomy* to the problem of organization is not, at least not *logically*, a "perfect and final" one.

The title page is an actual "face" for the book, a
picture of what is in it. Its proportions reflect the logical
proportions of the treatise: three horizontal divisions
corresponding to the three partitions of the whole, four
vertical stages corresponding to the four logical levels of
each major division—partition, section, member, and
subsection. The title in the middle makes the formulaic
statement of logical order for the treatment of the traditional subject. But the "ten distinct squares" do not
reflect the control of logic. All three kinds of Love-
melancholy are represented on one side (jealousy,
heroical love, and superstition); on the other we see
solitude (a cause of melancholy), hypochondriacus (a
particular kind of "definite" melancholy), and the mad-
man (who represents an "equivocation" of melancholy
[I.1.1.4;140], madness being an improper form of melancholy which the discourse is *not* designed to treat). In
the lower outside compartments are the two "sovereign
plants," borage and hellebore, both of which are remedies for the definite disease, but borage has no particular relationship to the Love-melancholics pictured above
it. The title page presents a conflation of the synoptic
tables and the index: ordered but not balanced, it is a
manifestatio of logical order modified by the not quite
logical associations of the emblems, as if one were to
view the perfect logic of a High Gothic facade only to
discover on closer inspection that the iconography
stretched or denied logical expectations, with the wise
virgins, perhaps, set opposite not foolish virgins, but
prophets and kings.

The title page represents the book in showing, as the
Anatomy shows, that the matter of melancholy is a
"variety and confused mixture" of causes, types, cures,

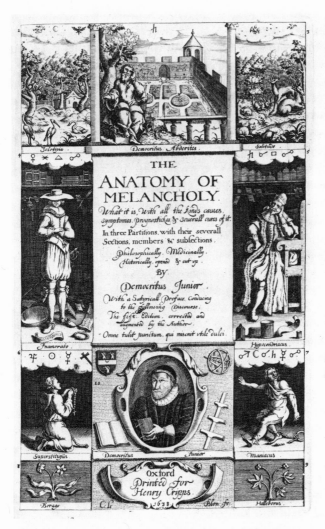

Title page from the *Anatomy of Melancholy,* Fifth edition, 1638. Reproduced by permission of The Huntington Library, San Marino, California. HM 120534.

and equivocations, yet by its form promising—"nevertheless I will adventure"—to array them all in the form of logic, to make no "labyrinth of doubts and errors" but by art to join everything into a totality even if the totality cannot be a perfect synthesis of matter ruled by form. Burton cannot show us in his title page a perfect series of emblems, four kinds of definite melancholy opposed to three of indefinite, or two emblems of causes balanced neatly by two of cures. For the melancholy of man is not, as the book will explicate, a matter of neat and well-defined equals and opposites. Whenever the book displays a series of opposites or a sequence of theses and antitheses, it does so by making confused categories and doubtful equivalents fit into the artificial neatness of the structure. So in the title page there is a kind of balance between the outer series of "distinct squares," which set indefinite melancholy generally opposite definite melancholy; yet the less logical associations—of borage and superstition for example—which are also in evidence, make of the whole an emblematic representation of what Burton both can and cannot do in his *Anatomy*.

The perfect synthesis and control of the Gothic Middle Ages will not work for Burton, for the truth that his structure has to express is confusion and diversity. We began by looking at the introductory member of the *Anatomy*, and we said that Burton leads through definition of disease to the disease of melancholy. But his definitions are very unsatisfactory: the body and mind distinction seems clear enough, except that the mental diseases turn out to be physically seated in the head (and later, of course, we find melancholy specified as of the head, of the hypochondries, or of the whole body),

and then all the diseases of fantasy, including melancholy, may or may not be distinguishable. By the time
Burton leads us to that "melancholy of which we are to
treat," we are certain of very little but that it is "an
habit" which is related to body and mind and which is
sometimes confused with various similar diseases. Even
when he later reaches the subsection on the "Definition
of Melancholy, Name, Difference," he is imprecise, for
his knowledge of melancholy tells him that he simply
cannot "perspicuously define" it.

I may now freely proceed to treat of my intended subject, to
most men's capacity, and after many ambages, perspicuously
define what this melancholy is, show his name and differences. The name is imposed from the matter, and disease
denominated from the material cause: . . . from black choler.
And *whether it be a cause or an effect, a disease or symptom,* let
Donatus Altomarus and Salvianus decide; *I will not contend
about it. It hath several descriptions, notations, and definitions.*
(I.1.3.1;169; my italics)

And despite confusion and indefinition, Burton proceeds to make a neat "distinct square" or "room" of his
treatise to contain the "Definition" which all his authorities cannot agree on and about which he will not
contend.

The structure does what the facade has announced it
can do: it rules what human reason and pure logic
cannot. Burton's emphatic adherence to the form of the
argument indicates that he is using the idea of manifest
order, and using it for all it is worth. Time and again a
subsection will begin by announcing that authorities
disagree, that there is some doubt or question about the
matter in hand, for doubt and question are the raw
material that Burton is working with. But as often as

disagreement and convincing but antithetical arguments threaten to topple the confused matter into
chaos, Burton makes art do what rationalization cannot:
he cuts out for himself a section or subsection, draws a
line from one topic to the next, fits a curly brace around
a series of ideas and aligns them in an order. He uses a
system which will let him set out, clarify, make unity
and order manifest for the sake of achieving unity and
order. That is the cutter's art: as Colie asserts (p. 436),
the *Anatomy* "is not quite a collection of essays. Burton
was bound by his material and his method to a more
complicated effort, to articulate, as anatomy does, the
disparate parts into a fitting whole."

Scholasticism, as Panofsky describes it (p. 64), had a
second "controlling principle," *concordantia* or the "AC-
CEPTANCE AND ULTIMATE RECONCILIATION OF CONTRA-
DICTORY POSSIBILITIES." Burton's matter has a myriad of
possibilities, as we have just seen with the basic definition of melancholy. Burton, however, cannot achieve
concordantia—he will not "contend"—and instead of trying to reconcile contradiction he accepts it and then goes
ahead and orders, defines, makes categories in spite of
it, letting others decide about causes, effects, or symptoms, and proceeding himself to draw out "descriptions, notations, and definitions." He makes a totality
out of the principle of *manifestatio* even though he
cannot arrive at *concordantia*, or, to put it another way,
he makes concord out of discord without resolving the
discord. This is indeed the implication of the last two
emblems of the title page. Democritus of Abdera,
Burton's forerunner in anatomizing melancholy, sits in
his garden cutting up animals, and around him are

scattered in disarray the carcasses which are his subject matter. But Democritus Junior—the author of this treatise in partitions, sections, members, and subsections which analyzes causes, symptoms, prognostics, and cures—appears holding his book. By the cutter's art he has devised a structure that will give him one finished view of the world of melancholy: whereas Democritus cuts things up, Democritus Junior joins them together by articulating them. And so he holds the finished book at the focal point of a design which comprehends not wholly rationalized relationships in a form of perfectly logical proportions, the ten distinct and diverse squares joined into one by the art, not just of an engraver, but of the anatomist of melancholy.

The outside of the *Anatomy of Melancholy* suggests, then, that Burton is not using form simply to disguise confusion, but to order it; that he is using the most explicit kind of structure as a model so that he and his readers will be able to understand and comprehend the nature of their disorder. The fundamental design of the book and the difficulties inherent, for Burton, in that design are to be accepted at face value—for, in fact, their value as a facade in which is to be seen the meaning of the book. I believe that the methodology of the book, and the form which that methodology lends to it, control and express Burton's meaning; that his continual reference to shaping his discourse points toward an understanding of its structure as necessary for an understanding of its idea; that the explicit *manifestatio* of the structure shows how, far from his being able to "write about life in general because of his lack of concern about methodology" (Finlay, p. 70), he uses the method of anatomy because it enables him to unify the diversity of human knowledge and reduce madness to method.

In the following chapters I shall be examining the ways in which Burton uses structure to clarify meaning by explicating those major portions of the book which cause it to be not a neatly ordered medical, philosophical, and historical exposition of a disease, but a tangled chain which exhibits the order and disorder essential to Burton's explanation of melancholy man. For as soon as one posits formality of structure as Burton's answer to disorder, obvious problems arise with the book's immediately apparent contradictions of order, notably those of the digressions, the discourse of indefinite melancholy in Partition III, and the "satyricall Preface," which is a different sort of anatomizing of the melancholy world. By studying these structural anomalies which seem to detract from order rather than conform to it, I shall hope to demonstrate that Burton realizes in the book the statements about order and disorder, diversity and totality which he makes manifest to his readers through the facade of his scholastic construct.

Unity that is organic implies the necessity of singleness of vision: the blind men in the old tale receive four entirely independent and incompatible impressions of the elephant because they cannot see the whole. But Burton's artificial structure implies unity of another sort: one can see a Gothic cathedral from innumerable vantage points and in each vision comprehend the meaning of the total form because the parts repeat and reflect in various combinations, through various contextual relationships, the proportions and patterns of the whole.

The book is, like the world, a tangled chain, for two structures, we shall see, coexist in its form and appear as one whole. The first is the chain itself, what the anatomy of man might be if in Adam's fall we had not all sinned: Partition I, Partition II, Partition III, with several sections, members, and subsections, an order confirming reason as man's mode of thought, indicating logic to be capable of expressing mankind. The second structure accepts the first but modifies it; the Preface stands at the head of the synoptic tables and, by establishing a second tripartite structure of Preface, Partitions I and II, Partition III, acknowledges human reason's tendency to stray from simply ordered logicality and accepts diversity as the definition of man. It is the second structure which is the *Anatomy* and which cures melancholy by giving to the understanding of life as it is the form which represents life as it should be.

Partitions I and II treat of man the rational animal and, through two systems of analysis, explicate both facts and the role question plays in human understanding. As systematic exposition defines causes and cures of a definite disease, a covert "system" of digression discloses that the overt one is an exemplum of the cure of life's miseries by the process of finding things out. Understanding mankind's diseased state depends on understanding that human knowledge, such as that displayed in Burton's sections and subsections, must be constantly weighed and constantly submitted to the test of wisdom. Burton's definition of man the rational animal frees the rooms of the treatise from the control of logical order and asserts that man's commonplace understanding of himself will cure the melancholy that learning, the "sciences" of medicine, philosophy, theology, and so forth, leaves festering in his body and mind.

Thus liberated from the necessity of corresponding to the logic of theses met and answered in appropriate antitheses, the treatise of melancholy may become, in Partition III, answerable to and definitive of the manifestations of passion in man. Man the passionate animal is defined according to type, and all his disease appears to be not strictly definable—"indefinite"—since it stems from his *primum mobile* which is love-and-hate, not reason. To the tangling of the chain of logic, which digression accomplishes in I and II, is added this of equivocation: symptom is cause is cure and all are species. And equivocation thus enables Burton to say not only *that* melancholy is the common disease of man's body and mind, but *how* it is so. For melancholy is universal defect of charity, which means that, however one views man's disorders—as symptoms of the world's miseries, as causes of the degradation of God's created perfection, as objects of all man's knowledge because all learning is trying to find things out about man in order to cure him—from whatever vantage point one sees melancholy, he is seeing nature fallen through defect of its essential sustaining force, love. To study Love-melancholy is to study man not "linked and touched with this charity," which is to know how man, and consequently, how the universe, the "golden chain" of love, are not what they should be. Yet Burton does not leave uncharitable man in chaos, for by the "engine" of art he puts the links together, forming his own chain of Love-melancholy out of the heroical

passion, the jealousy, the excessive and defective love
of God, all of which he makes equivalent and joins into
his treatise of liberal science.

"Anatomizing" in Burton's book is the continual
process of defining and dividing which results in form.
The three partitions of anatomy disclose man thinking
about what he is and is not, and they comprehend
things known, or "facts," in a structure which at once
limits the facts and liberates them. Matters of fact in
Partitions I and II and the facts of fiction in Partition III
describe the nature of melancholy man. Burton uses
those facts as his raw material and composes out of
them a dissection of mankind: this is the elucidation that
the Preface gives to the book, for Democritus Junior
shows through the Preface that out of various schemata
the artist can make a scheme. He announces that
deductive reasoning about the world may be inductive
reasoning, and that when a man sets out to satirize the
world he will end up anatomizing himself, for to see the
parts of the argument, to see foolish men, is to see the
whole of mankind, and, *nos numerus sumus, homo sum,*
I am mankind. The charity of Partition III begins in the
satire of the Preface, where Burton oversees the world
by envisioning it through a self who is also not himself,
and who sees in himself all that the world is not, and
through himself all that the world is. Men linked and
touched with charity are first expressed in the *Anatomy*
in Democritus Junior, who is actor and mere spectator,
the observer of all that the world is and the creator of all
that it should be. The Preface takes the three partitions
of anatomy and joins them in one: it gives to the
artificial construct of the *Anatomy*, with all its reiteration,

equivocation, and indefinition, the definition of unity in the collected self of Democritus Junior. So the *Anatomy* is a study of melancholy man from various viewpoints; its structure, in the broadest sense, allows for a total vision, yet suggests that the same truth can be seen from different angles. Partition III restates Partitions I and II, and the Preface conduces to the discourse by saying it all another way; and mirrored in this definition and redefinition of melancholy is the meaning that the order of anatomy, used as Burton uses it, gives to the *Anatomy of Melancholy*.

II. This New Science

For out of olde feldes, as men seyth,
Cometh al this newe corn from yer to yere,
And out of olde bokes, in good feyth,
Cometh al this newe science that men lere.
                    —CHAUCER, *The Parlement of Foules*

Robert Burton's book conforms to that traditional order
for the discussion of disease set forth in the title: *The
Anatomy of Melancholy. What it is, With all the kinds,
causes, symptomes, prognostickes, & severall cures of it. In
three Partitions, with their severall Sections, members, &
subsections.* The structure may be "imposed" on Burton
by the example of contemporary medical treatises
(Simon, pp. 422-423), but to admit that the order is not
of his invention does not force us to conclude, as Simon,
Finlay, and others do, that Burton does not use his
traditional structure to inform the *Anatomy* with its own
peculiar meaning. Most obviously, by confining himself
to the traditional schema of definition, cause, symptom,
cure, Burton seems explicitly to declare that the subject
of his discourse is the "causes, symptoms, cures" of a
definite "ordinary disease"—that he is dealing with the
matter of a material disease, the physical disorder of
humors. The traditional order proclaims it as certainly

as Democritus Junior does when he turns from the Preface to the *Anatomy* proper:

And although, for the above-named reasons, I had a just cause to undertake this subject, to point at these particular species of dotage, . . . yet I have a more serious intent at this time; and *to omit all impertinent digressions, to say no more of such as are improperly melancholy,* or metaphorically mad, lightly mad, or in disposition: . . . *my purpose and endeavour is,* in the following discourse *to anatomize this humour of melancholy,* through all his parts and species, *as it is an habit, or an ordinary disease,* and that philosophically, medicinally, to show the causes, symptoms, and several cures of it, that it may be the better avoided.   (Preface, 120; my italics)

Yet as he has already spoken of "such as are improperly melancholy" in the Preface, so Burton opens up the traditional schema, turning more than once, in the space of the "following discourse," away from the system which he has accepted for his book and from the subject matter the system defines for him. He digresses long and largely.

But we must recognize the portion of the *Anatomy* from which Burton turns aside, for the digressions exist only in the First and Second Partitions, which together complete his investigation of the "ordinary disease." From definition through cures, Partitions I and II fully describe humoral melancholy; they are together the whole anatomy of the disease which is "proper to parts" (Synopsis I), which allows him his traditional medical book schema, and from which he does not stray at random but digresses formally and purposefully. The medical treatise in I and II fulfills the expectations raised by the title for complete rehearsal of the physical disorder. In these partitions Burton selects and organizes the facts known about melancholy. He builds up vast lists of causes, symptoms, and cures in passages which seem to do little more than pad the citation in the synopsis with appropriate authors and a qualification or two, sometimes a tale. Indeed, in the last two sections of the Second Partition, Burton picks up speed with hurried incantations of facts about pharmaceutical and chirurgical cures. It was especially Partition II that Sir William Osler called a "strictly medical treatise, in which the author has collected all the known information about the treatment of mental disorders; the entire pharmacopoeia is brought in, and Burton writes prescriptions like a physician" (Osler, pp. 175-176). The two partitions make a complete system. There are three kinds of melancholy, and these are defined; general and particular causes, and these are set forth; common and peculiar symptoms, good and bad prognostics, cures lawful, unlawful, dietetical, pharmaceutical—all are distinguished, laid out in sections, confined by the structure to an order which perfectly encompasses all the indefinable material. If foods are causes and cures, then they are treated under cause and under cure. Fear is cause and symptom; purges are general and particular cures. Burton puts everything where it belongs in the design, physically capturing, in his sections and subsections, the physical disease. For melancholy's "perpetual fume and darkness," the system makes clear, is material, physical reality, an "object which cannot be removed" yet which must be removed before counsel or other "immaterial" cures can hope to have effect (I.3.3;421).

But in among the systematized facts of the matter of

melancholy are the digressions, and we must ask
whether they are pertinent to Burton's statement in the
Anatomy or merely "impertinent digressions," because
our answer will greatly qualify any estimation of
Burton's art. In the first place, hardly anyone concerned
with reading the *Anatomy* critically is now truly interested in black bile or hellebore. Scholarship is spent on
the Preface with its mask, on Love-melancholy, or on
the many stories that pack the book; or it is spent on the
Nature of Spirits, the Misery of Scholars, the Air, the
Consolation and Remedies of Discontents—all of these
last, of course, being digressions. And if one tries to
account for humoral psychology as the stated topic of
the *Anatomy*—if one deals with it at all—one will likely
end by agreeing with Babb's sentiment:

In composing *The Anatomy of Melancholy*, a scholar has drawn
upon the accumulated wisdom of mankind to present a
characterization and criticism of human nature and human
experience. In spite of the title, the primary theme is the
infelicity of man. . . . The lasting interest and value of the
book lie in its animated satiric representation of human life, in
its perceptive explanations of life's harshness, and in the
sympathetic counsel and consolation which the author extends to all whose burdens are too heavy.   (Babb, p. 109)

Nor, it must be admitted, was Burton himself seemingly very interested in the medical treatise. Expansion
through the six editions does not come in the information about the ordinary disease, but instead, the "discussions of geography and travel, of spirits and devils,
and of every sort of love matter were greatly enlarged,
and . . . constantly increasing stress was laid upon the
social and moral criticism in the book" (Hallwachs, p.
v). There is something static, for Burton as well as for

us, about the very discussion which gives rise to his book. We look at the assumptions underlying the book's makeup—the facts about the physical disease, anatomy, the form of a scholarly treatise, all the jargon and the painstaking accumulation of authority—and we agree that the "lasting interest and value of the book" do not lie here. The digressions, I shall hope to show, point up Burton's own awareness of his "primary theme, the infelicity of man," by creating tension within the more stolid medical discourse, tension between matter and mind, between physical "ordinary disease" and "improper" or "metaphorical madness," tension finally between the medical book itself and questions about the very trustworthiness or usefullness of human knowledge which makes possible the writing of textbooks in traditional schemata designed to transmit accepted fact, or Truth.

Digression becomes, in Burton's art, necessary to the transmission of knowledge because it makes us question and see what knowledge is. But in not noticing the context of the digressions (Partitions I and II in general, and, in particular, certain sections of those partitions), critics have most often missed Burton's way of locating for us the "true matter and end" of his traditional discourse as well as of the digressions from that discourse.

The digressions have been seen as pleasant side trips unrelated to the central issues of the *Anatomy*, as "resting-points" on our "orderly march through [Burton's] melancholy terrain."[1] Now a digression, certainly, is a turning aside of some kind, one which defies or inter-

---

1. John L. Lievsay, "Robert Burton's *De Consolatione*," *South Atlantic Quarterly*, 55 (1956), 329.

rupts a literary work's ordered progression and in general indicates a straying from the main theme. This is not to say that digression cannot be an artistic means of opening up the statement of a work, but it does so by way of addition; and there is, I think, in the term an assumption that the additive is not inherent in or necessary to the statement, no matter how much it may modify the given work. For the most part, Burton's digressions have been accepted as this kind of addition. Lievsay calls them "resting-points"; Simon suggests that they are "autant de parenthèses, dûment ouvertes et dûment refermées, qui n'altèrent nullement la régularité de la construction" (p. 423). King feels that digression conflicts with the planning evident in the synopses and so indicates an "almost comic inability to manage the most fundamental problems involved in writing a book," and he cannot allow the Burtonian digression to be other than, at worst, a "free ride on a hobby horse," wholly irrelevant to the "structural fabric" of the book (King, pp. 82-84). But Burton's digressions have their planned places in the structure. They are part of the order, occupying, as their very presence in the synoptic tables indicates, positions within the formal structure of the book. Burton has no unit of his structure made especially for use when he wishes to turn aside; a digression occupies whatever existing forms fit its breadth and length. There are digressions filling out a whole section, like the Consolatory Digression; or a member, like the Digression of Anatomy; or a part of a subsection, like the Digression of Compounds. Thus the digressions are built into the structure of the first two partitions, not inserted like so many afterthoughts—or interruptions of thought (parentheses)—but woven in as threads of the discourse. Simon is right that the digressions do not alter the lines of construction; from a purely formal standpoint, they are part of Burton's very formal construct, and I hope to show that they are also essential thematic constituents of the *Anatomy*.[2]

Still, the digressions do digress from something: they turn aside from the sequence of definition, cause, symptom, cure. From the point of view of the orderly exploration of humoral psychology, they are, in fact, digressions. But even as they digress, thus apparently denying the massive and painstaking organization of the book, they become part of the organization by being shaped into the forms of the ordered progression which they would seem to defy.

And they are not, from the point of view of the whole matter of the *Anatomy*, "so many closed parentheses." The discontinuity of subject matter suggested by calling them digressions is, to the reader who has been "fore-possessed" of Burton's method by the book's apparatus, simultaneously revealed to be continuity in the broader vision of the entire book. The careful reader is always made aware, by section heading if not by overt statement in the text, when Burton is going to digress and into what territory he will divert his discussion. And, thus alerted, one discovers in Partitions I and II a complex interrelationship between the system stated in the title, and a "system" implied in the progression from one digression to the next. As the section titles in

2. Lyons (pp. 126-130) suggests readings of the digressions more sensitive than those of the critics cited above. She sees them as "variations or elaborations on the outline plan" and notices that they are "far better integrated into the treatise than is sometimes thought" (p. 127).

this chapter suggest, a discourse on knowledge, its causing and curing of the disorders of post-lapsarian man's life, intermingles with and counterbalances the *Anatomy's* "proper" investigation of humoral psychology, that presentation of facts which make up Burton's traditional discourse.

The form and content given him by his title and his overt methodology, which commit Burton to finding and ordering facts, is (most emphatically in the Digression of the Air) opposed to or superseded by a new understanding of what such methodologies imply. Ordered human thought through the ages, *auctoritas*, is not final and total; but the necessary roving from formal artificial limits into digression shows us that such ordered "knowledge" *is* the firm groundwork upon which new and always possible truth can be learned, tested, transmitted as "science." Authority is less undermined than it is redefined as knowledge's starting place, as rational man's textbook rather than his *summa* or his Scripture. Following the introduction in I.1.1, which places melancholy in the context of man's fall from perfection, Burton begins his *Anatomy of Melancholy* by making—of all things—a *Digression* of Anatomy. Each successive digression is then as pertinent and necessary to our understanding of the science of the *Anatomy* as this first one, for while the formal progression of the book is concerned with all the facts that men know about melancholy's definition, causes, symptoms, and cures, the "system" of the formal digressions is concerned with definitions of knowledge itself, with man's failure to know and his hopes for achieving understanding. Man asks what he can know, falls short of knowing all he can, discovers answers in the form of both statements and more questions. And so the digressions allow the reader learning about melancholy to learn as well what it means for him to be man, the rational, learning, knowing animal.

KNOWLEDGE AS QUESTION: DEFINITION

The Digression of Anatomy must certainly be seen as essential to the whole book. The first synopsis describes this digression as being "To [melancholy's] explication," and in the opening sentence Burton declares, "Before I proceed to define the disease of melancholy, what it is, or to discourse further of it, I hold it not impertinent to make a brief digression of the anatomy of the body and faculties of the soul, for the better understanding of that which is to follow" (I.1.2.1;146). While the *Anatomy* is not argumentative discourse, Burton's references to this digression show that he thinks of it as the "narration" of the book, that he intends it to give the "story" or statement of fact necessary for what is to follow. Man is what we start with, the object of the disease and the subject, in the broadest sense, of the *Anatomy*. Burton is specific about why he considers the digression pertinent: it gives facts necessary to the discourse—"hard words will often occur . . . which by the vulgar will not so easily be perceived"; and it calls for the appropriate attitude toward the facts set forth—it may cause men to "search farther into this most excellent subject, and . . . to praise God" (I.1.2.1;146).

Thus the digression prepares for the discourse first by taking care of all those "hard words." From humors and spirits to understanding and will, Burton anatomizes man's anatomy. What man is should be understandable in terms of the enumeration of his parts, physical and spiritual; articulation is straightforward, specification exact:

Containing parts, by reason of their more solid substance, are either homogeneal or heterogeneal, similar or dissimilar. . . . Similar, or homogeneal, are such as, if they be divided, are still severed into parts of the same nature, as water into water. Of these some be spermatical, some fleshy or carnal. Spermatical are such as are immediately begotten of the seed, which are bones, gristles, ligaments, membranes, nerves, arteries, veins, skins, fibres, or strings, fat.

The bones are dry and hard, begotten of the thickest of the seed.   (I.1.2.3;148-149)

And so on. The most obvious function of the Digression of Anatomy lies in such spelling out of distinctions necessary to the explication of the rest of the *Anatomy*.

But the explanation is not always so clear-cut as in the case of bones and gristle. The Digression of Anatomy not only gives the known facts, it raises the right questions, for to Burton it is pertinent that his audience should be wondering how man is man: "for such matters as concern the knowledge of themselves, they are wholly ignorant and careless; they know not what this body and soul are, how combined, of what parts and faculties they consist, or how a man differs from a dog" (I.1.2.1;146-147). "To stir them up therefore to this study," he digresses. Burton asks us to investigate at the same time that he defines and answers questions for us. The method of turning statements into questions and questions into statements is one of his chief means of stirring up his readers to participate in his inquiries, both in this digression and throughout the *Anatomy*.

One way Burton makes his statements questionable is by epitomizing. The *Anatomy* is full of epitomies—is itself an epitome—and the first digression is formed as "some small taste, or notice of the rest" to be found in "Wecker, Melancthon, Fernelius, Fuchsius, and those tedious tracts *de Anima*" (p. 147). Sometimes Burton merely sets down a generally received opinion, like that "most approved" division of the parts of the body (p. 147). Or he decides to leave out a discussion which is impertinent, like that of the "members of generation" (I.1.2.4;152), or which, like the motion of the pulse, has had whole books written about it (I.1.2.8;162). Or he chooses to include a particular explanation, like that of the conscience (I.1.2.10;166). Such explicit picking and choosing among authorities and topics makes us immediately aware of the author behind his book, sorting out his facts and figures, poring over his "old books" in order to put together his new scientific treatise. Instead of simply telling his readers what the body and soul are, Burton tells us what pieces of knowledge, out of the many available pieces of knowledge, he is going to set down. His epitomizing makes plain that the definition of a "hard word" or a statement of fact about man's nature is not an end product, but is part of an endless process of individual men reasoning about themselves and choosing or not choosing whether to agree with each other about what they know, or even whether to take part in the discussion. So Burton does not merely give us certain facts, but makes us understand that facts are simply those things we now know or think we know, and so he is talking about knowing, about what "facts" are, even as he instructs us in the things we must know.

The underlying investigation of epistemology is more

apparent when in epitomizing Burton sets the differences among the best writers in high relief. He begins
his anatomy of the soul (I.1.2.5;154-157) with expression
of all the doubts about the soul:

"We can understand all things by her, but what she is we
cannot apprehend." Some therefore make one soul, divided
into three principal faculties; others, three distinct souls:
which question of late hath been much controverted by
Piccolomineus and Zabarel. Paracelsus will have four souls,
adding to the three grand faculties a spiritual soul: which
opinion of his Campanella, in his book *de sensu rerum*, much
labours to demonstrate; . . . and some again, one soul of all
creatures whatsoever, differing only in organs. . . . Others
make a doubt whether it be all in all, and all in every part;
which is amply discussed in Zabarel amongst the rest.

Then he seems to resolve the differences by one of his
appeals to what is most accepted: "The common division of the soul is into three principal faculties—vegetal,
sensitive, and rational," but then he proceeds to more
impossible knowledge—how the faculties are connected
and distinguished. Finally, on top of all this foundation
of indecision, Burton begins immediately to build his
cryptic definition of the vegetal faculty, with all its
functions neatly set out: his system is designed to
impress the reader with the idea that knowledge is
disputed, that fact is hypothesis, assertion, or conclusion built on other hypotheses, assertions, and con-
clusions—and thus that fact is "fact," not Truth.

No discussion exhibits the indefinite quality of knowledge more than the subsection on the rational soul
(I.1.2.9;162-165) in which Burton takes one of his more
unequivocal stands: "Out of which [philosophers' defi-
nition] we may gather that this rational soul includes the

powers, and performs the duties, of the other two which are contained in it, and all three faculties make one soul, which is inorganical of itself, although it be in all parts, and incorporeal, using their organs, and working by them." But this decision on "a pleasant but a doubtful subject" follows two and one-half pages of citation of arguments on the essence, seat, origin, and immortality of the soul, in which Burton mentions at least fifty-three specific authorities, together with Chaldees, Egyptians, Pythagoreans, Stoics, Church Fathers, and "others," and uses numerous examples, from Lucian's cock to Leo Decimus. Questions are resolved in statement, but statement is tempered by the bulk of the preceding question. Burton's effect may perhaps be seen more clearly if we compare with his definition a short passage on the same subject from Timothy Bright's *Treatise of Melancholie*. In a chapter on "How the bodie affecteth the soule," Bright explains the nature of the soul:

The soule, as the substance therof is most pure, and perfect, and far of remoued from corruption; so it is endued with faculties of like qualitie, pure, immortall and answerable to so diuine a subject; & carrieth with it, an instinct science, gotten, neither by precept, nor practise; but naturally therewith furnished; whereby it is able, with one vniuersall, and simple facultie, to performe so many varieties of actions . . . I say the facultie, and not faculties. For if we plant so many faculties in the soule, as there be outward, and inward actions performed by vs, it certainly could not be simple, but needes must receiue varietie of composition.   (Bright, p. 42)

Where this passage concerns Truth and presents what its author knows, Burton's statement concerns truth which may be gathered from all the knowledge that men have. Bright talks about the soul, Burton about our knowledge of the soul: "The aim is to show that . . . the whole subject under consideration is far more complicated than might at first appear" (Lyons, p. 131).

Epitome coupled with precision of classification and division can also lead to confusion in the definition of hard words. When Burton defines the understanding, he carries out analysis in several directions at once, noting three distinctions between man and beast, three steps in the process of understanding, eight (possibly seven) of its actions, four separate divisions. Then he begins to sort out the divisions, and in the climax of the subsection he throws out lists of words and varying accounts of numbers and distinctions:

Some reckon up eight kinds of [habits]: sense, experience, intelligence, faith, suspicion, error, opinion, science; to which are added art, prudency, wisdom; as also synteresis, *dictamen rationis*, conscience; so that in all there be fourteen species of the understanding, of which some are innate, as the three last mentioned; the other are begotten by doctrine, learning, and use. Plato will have all to be innate: Aristotle reckons up but five intellectual habits: two speculative, as that intelligence of the principles and science of conclusion; two practic, as prudency whose end is to practise, art to fabricate; wisdom to comprehend the use and experiments of all notions and habits whatsoever. Which division of Aristotle (if it be considered aright) is all one with the precedent; for three being innate, and five acquisite, the rest are improper, imperfect, and in a more strict examination excluded. Of all these I should more amply dilate, but my subject will not permit. Three of them only I will point at.   (I.1.2.10;166)

One hard word becomes a score as Burton allows clarification to melt into cloudiness.[3]

_____

3. The sort of "taking back" of statement I am noting here is certainly prevalent in Burton's method throughout the *Anatomy*, as

In anatomizing man, moreover, Burton confronts what we know should be, as well as what we know, or think we know, is. The theme of the digression gradually shifts from statement to preachment as he explains how a man differs from a dog. From bones to brain, the body exists—it *is*—but along with its physical reality, we can consider the quality of that existence: the brain is "the most noble organ under heaven, the dwelling house and seat of the soul, the habitation of wisdom, memory, judgment, reason, and in which man is most like unto God" (I.1.2.4;153). Furthermore, we consider not only what the body is, but from whom and how it is: preparing to anatomize man's gut, Burton warns us "to behold not the matter only, but the singular art, workmanship, and counsel of this our great Creator" (I.1.2.4; 151). All of this is fact. But as soon as he begins to talk of the rational and sensible souls, he is speaking of what is potential but is not: imagination in men is governed by reason, "or at least should be" (I.1.2.7;160); and he is speaking of what men think is, but is not: "all things seek their own good, or at least seeming good" (I.1.2.8; 161). This shift in the explanation culminates in the last subsection of the digression, "Of the Will" (I.1.2.11;167-169), where the definition of man which started in the facts of matter ends in a "confusion in our powers": "[Appetite] was (as I said) once well agreeing with reason, and there was an excellent consent and harmony betwixt them, but that is now dissolved, they often jar, reason is overborne by passion. . . . Lust counsels one

---

Stanley Fish argues. I see, however, a final completion of statement in the completion of the book, whereas Fish concludes that, *if* the book is finally a "mercy," the "unbuilding" that takes place in individual arguments nevertheless destroys the artifact itself or its "superstructure" (see above, page 000).

thing, Reason another, there is a new reluctancy in men. . . . Those natural and vegetal powers are not commanded by will at all; for 'who can add one cubit to his stature?' These other may, but are not." So anatomy of man leads Burton away from simple statement to statement which involves facts about what is not. The development is inherent in the subject matter; the state of man's soul requires sermons. And the digression ends looking from what man is, or should be, across the boundaries of this book toward other books about what man does, or should do: "The principal habits are two in number, virtue and vice, whose peculiar definitions, descriptions, differences, and kinds are handled at large in the ethics, and are, indeed, the subject of moral philosophy."

As simple narration elucidating man's anatomy, the Digression of Anatomy would no more be digression than is the first member, the introduction. Man is an ordered being, made of body and mind, the order being understood in terms of elements and faculties of body and soul. But in analyzing man Burton gives answers and raises questions simultaneously. The methods of qualifying statement of fact which I have been examining are not limited to this digression: epitome with its implicit arguments over what is fact, definition or indefinition by means of analysis, juxtaposition of what is with what should be—all of these methods Burton uses throughout the book to call attention to the fact that his subject matter is not so much man as it is man's knowledge of himself. I have been interested in pointing them out here, however, because they modify significantly the digression's function as the narration of this discourse. Again, though the *Anatomy* is not structured as an oration, this digression should work, Burton has said, to inform us of necessary facts of the matter. But Thomas Wilson warns the writer of a narration:

"And surely if the matter be not so plainely told that all may understand it, wee shall doe little good in the rest of our report, for in other partes of the Oration if we be somwhat darke, it is lesse harme, wee may be more plaine in an other place. But if the Narration, or substance of the tale be not well perceived, the whole Oration besides is darkned altogether. For to what ende should we goe about to proue that, which the hearers know not what it is?"[4]

Burton has deliberately made his narration "somewhat dark." Even as he has prepared his readers for the explication of the ordinary disease by telling us what humors and spirits and sense and reason are, he has turned the narration on itself, defining not quite definitely, suggesting that we know not all that man is, stirring us up to wonder how a man differs from a dog even as he tells us how. And so the whole massive analysis of the *Anatomy*, beginning in the very next subsection with Burton's not very clear definition of melancholy, rests not on preparative statement of fact, but on statement of fact which is at one and the same time question of fact. Because he made this peculiar narration a digression away from his orderly scheme, Burton alerts us to the notion that as we begin to "learn" about the quintessential human disorder, melancholy, we will do so despite not knowing for sure that we understand the "substance of the tale," man himself.

The Digression of the Nature of Spirits, like the Digression of Anatomy, deals with man's knowledge of

4. *Arte of Rhetorique: 1560*, ed. G. Mair (Oxford: Clarendon Press, 1909), p. 106.

essences. Burton has asked, pertinent to his discussion
of man's diseases, what man is; he now asks, pertinent
to his discussion of how spirits cause the disease, what
spirits are.

The digression never asks *if* there are spirits, but what
they are like and what we can know about them.
Though Burton always makes plain what is and is not
digression, we should note the boundaries of this digression, for it leads right into the rest of the subsection,
which is proper to the *Anatomy* itself. "How far the
power of spirits and devils doth extend, and whether
they can cause this, or any other disease, is a serious
question, and worthy to be considered: for the better
understanding of which, I will make a brief digression
of the nature of spirits" (I.2.1.2;180). This opening
sentence of the subsection clearly assigns the extent
of spirits' power and their effecting melancholy to the
partition itself, their nature to the digression; and so the
synopsis: "Or from the devil immediately, with a digression of the nature of spirits and devils." Thus with
the paragraph beginning, "How far their power doth
extend it is hard to determine" (p. 197), Burton turns
back to the discourse from the digression, the limits of
which should be noted if we are to understand the very
close relationship between it and the *Anatomy* proper.

This digression inquires into the nature of beings
unlike man but effective in his life. Spirits are difficult to
know; our nature makes their nature obscure to us, but
Burton does not balk at what is "beyond the reach of
human capacity": "our subtle schoolmen, Cardans,
Scaligers, profound Thomists, *Fracastoriana et Ferneliana
acies*, are weak, dry, obscure, defective in these mysteries, and all our quickest wits, as an owl's eyes at the
sun's light, wax dull, and are not sufficient to appre-

hend them; yet, as in the rest, I will adventure to say something to this point" (p. 180). Like human nature, the nature of spirits is indefinable but open to definition. Though knowledge may never be complete or completely right, we can know and say something, and Burton says about spirits, in sum, that they affect man.

He tackles all the "subtle schoolmen's" ideas. His epitome is comprehensive of every question of form and matter that could be asked about spiritual beings, and he punctuates the discussion with comments on this blinding mass of "knowledge." Talmudists say that devils were begotten by Adam of Lillis, and "The Turks' Alcoran is altogether as absurd and ridiculous in this point" (p. 180). That spirits are dead men's souls is a "foolish opinion" (p. 181). Platonists have "altogether erroneous" ideas about good and bad devils (p. 186); that spirits reward men when pleased or send plagues when displeased is "as vain as the rest" (p. 187). Often Burton stays outside the argument. He will spread out the answers that men give and let them fight it out amongst themselves: some prove angels and devils corporeal while others laugh them to scorn (p. 182). He will pay minute attention to a question but let it remain a question: some hold the number of spirits to be infinite, but if we figure the distance from heaven to earth, "as some say, 170 millions 803 miles," how many would that hold? and in any case Thomas and others agree that "there be far more angels than devils" (p. 189). He will build up a list of statements that begins to sound like affirmation on his part, then lay the beliefs at others' feet:

That they can assume other aerial bodies, all manner of shapes at their pleasures, appear in what likeness they will themselves, that they are most swift in motion, can pass many miles in an instant, and so likewise transform bodies of others into what shape they please, and with admirable celerity remove them from place to place; . . . that they can represent castles in the air, palaces, armies, spectrums, prodigies, and such strange objects to mortal men's eyes, cause smells, savours, etc., deceive all the senses; *most writers of this subject* credibly believe. (P. 183; my italics)

Burton lets the argument rock back and forth over spirits' number, corporality, mortality. He acknowledges probability, sniffs at absurdity, but takes no stand on the nature of spirits in themselves, only at last on their nature *in respect to* man.

To reach his position, Burton first discusses the spiritual nature itself, then spirits' kinds and numbers—their organization. In the quotation just cited, Burton hedges about whether spirits deceive man, but he finally *decides*— sliding into the decision, typically, through the midst of disagreement which constitutes men's "knowledge" of spirits. First he says that all the "paradoxes of their power, corporeity, mortality" are confuted in various authors; then that spirits may deceive men's eyes without true metamorphosis; then that "this, no doubt, is as true as the rest" (pp. 185-186). Having only doubt about how true the rest is, we are left unsure about both paradoxes and confutations: in other words, the nature of spirits *per se* is left unclarified. But Burton then shows what others believe "in general"—beliefs having to do with spirits' relations with man: they have greater understanding than man, they can deceive him and are more skilled in arts than he, they know and can apply the "virtues of herbs, plants, stones, minerals, etc.," they "deceive all our senses, even our understanding itself at once," they can "conquer armies, give victories, help, further, hurt, cross, and alter human attempts and projects" (p. 186). Only at last does Burton himself off-handedly accept these accumulated general opinions: "Such feats can they do."

Inquiring then into the number and kind of spirits, Burton quickly reveals that he does not care to decide about infinities or even about guardian angels (though he finds the unorthodox notion of good devils absurd). Instead, what is pertinent to his book (and thus to his digression) is devils' interference with men. Their number is *"nihil ad nos,"* and the divines, if they wish, may argue whether spirits rule the moon (p. 190). Our concern is rather that "they are confined until the day of judgment to this sublunary world, and can work no farther than the four elements, and as God permits them" (p. 190). And so Burton follows Psellus: the classification of spirits is according to the four elements, and the explanation of each kind is according to man. Spirits, for Burton, never become mere modernistic metaphors for psychic human disorders, but as essences different from us, they are important insofar as they affect us. Fiery spirits "sit on shipmasts" and signify mischief (p. 190); aerial spirits cause tempests and make it rain stones (p. 191); water devils cause floods; and terrestrial spirits, "as they are more conversant with man, so they do them most harm" (p. 192). "Thus the devil reigns, and in a thousand several shapes; . . . but be where he will, he rageth while he may to comfort himself, as Lactantius thinks, with other men's falls, he labours all he can to bring them into the same pit of perdition with him" (p. 196).

The theme of the Digression of the Nature of Spirits, as that reference to Satan's working "other *men's* falls" implies, is the theme of Burton's earlier Digression of Anatomy: the theme of knowledge of man. For man's knowledge of spirits lies in his knowledge of himself. The digression concludes by defining spirits in terms of man: "He studies our overthrow" is the closest Burton will come to saying what spirits are. They are those beings which deceive man's understanding, making it hard for him to know; they are impurity, perniciousness, heresy, superstition working *in men* to their confusion. For Burton, to ask what we know about spirits is not to decide on the niceties of spiritual essence: it is not to consider endless *quaestiones* like *"Si spiritus sunt quanti, erunt corporei: At sunt quanti, ergo,"* and so forth. That would be merely parenthetical, "impertinent" digression. Instead, to digress far enough into the question of the Nature of Spirits is, for Burton, to ask more about what we know about ourselves and *our* disorder.

Burton goes from the digression, then, back to his anatomy of melancholy, and sees the extent of spirits' power: " 'Tis true they have, by God's permission, power over us, and we find by experience that they can hurt not our fields only, cattle, goods, but our bodies and minds" (p. 199). The Nature of Spirits, which, the digression said, is to act against man, is now realized in their actions: they rule him; they captivate his soul. The relationship of spirits to man is analogous to the relationship of man's body to his mind. Man is not *simply* affected. Melancholy is the graphic representation of mind subjected to body subjected to indwelling devil: "And Jason Pratensis [proves] 'that the devil, being a slender incomprehensible spirit, can easily insinuate and wind himself into human bodies, and cunningly couched in our bowels, vitiate our healths, terrify our souls with fearful dreams, and shake our minds with furies' " (p. 200). The later part of the subsection, being part of the *Anatomy* proper, is, as it were, exemplification of the digression. And so does the following subsection exemplify and depend upon the whole preceding discussion—the subsection, that is, on witches and magicians in which Burton shows spirits causing melancholy in man by means of man.

But the image of the devil sneaking into our bowels to torment us is not all that the digression allows to the *Anatomy*. More important is what digression is doing to the analysis of the disease in general. We have seen the pertinent digressions putting questions in the way of the facts of the disease, for the digressions stand aside from facts, pointing to knowledge and asking what it is. The discussion of the ordinary disease is not faulted; when Burton writes that the devil affects the fantasy, but "not without the humour" (p. 200), we cannot assume that he does not mean what he says, that it is all metaphor. But we are seeing melancholy as a particular exemplify the general post-lapsarian confusion of the man-devil antagonism. And we know by now that fact is not always Truth, but is also Question.

The nature of man and the nature of spirits are finally less clear in these digressions than is man inquiring into what he knows about himself. And to the degree that inquiry displaces statement, the facts of the ordinary disease to which the digressions pertain are abstracted from their particular framework and referred to a broader disorder. Having come no farther than the first member of the second section of the First Partition, we find that Burton's inclusion of digression in the context of the discussion of humoral man is turning that discus-

sion away from itself and making the disease of humors
pertinent to a larger discussion of knowledge and of
facts which are not necessarily facts of matter.

KNOWLEDGE IN DEFECT: CAUSE

Whatever may be the truth about his nature, man
has—in being man—to make out of body and soul a
working union. However much or little he may understand of himself, he has to live from day to day; and
whether or not he ever ponders the tripartite nature of
the soul, he must function, for better or worse, as a
man. And this means that he must eat, he must assimilate and evacuate matter, he must breathe, exercise,
sleep and wake, and he must react positively or nega-
tively with his mind to life around him. These are the
"six non-natural things." Few of Burton's sections are
so bound up with the material reality of man and his
disease as are his discussions of "those six non-natural
things," and the discourse on them as causes of melancholy begins, in I.2.2.1, with unequivocal obedience to
the form and matter of the medical treatise. Burton
reminds us of the textbook rules he is following:

According to my proposed method, having opened hitherto
these secondary causes, which are inbred with us, I must now
proceed to the outward and adventitious, which happen unto
us after we are born. And those are either evident, remote, or
inward, antecedent, and the nearest: continent causes some
call them. These outward, remote, precedent causes are
sub-divided again into necessary and not necessary. Necessary (because we cannot avoid them, but they will alter us, as
they are used or abused) are these six non-natural things, so
much spoken of amongst physicians, which are principal

causes of this disease. For almost in every consultation, whereas they shall come to speak of the causes, the fault is found, and this part most objected to the patient: . . . he hath still offended in one of those six.   (I.2.2.1;216)

The anatomist's "proposed method," however, leads him through well-ordered steps and brings him out where he did not seem to be headed. Beginning with food and drink which cause melancholy in men, the discussion of the non-natural things as roots of the material disease ends with the mistreatment of man by man which causes melancholy in society. The Digression of the Force of Imagination opens Burton's discourse on "perturbations of the mind," while the Digression of the Misery of Scholars—so often simply accepted as Burton's autobiographical complaint—concludes his treatment of this sixth non-natural thing, mental perturbation. The two digressions thus serve as boundaries to the "methodical" discussion of perturbations of the mind, and this fact seems to require that we read them in relation to each other and in the context of this last and most influential non-natural thing. These digressions begin Burton's "not impertinent" investigation of causes, not just of "material" melancholy, but of that melancholy which grows out of and is defined by lack of human knowledge. As men's minds are "perturbed" by irascible and concupiscible reactions to life, the two digressions together diagnose the cause of men's individual and social ills to lie in matters which are more important to them, and more pertinent to Burton's essential meaning, than overeating or lack of exercise or even emotional disturbance itself. The Force of Imagination and the Misery of Scholars open the system up, making the causes of material disease in body and mind attributable to a disorder more destructive of the nature of things than a malady caused by any amount of beef, Venus, thick air, idleness, envy, anger, or self-love. Behind man functioning as man there must be knowledge—information about outside objects to be subjected to reason. But behind his malfunctioning there is the day-in and day-out corruption of his "good parts and profitable gifts" by his acceptance of *mis*information.

The theme of moderation cloaks the second and third members of Partition I, section 2, of the physician's discourse with the fairly homely garb of common-sense practicality. Member 2 treats the first five non-natural things, and in explaining their relationship to melancholy, Burton ticks off the extremes of abuse whereby man submits his body to the necessity of disease. Every food or drink has been condemned by some authority (I.2.2.1), and too little food is as bad as too much (I.2.2.2). "Venus omitted" is one thing, but "Intemperate Venus is all out as bad in the other extreme" (I.2.2.4;235). Air is harmful if too hot, cold, tempestuous, impure, wet, dry (I.2.2.5). And the same may be said of sleeping and waking (I.2.2.7) as of exercise and idleness: "Nothing so good but it may be abused" (I.2.2.6;214). By his conscientious analysis according to his "proposed method," Burton turns the list of causes into a recommendation for moderation in all things. For although he is not yet concerned with cures, in noting causes he pits the necessity of the functions ("we cannot avoid them, but they will alter us") against his careful recording of the objections to almost every use of them. And if eat we must, but every food is bad, then reasonableness is our only hope; therefore, the upshot of the learned catalogue is but a friendly warning: "but to such as are wealthy, live plenteously, at ease, may take their choice, and refrain if they will, these viands are to be forborne, if they be inclined to, or suspect melancholy, as they tender their healths: otherwise if they be intemperate, or disordered in their diet, at their peril be it. *Qui monet amat, Ave atque cave*" (I.2.2.3;233). Ultimately, right use of the body involves responsibility more than rules, and in analyzing men's abuse of their bodies, Burton blames them for being irresponsible. Nature may rightly complain, he says with Mercurialis, that we have corrupted and perverted the "many good parts and profitable gifts" bestowed on us in our creation and have become traitors to God, to nature, and to the world by not caring for ourselves (I.2.2.6;249).

Turning then from the causes seated in man's body, Burton deals in member 3 with those stemming from misuse of the mind. He has more than twice as much to say about the "thunder and lightning of perturbation" as he does about the first five non-natural things put together, since "this of passion is the greatest of all" (I.2.3.1;250). Burton indicts the rational soul, handing down a single clear judgment throughout his anatomy of passions: that what makes man man, his very reason, is also—by its "supine negligence"—what makes him universally diseased. We have been over this ground before in the Digression of Anatomy, but Burton is talking here not in terms of theory but of experience: "All philosophers impute the miseries of the body to the soul, that should have governed it better, by command of reason, and hath not done it. . . . But let them dispute how they will, set down *in thesi*, give precepts to the contrary; we find that of Lemnius true by common experience: 'No mortal man is free from these perturbations: or if he be so, sure he is either a god or a block' " (I.2.3.1;251). As the body is punished by extremes of abuse, so the mind is diseased by intemperate passions. And while he includes theoretical explanation—"If the imagination be very apprehensive, intent, and violent, it sends great store of spirits to or from the heart, and makes a deeper impression and greater tumult" (I.2.3.1;252)—nonetheless Burton puts the main weight of the discussion on *what we see around us.* Everyone has witnessed the working of envy: "He tortures himself if his equal, friend, neighbour, be preferred, commended, do well" (I.2.3.7;265); and immoderate pleasure preaches its moral daily: "It is a wonder to see how many poor, distressed, miserable wretches one shall meet almost in every path and street, begging for an alms, that have been well descended, and sometime in flourishing estate, . . . and all through immoderate lust, gaming, pleasure, and riot" (I.2.3.13; 287).

The portion of the *Anatomy* given over to the six non-natural things as causes thus emphasizes the responsibility man has simply to be himself. Not immediate to his nature, but necessary for his daily life, the functions of body and mind have to be controlled by man, and to a great extent they control what he makes of himself.

Immediately after Burton has introduced the working of mind upon body in subsection 1 of member 3, he digresses. The passions "overwhelm reason," he says in the introductory subsection, and he says it again and again in the subsections which enumerate the extremes of men's loving and hating. But man's passions overwhelm him because his imagination "misinforms" the heart, "misconceiving or amplifying" an "object to be known" (I.2.3.1;252), and before Burton shows the passions at work, he digresses to show the effects of such misinformation:

Of which imagination, because it hath so great a stroke in producing this malady, and is so powerful of itself, it will not be improper to my discourse to make a brief digression, and speak of the force of it, and how it causeth this alteration. Which manner of digression howsoever some dislike, as frivolous and impertinent, yet I am of Beroaldus his opinion, "Such digressions do mightily delight and refresh a weary reader, they are like sauce to a bad stomach, and I do therefore most willingly use them." (I.2.3.1;253)

The Digression of the Force of Imagination is, as Burton says here, delightful, but it is also, and primarily, pertinent to his discourse of how men turn their minds over to passion's control. It is thus, "like sauce to a bad stomach," an important part of the meal we consume in this section of causes—important, we shall discover, for its ability not only to refresh us, but to make us taste and see the full course dinner laid out in the *Anatomy*, digressions and all. Burton often refers to the delightfulness of his digressions, but seldom without, as here, also implying that they are "not improper" to the broadest meaning of his systematic perusal of melancholy, and the pertinence of that systematic perusal to our full understanding of his book, with its covert structure of digressions intermingled with the overt structure of Partitions I and II.

Burton has already "sufficiently declared" what imagination is, and he is content now to "point at the wonderful effects and power" of the fantasy (I.2.3.2;

253) by telling tales of what "we see verified" daily in
men's lives, that men live by making fiction into fact.
Remember the people you have seen or heard about,
Burton says, who have lain choking because they
thought witches pressed down on them (p. 253), who
have borne monstrous children because of monstrous
fantasies (p. 255), who have died of plague from thinking of plague (p. 256). All around us, men are over-
whelmed by falsehood.

We see commonly the toothache, gout, falling sickness, biting
of a mad dog, and many such maladies cured by spells,
words, characters, and charms, and many green wounds by
that now so much used *unguentum armarium* magnetically
cured. . . . All the world knows there is no virtue in such
charms or cures, but a strong conceit and opinion alone, as
Pompanatius holds, "which forceth a motion of the humours,
spirits, and blood, which takes away the cause of the malady
from the parts affected." The like we may say of our magical
effects, superstitious cures, and such as are done by mountebanks and wizards. "As by wicked incredulity many men are
hurt" (so saith Wierus of charms, spells, etc.), "we find in our
experience, by the same means many are relieved." An
empiric oftentimes, and a silly chirurgeon, doth more strange
cures than a rational physician.   (Pp. 256-257)

Cures work, but they work although they should not
work. What is not true in fact becomes, in fact, true; and
all of this because men believe what is not so.
    Living is the stuff of fairy tale and fable, for the truth
is twofold: men believe what is not, or may not be, so;
and what is not so can have very real effects: "Some will
laugh, weep, sigh, groan, blush, tremble, sweat, at such
things as are suggested unto them by their imagination," while others get palsy or stigmata, mimic birds or
become beasts, or undergo other "famous transforma-

tions" by the force of imagination (p. 255). For Burton, however, the objective truth of stigmata and were-wolves is only a secondary matter; rather, it is important that men change themselves or believe themselves changed by force of "absurd and prodigious things" (p. 253). Fact and fiction are a wonderful hodgepodge, and we must all agree on that, from common experience: "as he falsely imagineth, so he believeth; and as he conceiveth of it, so it must be, and it shall be, *contra gentes*, he will have it so" (p. 254).

At the beginning of the digression we are reminded that Burton has defined imagination in the Digression of Anatomy, and we remember that this "inner sense which doth more fully examine the species perceived by common sense" differentiates, being the highest power of the sensible soul, men from beasts: "In men it is subject and governed by reason, or at least should be; but in brutes it hath no superior, and is *ratio brutorum*, all the reason they have" (I.1.2.7;159-160). The Digression of the Force of Imagination, however, shows through its stories all the events of men's lives ruled by the absurd imaginings of their "unapt, hindered, and hurt" fantasies: "Some ascribe all vices to a false and corrupt imagination, anger, revenge, lust, ambition, covetousness, which prefers falsehood before that which is right and good, deluding the soul with false shows and suppositions" (I.2.3.2;254). Burton constructs a picture of life in general based on and growing out of falsehood rather than out of the "right and good." Conception and birth are ruled by fantasy: an Ethiopian princess bears a "fair white child"; a Pope's concubine is "brought to bed of a monster"; and if these appear too farfetched, "Great-bellied women, when they long, yield prodigious examples in this kind, as moles, warts, scars, harelips, monsters, especially caused in their children by force of depraved imagination" (p. 254-255). Not only are we moved to "laugh, weep, sigh, groan, blush, tremble, sweat" by our imagination, but we make ourselves sick, we cure ourselves, we kill ourselves by means of an overwhelming fantasy. We are as monstrous as we think we are, and so, for a whole lifetime, we are not what we should be, rational men.

Generally speaking, mankind has this disease—an unnatural love of misinformation that necessarily affects the nature of man. The stories point out this general force of imagination that cannot be denied because it is everywhere. And so does Burton's conclusion. He has used anecdote and authority; he ends with a stream of questions which are rhetorical and therefore really statements, having only one answer implicit in them— Burton's answer, which must also be ours as it is that of the authorities:

So diversely doth this phantasy of ours affect, turn, and wind, so imperiously command our bodies, which "as another Proteus, or a chameleon, can take all shapes; and is of such force" (as Ficinus adds), "that it can work upon others as well as ourselves." How can otherwise blear eyes in one man cause the like affection in another? Why doth one man's yawning make another yawn? one man's pissing provoke a second many times to do the like? Why doth scraping of trenchers offend a third, or hacking of files? Why doth a carcass bleed when the murderer is brought before it, some weeks after the murder hath been done? Why do witches and old women fascinate and bewitch children? but as Wierus, Paracelsus, Cardan, Mizaldus, Valleriola, Caesar Vaninus, Campanella, and many philosophers think, the forcible imagination of the one party moves and alters the spirits of the other . . . So that I may certainly conclude this strong conceit or imagination is *astrum hominis*, and the rudder of this our ship, which reason should steer, but overborne by phantasy, cannot manage, and so suffers itself and this whole vessel of ours to be overruled, and often overturned.   (P. 257)

You can read, he says, more elsewhere; but we need no more to understand the extent to which a "strong conceit" underlies the mind's malfunctions.

The definition of much of what man is—the Digressions of Anatomy and of the Nature of Spirits have shown us—is tentative, questionable, because all facts are not material and provable, and even material facts are open to question. Yet whether or not we understand ourselves philosophically, we have to know what we are well enough to act as men in daily life. That kind of self-knowledge, at least, is vital to our nature. But the Digression of the Force of Imagination shows us that it is our nature constantly to get things, and ourselves, all confused: we pervert our "good parts and profitable gifts" by "misinforming our hearts" and by believing, all the world to the contrary, what is not true. Thus if—as the sections on the non-natural things declare— we have continually to take care to be ourselves rather than corrupt images of humanity, nonetheless—the digression relentlessly documents—we forcibly metamorphose the nature of rational man into the freakishness of absurd men who substitute imagination for reason, fiction for life. The Digression of Anatomy was intended to stir us up to wonder how a man differs from a dog; this digression confirms that we do not ordinarily care to differentiate ourselves from the beasts whose only "reason" is imagination.

In the thirteen subsections which follow, Burton enumerates the perturbations of the mind, but the digression has discovered the root of the problem in those sometimes violent, sometimes merely vexing misapprehensions which destroy man's nature in that they make him follow his sensible rather than his rational soul. Natural and non-natural are not so distinct as that introduction to the non-natural things suggested. For if the "physician objects to us" that we offend in extremes of passions, we must see that we have been denying our humanity by ignoring reason in favor of fancy. Joy and anger, emulation and jealousy affect man through that imagination which misinforms his heart, and he mistakes himself—he is not what he should be—when he mistakes fact and fiction, so that, "*contra gentes*, he will have it so" when it is not so.

It is man's responsibility to mark out a way of living which makes of his "many good parts and profitable gifts" a workable union; yet as he must use body and mind, it would seem, he will abuse them, abandoning moderation in favor of intemperance: this is the essence of members 2 and 3 of the causes of melancholy. But the digression at the beginning of member 3 interrupts the orderly catalogue of physical and mental intemperance to suggest a kind of fantastic influence of non-natural on natural, putting the extremes of passion into a context of lifelong denial of human nature through man's tendency to make fiction the fact of life. And Burton concludes the member with the Digression of the Misery of Scholars, and Why the Muses are Melancholy—a digression which shows that misinformation is not only the cause of passion-ruled behavior in individual men, but also the result when such behavior affects, as it must do, the social organization of men. Burton diagnoses, in this digression, society's abuses of its good parts and profitable gifts, for scholars are the mind, the rational faculty, of the social body (or at least they should be), but corporate man is as irresponsible for the well-being of his reason as are individuals:

But our patrons of learning are so far nowadays from respecting the Muses, and giving that honour to scholars, or reward, which they deserve and are allowed by those indulgent privileges of many noble princes, that after all their pains taken in the universities, cost and charge, expenses, irksome hours, laborious tasks, wearisome days, dangers, hazards, (barred interim from all pleasures which other men have, mewed up like hawks all their lives), if they chance to wade through them, they shall in the end be rejected, contemned, and, which is their greatest misery, driven to their shifts, exposed to want, poverty, and beggary.   (P. 305)

The world itself, Burton has said within the treatise, "is a maze, a labyrinth of errors, a desert, a wilderness, a den of thieves, cheaters, etc." (I.2.3.10;274), because men are made by Care, and so discontents and miseries are "an inseparable accident to all men" (I.2.3.10:271-272). The misery spoken of in the digression, however, is not accidental to men, but is caused by men and happens to all Man. Burton sets out to blame men for the injury they do to the nature of society. Two judgments of scholars, diametrically opposed in tone, mark the limits of this digression, and the differences between them indicate the distinctions between cure of the ordinary disease and the difficulties facing the physician who would treat the very soul of mankind.

As physician of the ordinary disease, Burton knows leniency; just before departing on his digression, he speaks of scholars who get melancholy by neglecting the care of "that instrument (their brain and spirits I mean) which they daily use" (I.2.3.15;302). Yet they are endearing men, and the judgment is kind.

> Your greatest students are commonly no better, silly, soft fellows in their outward behavior, absurd, ridiculous to others, and no whit experienced in worldly business; they can measure the heavens, range over the world, teach others wisdom, and yet in bargains and contracts they are circumvented by every base tradesman . . . To say the best of this profession, I can give no other testimony of them in general, than that of Pliny of Isaeus: "He is yet a scholar, than which kind of men there is nothing so simple, so sincere, none better"; they are most part harmless, honest, upright, innocent, plain-dealing men.   (P. 304)

But with the next sentence Burton is off on his digression, and as judge of the community he bars no holds. The digression leaps from judgment on patrons, through blame hurled this way and that, to a final long condemnation of academicians and clergy, so violent that Burton will not English it. We cannot avoid juxtaposing that loving sentence on scholars with the concluding lines of the digression:

> But I will stir up these foul waters no more. Hence our tears, hence it is that the Muses are in mourning, and that religion itself, as Sesellius says, is brought into ridicule and contempt, and the clerical calling is rendered vile. And in view of these facts, I venture to repeat the abusive expressions which some vulgar fellow has applied to the clergy, that they are a rotten crowd, beggarly, uncouth, filthy, melancholy, miserable, despicable, and contemptible.   (P. 330, Jackson's translation)

Society's faults, like those of individuals, result from the skewing of the order of things. With patrons and scholars, it is a question of the first being last and the last first, even when that is not the morally just order. Scholars "prostitute themselves" to great men, who "have their best education, good institutions, sole quali-fication from us, and when they have done well, their honour and immortality from us . . . They are more beholden to scholars, than scholars to them; but they undervalue themselves, and so by those great men are kept down" (p. 308). "Poverty is the Muses' patrimony" (p. 309); by it men are animals, and asses themselves (p. 306), they make of knowledge a mere beast of burden: "for being as they are, their 'rhetoric only serves them to curse their bad fortunes,' and many of them, for want of means, are driven to hard shifts; from grasshoppers they turn bumble-bees and wasps, plain parasites, and make the Muses mules, to satisfy their hunger-starved paunches and get a meal's meat" (p. 307). Thus an order which puts the important things last degrades them *really*. Knowledge ceases to be art; it is the basis still of ways of life—of professions—but only in that it is bastardized. It is misinformation at the heart of society, its ends but fictional fantastic versions of the true objects of study: "he that can tell his money hath arithmetic enough: he is a true geometrician, can measure out a good fortune to himself; a perfect astrologer, that can cast the rise and fall of others, and mark their errant motions to his own use. The best optics are, to reflect the beams of some great men's favour and grace to shine upon him" (p. 309).

Such conditions call for satire, and the digression seems at first headed in that direction. But as much as Burton blames in this digression, he does not fix blame finally. He points to scholars' poverty and he condemns patrons. He points to "all-devouring municipal laws" and to "mountebanks, empirics, quacksalvers" (p. 310), and he condemns law and medicine. Then he points to divinity.

In the beginning of the digression, Burton has kept his customary distance from the ills he describes. He blames from outside any group: patrons and scholars, both are "they." If Burton has a position within the picture he is presenting, it is the unspecified position of a member of the community.

> . . . we can make mayors and officers every year, but not scholars: kings can invest knights and barons, as Sigismund the emperor confessed; universities can give degrees; . . . but he, nor they, nor all the world, can give learning, make philosophers, artists, orators, poets. We can soon say, as Seneca well notes, *O virum bonum! o divitem!* point at a rich man, a good, a happy man, a prosperous man; . . . but 'tis not so easily performed to find out a learned man.   (Pp. 305-306)

He has set up both patrons' scorn and scholars' plight while standing aside: scholars, the story goes, were once grasshoppers, "and may be turned again, . . . for any reward I see they are like to have" (p. 307). But he is soon drawn into the dispute. Without warning, "they"—scholars—become "us," and "they" are the opposition: "They are like Indians, they have store of gold, but know not the worth of it; . . . they have their best education, good institutions, sole qualification from us, and when they have done well, their honour and immortality from us" (p. 308). Burton is involved in the miserable state of things he is describing, and he is involved as a partisan. From now on in the digression, whenever "they" refers to scholar-divines, it refers to "us," for Burton is one of them. And so when he points to divines, he cannot blame objectively as he did with patrons, lawyers, and doctors. He lets a "reverend bishop of this land" point out the distress of ministers for him, and then he calls his fellows to arms:

> If this be all the respect, reward and honour we shall have, . . . let us give over our books, and betake ourselves to some other course of life. To what end should we study? . . . If there be no more hope of reward, no better encouragement, I say again, . . . let's turn soldiers, sell our books and buy swords, guns, and pikes, or stop bottles with them, turn our philosophers' gowns, as Cleanthes once did, into miller's coats, leave all, and rather betake ourselves to any other course of life than to continue longer in this misery.
> (P. 312)

He cannot be a satirist; he has not got the distance. Instead, Burton speaking as a divine is moved by the same desires—extreme desires—which move the other men and groups of men whom he judges. He cries out for respect, reward, and honor; he bemoans lack of preferment. He is being a true divine in the same way that "he is a true geometrician, can measure out a good fortune to himself." Divinity is distorted by his complaint as those other studies of optics and engineering are distorted by men who "apply themselves in all haste" to getting reward, "rejecting these arts in the meantime."

Burton wants us to see the distortion in himself as well as in those he condemns. The digression lasts too long, gets bogged down in its accusations, hedges about admissions of guilt by adding too many qualifications, by mixing in too many excuses:

> That there is a fault among us, I confess, and were there not a buyer, there would not be a seller: but to him that will

consider better of it, it will more manifestly appear that the fountain of these miseries proceeds from these griping patrons. In accusing them I do not altogether excuse us; both are faulty, they and we: yet in my judgment, theirs is the greater fault . . . For my part, if it be not with me as I would, or as it should, I do ascribe the cause . . . to my own infelicity rather than their naughtiness: although I have been baffled in my time by some of them, and have as just cause to complain as another: or rather indeed to mine own negligence. (P. 313)

Condemnation is diluted throughout the digression because this voice proclaiming evils does not represent good and reasoned right. It is a self-interested voice, complaining of its hurts.

The digression wears on. Burton condemns rich men for perpetuating their prime faults of covetousness and ignorance, and he is never far from bitter contempt—as when he cites the eagle in Aesop who destroyed her own nest and young by her pilfering: "Let our simoniacal church-chopping patrons and sacrilegious harpies look for no better success" (p. 316). But responsibility for the state of things becomes harder to pin down as he gets more involved in watching his step.

Yet oftentimes, I may not deny it, the main fault is in ourselves. Our academics too frequently offend in neglecting patrons, as Erasmus well taxeth, or making ill choice of them . . . So some offend in one extreme, but too many on the other, we are most part too forward, too solicitous, too ambitious, too impudent; we commonly complain . . . of want of encouragement, want of means, whenas the true defect is in our want of worth, our insufficiency . . . *So we offend, but the main fault is in their harshness,* defect of patrons.   (Pp. 318-319; my italics)

He begins to be repetitious: "Let me not be malicious, . . . I may not deny but that we have a sprinkling of our

gentry, here and there one, excellently well learned. . . .
Mistake me not (I say again) . . . you that are worthy
senators" (p. 320). He knows his worth, knows he is
being tiresome in defending it, but has to go on: "*I have
not yet said*. If after long expectation . . . we obtain a
small benefice at last, our misery begins afresh; we are
suddenly encountered with the flesh, world, and devil"
(p. 323; my italics). Burton exemplifies, through his own
voice as well as through what he says about other men,
that the true misery of scholars is not poverty and stingy
patrons, but the mess that is made of knowledge by the
prostitution of the profession of scholarship. He shows
us how scholars have to be what they are not, self-
seekers burning themselves out in the search for preferment rather than voices of reason guiding men by the
"fair light" of true knowledge. And it is no small part of
the misery of scholars that a scholar cannot with a
simple knowledge of right challenge wrong.

The digression is "Of the Misery of Scholars, and
Why the Muses are Melancholy." Knowledge itself is
sick and bears ill-formed, misbegotten monsters. As
imagination ruling in individual men breeds ugliness,
confusion, and false nature, where reason would breed
truth, so when scholars look not for truth but for
position, then universities produce philosophasters and
theologasters, society itself is misgoverned, knowledge
is a fiction, scholarship but quackery.

I say this is the fault of all of us, and especially those of us who
belong to a university. It is we who are the ultimate cause of
the evils under which the State is labouring. We have actually
introduced these evils ourselves, though there is no reproach
and no suffering we do not deserve for not having used all our
might to oppose them. . . . Hence it comes that such a pack of

vile buffoons, ignoramuses wandering in the twilight of learning, ghosts of clergymen, itinerant quacks, dolts, clods, asses, mere cattle, intrude with unwashed feet upon the sacred precincts of Theology, bringing with them nothing save brazen impudence, and some hackneyed quillets and scholastic trifles not good enough for a crowd at a street corner.   (Pp. 327-328, Jackson's translation)

The tone has changed, for Burton's position has changed; he is now speaking to his fellow scholar-divines in Latin. Being one of them, he knows their part in the state of things, and looking sharply on them, he can blame—but blame them only in their own eyes, not in the vernacular and in view of the world, not absolutely. The position has changed, but he is not yet freed from the working of the opposition between "us" and "them." If he castigates instead of complaining, if he has reassumed the role of diagnostician of ills, we continue to see the symptoms *in* as well as *through* him, in the extreme abuse he hurls but coyly, so that learned men only may understand. The digression ends with the Muses in mourning for their children because true knowledge is condemned and oppressed while false show is praised and preferred. Through the workings of society, men together live by false knowledge, just as they depend, as individuals, on imagination's misinformation for guidance.

The digression closes the discourse on the non-natural things, and in doing so concludes a major step in Burton's process of modifying his subject by pertinent digression. From ordinary melancholy caused by overeating and lack of sleep, we have come to melancholy of the Muses caused by the disregard of knowledge. At the beginning of the discourse on the six non-natural things as causes of material melancholy, Burton called attention to the "proposed method" which would govern it. In the middle he digressed and called attention to the fact that he had some pertinent things to say which the method did not allow for. In the end he digressed expansively on a topic not at all inherent in the method, and he did not make any motion of apology for turning aside. (It is not unimportant that this seemingly most parenthetical of digressions is the only major one not carrying any apologetics: Burton gives only the formal notice of the digression in the synopsis—"Love of learning, study in excess, with a digression of the misery of scholars, and why the Muses are melancholy"—and that, with similar wording, in the subsection heading.) And having finished his discourse, he again calls attention to method as he prepares for a new topic, but only in order to say that the method cannot truly rule his treatise, that it is being used despite its inadequacy:

Of those remote, outward, ambient, necessary causes, I have sufficiently discoursed in the precedent member. The non-necessary follow; of which, saith Fuchsius, *no art can be made*, by reason of their uncertainty, casualty, and multitude; so called "not necessary" because, according to Fernelius, "they may be avoided, and used without necessity." *Many of these accidental causes, which I shall entreat of here, might have well been reduced to the former*, because they cannot be avoided, but fatally happen to us, though accidentally and unawares, at some time or other: the rest are contingent and inevitable, and more properly inserted in this rank of causes.   (I.2.4.1;330; my italics)

Out of the general malfunctioning of mankind, elucidated by Burton in the Digressions of the Force of Imagination and of the Miseries of Scholars, there grows a general detestation of knowledge itself, out of every man's diseased self a universal social corruption of truth. Illness may begin in extremes of action and emotion, but those extremes themselves begin with fiction imagined as fact, and they end in man as a corporate being officially applauding quackery and veiling truth in obscurity while the Muses mourn.

KNOWLEDGE AS ANSWER: CURE

Digression in Partition I of the *Anatomy* qualifies man's ability to define and to state facts about causes and effects, and makes the study of ordinary disease relevant to a study of studies—to questions about the place of knowledge in life. And in Partition II, where Burton examines the cures of ordinary disease, he allows digression to turn question into answer and to suggest ways of living which define right knowledge. The great digressions of Partition II respond to the questions presented through the preceding digressions. What is true knowledge and what are its ends?—the Digression of the Air sweeps the height and breadth of curiosity, awakening the mind to the possibilities of questions about outside objects to be known and providing an answer which is not the fiction of *ratio brutorum*. And what does right living from day to day involve?—the Consolatory Digression, containing the Remedies of all manner of Discontents, is an epitome of wisdom which predicates reason as a way of life.

Cure of melancholy is cure of more than melancholy:

So that in a word I may say to most melancholy men, . . . the six non-natural things caused it, and they must cure it. Which howsoever I treat of as proper to the meridian of melancholy, yet nevertheless, that which is here said, with him in Tully, though writ especially for the good of his friends at Tarentum and Sicily, yet it will generally serve most other diseases, and help them likewise, if it be observed.   (II.2.1.1;22)

The book of cures is proper to more than its own subject, and by digression, once again from the material core of the six non-natural things, the order comprehends more than its nature as medical treatise would allow, and the system is closed by enclosing more than the proper boundaries could surround.

The Digression of the Air heralds both an escape from and a confirmation of the form and substance of Burton's discourse. We start, predictably, with the often quoted passage wherein Burton declares his intention to rove:

As a long-winged hawk, when he is first whistled off the fist, mounts aloft, and for his pleasure fetcheth many a circuit in the air, still soaring higher and higher till he be come to his full pitch, and in the end when the game is sprung, comes down amain, and stoops upon a sudden: so will I, having now come at last into these ample fields of air, wherein I may freely expatiate and exercise myself for my recreation, awhile rove, wander round the world, mount aloft to those ethereal orbs and celestial spheres, and so descend to my former elements again.   (II.2.3;34-35)

But we have to notice two things. First, of course, that it is by reference to his discourse that Burton gets where he is going: "The logic of the structure of his book had brought him to the point where he was to consider the effect of air and climate upon the constitution, and with some relief he relaxes from the close work of dissection and roams at will in the exciting air of speculation."[5] "Relaxes" is perhaps not quite the word for so exhausting an exercise as the Digression of the Air, but certainly Burton starts on his exploration by pushing off from the realities of form and matter. It is his simile that lets him put the digression here; the substantial fields of air through which he roams are elusive questions about physical realities, and so he puts aside for a moment the rectification of elemental air and the opportunity to discuss climate and geography as they affect cure of material melancholy. The medical treatise becomes a hunt, the hawk's flight a voyage; the voyage is itself metaphorical, seeing is believing—and all because the "thing" that is air is ample, almost unbounded. By playing with words, with "air," Burton grounds his discourse on speculation in the discourse on material disease.

Further, we have to see that it is by reference to his digression that Burton gets back to his discourse. If the circuits he fetches are for pleasure, mounting aloft is nonetheless the necessary prelude to stooping. Burton does not digress *from* Air Rectified; he digresses to get to it: "and *so* descend to my former elements again." He lets metaphorical air lead him to real air and to cures for ordinary melancholy. But that is answer, and we have first to look at the questions.

The digression is composed of questions. There is barely an independent indicative mood, hardly a simple statement in the long progress of inquiring and suppos-

5. F. P. Wilson, *Elizabethan and Jacobean* (Oxford: Clarendon Press, 1945), p. 10.

ing. Even the context of the digression is the simile, which is an hypothesis. Like a hawk, I will rove; and as I rove, I will see if I can tell: whether, how, why. And if I find one thing, then I would see the next. Burton's is the flight of fancy, but this fancy is about subjecting objects to reason, for the questions that make up the digression are questions about questions of knowledge.

The digression is only secondarily about the magnetic field, climatology, the center of the earth, or the arrangement of the heavens. Primarily it is about opinions and what men will have to be.

In which progress I will first see whether that relation of the friar of Oxford be true, concerning those northern parts under the Pole . . . whether there be four such euripes, and a great rock of loadstones, which may cause the needle in the compass still to bend that way, and what should be the true cause of the variation of the compass; is it a magnetical rock, or the polestar, as Cardan will; or some other star in the Bear, as Marsilius Ficinus; or a magnetical meridian, as Maurolicus; *vel situs in vena terrae,* as Agricola; or the nearness of the next continent, as Cabeus will; or some other cause, as Scaliger, Cortesius, *Conimbricenses,* Peregrinus contend?   (II.2.3;35)

With the simile of the hawk Burton says that he will "wander round about the world," but from the moment the flight begins we see that he is looking down on the human mind. It is not mere accident that the friar is "of Oxford" in the first thesis of the digression. The place of the maker of opinion is as specified as the place of opinion's object, for the thinker is thinking about thinkers thinking. One primary answer or "cure" for lack of, or disorder in, human knowledge that Burton will elucidate through his digressions will be the community of scholarship that allows all knowledge, all opinion—contrary or otherwise—to come together into a compendium of truths which can be stated, even if they cannot be capitalized into abstract, perfect Truth. And the Digression of the Air first leads us toward this cure by locating *place where*, the focus of the digression, in mind questioning rather than in the question itself or in the truth of any opinion.

Thus Burton is the center of the digression: "The actual voyage of discovery is only apparently through the sensible world. Actually the voyage is inward, through the fantastic worlds the imagination creates" (Colie, p. 453). But the voyage, I think, *appears* to be inward, does not even seem to be one through the "sensible world." For one thing, the grammatical mood of the digression, as I have suggested, is largely interrogative, subjunctive, seldom indicative, so that one rarely has the feeling of being shown anything. Always we read: " 'Tis fit to be inquired whether . . ."; "I would examine . . ."; "Is it the sea that causeth . . . ?" Statement comes in the form of testimony of what is thought and written: "The philosophers of Coimbra will refer this diversity . . ."; "It is much controverted . . ."; ". . . he makes the earth as before the universal centre." Things are written somewhere or have been read in such a book. Statement is the expression of unsolved controversy. Never do we look down on the sensible world without the questioning mind that avoids the indicative mood interposed between us and experiential "reality." There is no appearance of fact in the Digression of the Air, but only the fact of question. Foremost in the digression is always the *I*—thinking about knowing, if it were possible.

Burton feints a development in his "progress" from the inside to the outside of the sensible universe. From poles to planets, he would know. But the progress, while giving a geographical reference to the questions, does not really make of the digression an armchair voyage, for the simple reason that what is being "seen" is opinion, which cannot be realized as "sensible" perception, even with the imagination. There are moments of travelogue-like description, in which political and geographical boundaries function, as when the regions of Spain are enumerated to exemplify the curious fact that "we find great diversity of air in the same country, by reason of the site to seas, hills, or dales, want of water, nature of soil, and the like" (p. 45). But the progress itself more often deliberately defies the arrangements of geography: in a passage typical of the digression's "world" of unbounded thought, questions about similarities and dissimilarities of climate pile Norembega, New England, the "island of Cambriol Colchis," "Little Britain in France," the Arctic Circle, Hungary, and Ireland all together in one extended sentence (p. 44).

Burton's progress is thus more a cogitative than a spatial one, from questions about things under the earth, to questions about infinite worlds, to questions about God's daily regimen—a progression actually from what is more potentially knowable to what is less open to answer. He moves from "I would see" and "I would examine" (phoenix, pelican, and pyramid, hibernating men, and ships buried in mountains) to why and how are climates differentiated, the heavens irregular. He gets further removed from certainty as his wings carry him from mundane experience to the heavens of astronomical theory and conjecture:

If the heavens then be penetrable, as these men deliver, and no lets, it were not amiss in this aerial progress to make wings and fly up, . . . or if that may not be, yet with a Galileo's glass, or Icaromenippus' wings in Lucian, command the spheres and heavens, and see what is done amongst them. Whether there be generation and corruption, as some think, by reason of ethereal comets, that in Cassiopea, 1572, that in Cygnus, 1600, that in Sagittarius, 1604, and many like. . . . Whether the stars be of that bigness, distance, as astronomers relate, so many in number? . . . Whether the least visible star in the eighth sphere be eighteen times bigger than the earth? . . . Whether they be thicker parts of the orbs?   (Pp. 50-51)

Burton basks in the multiplicity of "whethers" as he progresses from theory to theory. Even his delight in the absurdity of the theorists' posture cannot dampen his enthusiasm for question.

In the meantime, the world is tossed in a blanket amongst them, they hoist the earth up and down like a ball, make it stand and go at their pleasures: one saith the sun stands, another he moves; a third comes in, taking them all at rebound, and lest there should any paradox be wanting, he finds certain spots and clouds in the sun, by the help of glasses, which multiply (saith Keplerus) a thing seen a thousand times bigger *in plano*, and makes it come thirty-two times nearer to the eye of the beholder. . . . Fabricius puts only three, and those in the sun: Apelles fifteen, and those without the sun.   (P. 57)

But theory and question about outside objects to be known, be they pyramids or comets, can lead past reason to uncontrolled fantasy, and the progress ends with Burton seeing the monstrous questions of "these gigantical Cyclopes" who will "soar higher yet, and see what God himself doth":

Some, by visions and revelations, take upon them to be familiar with God, and to be of privy council with Him; they will tell how many, and who, shall be saved, when the world shall come to an end, what year, what month, and whatsoever else God hath reserved unto Himself, and to His angels. Some again, curious phantastics, will know more than this, and inquire with Epicurus, what God did before the world was made? was He idle? Where did He bide? What did He make the world of? Why did He then make it, and not before? (Pp. 58-59)

Burton's digressive flight teaches that speculation is potentially nonsense if it gets outside all boundaries of the knowledge with which men should be concerned. Fantasy, not reason, makes men want to answer questions reserved to God.

Still, the aim of a progress composed of questions has to be answer. "I would know" is the point of the flight, the end of reasonable question. And the long hypothetical view of all kinds of theory answers, in a way, the questions about human knowledge which Burton has been asking through this and the preceding digressions. The first answer is implicit in Burton's epitome of theories, the obvious answer of doubt. Where do the birds go in winter?—"I conclude of them all, for my part, as Munster doth of cranes and storks; whence they come, whither they go, *incompertum adhuc*, as yet we know not" (p. 38). When one man wills one answer and another wills another, the judicious man simply continues to wonder: "I will end the controversy in Austin's words, 'Better doubt of things concealed, than to contend about uncertainties, where Abraham's bosom is, and hell-fire'; . . . scarce the meek, the contentious shall never find" (p. 42). Burton's benignant skepticism that underlies the tone of this digression lets him enjoy the spectacle of blanket-tossing while he savors the extent to which, because his flight is fanciful, answer is bound to be elusive. Is the earth full of wind?—"Let Lucian's Menippus consult with or ask of Tiresias, if you will not believe philosophers; he shall clear all doubts when he makes a second voyage" (p. 43). The *a priori* answer to "If it be possible" is, after all, in terms of the hypothetical imaginary voyage, "But it is not possible."

Yet skepticism tempered by delight in theory is not the only answer to Burton's "I would know," for the flight is an *arrangement* of knowledge. Burton works with and characterizes theories and questions; he estimates their worth. And so, point of view in this digression is not only a source of question, but a part of the answer. If, *a priori*, it is not possible to know the final answer, there is nonetheless an element of answer in seeing the possibilities, in knowing theories and asking reasonable questions. In the progress from the more to the less potentially knowable, the questions are all "seen" by the *I*, and "(I say)" must be, from our viewpoint, the expression of one who understands.

The causes of these alterations are commonly by reason of their nearness (I say) to the middle region.   (P. 45)

. . . .

But *hoc posito*, to grant this their tenent of the earth's motion: if the earth moves, it is a planet. . . . Then (I say) the earth and they be planets alike, inhabited alike, moved about the sun, the common center of the world alike, and it may be those two green children which Nubrigensis speaks of came from thence.   (Pp. 53-54)

Burton does not commit himself to a view of the universe; he would rather doubt of things concealed and wait with the meek to know truth when it is told. In seeing him question, however, we see him thoroughly explore the "knowledge" which is other men's reasoning: "But this reason is weak and most insufficient"; "Clavius conjectures otherwise, but they be but conjectures" (pp. 46-47). He analyzes the relationships of theories: "Tycho will have two distinct matters of heaven and air; but to say truth, with some small qualification, they have one and the self-same opinion about the essence and matter of heavens" (p. 49); "Howsoever, it is revised since by Copernicus, not as a truth, but a supposition, as he himself confesseth, . . . but now maintained in good earnest by Calcagninus, Telesius, Kepler, Rotman, Gilbert, Digges, Galileo, Campanella, and especially by Lansbergius" (p. 52).

Burton not being contentious, the flat judgments and personal intrusions are few, but they remain important in that they uphold man's ability to know something. He can know the theories and know, as a man, when he sees other men go astray. Through him we see the stupidity of theologasters who would assign part of God's day for playing with Leviathan (p. 58). He is authority working with authorities; through him we see that hypothesis can be laughably vain: "But to avoid these paradoxes of the earth's motion . . . our latter mathematicians have rolled all the stones that may be stirred: and to solve all appearances and objections, have invented new hypotheses, and fabricated new systems of the world, out of their own Daedalian heads" (p. 56). And through him we see that hypothesis—inconclusive but reasonable "*hoc posito*"—can be useful when we understand it as possibility, as "no otherwise" than imagined fact which can work in helping us understand outside objects. Burton exemplifies man knowing what can be known when he sees in theory workable truth:

Tycho Brahe, Nicholas Ramerus, Helisaeus Roeslin, have *peculiar hypotheses of their own inventions;* and *they be but inventions,* as most of them acknowledge, as we admit of equators, tropics, colures, circles arctic and antarctic, *for doctrine's sake* (though Ramus thinks them all unnecessary), *they will have them supposed only for method and order.* Tycho hath feigned I know not how many epicycles in epicycles, etc., to calculate and express the moon's motion: *but when all is done, as a supposition, and no otherwise;* not (as he holds) hard, impenetrable, subtile, transparent, etc., or making music, as Pythagoras maintained of old, and Robert Constantine of late, but still quiet, liquid, open, etc.   (P. 50; my italics)

As we see Burton seeing, we understand that each opinion in itself—what any particular man wills to be so—is not knowledge; but Burton has a kind of knowledge because through his judging mind, all men's ideas about outside objects are subjected to reason. In him particular opinion becomes common knowledge, known possibility.

Nonetheless, the Digression of the Air ends in not knowing, or in knowing what is impossible to know. There is the absolute boundary of curiosity, which is God. Burton's oft-quoted "But hoo!" has to be put in context, for it is not simply good-natured amusement with his own far-out flight, but a stand which gives man a firm position in regard to knowing. Men "prodigiously inquire," he says:

If God be infinitely and only good, why should He alter or

destroy the world? . . . If He pull it down because evil, how shall He be free from the evil that made it evil? etc., with many such absurd and brain-sick questions, intricacies, froth of human wit, and excrements of curiosity, etc., which, as our Saviour told His inquisitive disciples, are not fit for them to know. But hoo! I am now gone quite out of sight, I am almost giddy with roving about: I could have ranged farther yet, but I am an infant, and not able to dive into these profundities or sound these depths, not able to understand, much less to discuss. I leave the contemplation of these things to stronger wits, that have better ability and happier leisure to wade into such philosophical mysteries; for put case I were as able as willing, yet what can one man do?   (Pp. 59-60)

The last answer is conservative, but it is only conservative by way of the long flight: about all of this we can ask, about all of this we can want to know, of all of this we can judge. Then, "He reveals and conceals to whom and when He will." And finally, from all times, places, facts, and theories, Burton has come back to *this* knowledge, the *Anatomy of Melancholy*.

The final answer flushes out the game: "so kingdoms, men, and knowledge ebb and flow, are hid and revealed, and when you have all done, as the Preacher concluded, *Nihil est sub sole novum*. But my melancholy spaniel's quest, my game, is sprung, and I must suddenly come down and follow" (pp. 60-61).

What can one man do to know? He can follow the melancholy spaniel's quest; he can go back to his "game," to the form and substance of the discourse. If all were absolute not-knowing, then Burton would have nowhere to go. There would be no point in judging possibilities, and the "But hoo!" would speak his final estimation of the giddy roving represented by the Digression of the Air. But the digression is, finally, answer made of question, in that the exploratory progress through the realm of curiosity goes past the froth of human wit with its brain-sick questions, to end in the *Anatomy*. There is possibility here, and workable knowledge: "As a long-winged hawk . . . in the end when the game is sprung, comes down amain, and stoops upon a sudden: so will I . . . descend to my former elements again." Burton does not flop to the earth; he stoops to the game. He turns back to the framework of this *hoc posito*, working with his facts, suggesting cure. And because of digression, the framework itself is part of the cure: following the spaniel's quest is answering what can be answered in terms of what men can know. The "new science" of the *Anatomy* does not come in the form of Burton's acceptance of new cosmological theories; he is not modern in that sense. Instead he is modern in Chaucer's sense, extracting new knowledge from old authors, gaining not new certainty of things never before understood, but fruitful questions and hypotheses which are the source of human knowledge.

"What can one man do?" Burton asks, and he concludes with Scaliger that "we are not whole men, but parts of men; from all of us together something might be made and that not much; from each of us individually nothing" (p. 60, Jackson's translation). When he goes back to his "former elements," the medical treatise, he goes back by way of authority, emphatically getting his "new science" at two removes by learning from "old books."

Jason Pratensis, in his book, *de morbis capitis*, and chapter of melancholy, *hath these words out of Galen*, "Let them come to me to know what meat and drink they shall use, and besides that, I will teach them what temper of ambient air they shall make choice of, what wind, what countries they shall choose, and what avoid." *Out of which lines of his thus much we may gather*, that to this cure of melancholy, amongst other things, the rectification of air is necessarily required.   (P. 61; my italics)

With the end of the Digression of the Air—with its progression back to the *Anatomy*—we understand for the first time the full meaning of Burton's use of authority throughout the book: he is making something with all men which pretends to be neither something new under the sun, nor final unassailable fact. That this digression leads away from the formulaic presentation of facts and moves through speculation *in order to get back to* the structured progression, testifies that Burton's *Anatomy* is a *summa* of the only sort melancholy mankind can hope to make: an accumulation and arrangement of the best possible estimations of truth, set down in the light of men's rational awareness of their own limitations and of knowledge's ebb and flow.

Air Rectified—the collection of facts (or "facts") ranging from Périgord in France to Coldfield in Warwickshire, from the sites of houses to real voyages for health—is part of a system derived from the lines of many authors in many books, and that system is the quest of one who knows how to rove and range amidst the possibilities of philosophical mysteries, but who comes back always to the thing that, at least, "we may gather." The Digression of the Air, more than any other element in Burton's systematic perusal of the ordinary disease, teaches us that roving is not just pleasant but necessary if we are to stand far enough out from the collected statements of truth we think of as books of knowledge; far enough out, that is, to see their limitations and their worth. Now Burton can "rove" even within the proper boundaries of the discourse, for we have been led to see that roving is looking out only so that we may return to the generalized sum and substance of a knowledge which is not new, but has been found to work: "But I rove: the sum is this, that variety of actions, objects, air, places, are excellent good in this infirmity and all others, good for man, good for beast" (p. 69).

The last of the major digressions, and the longest, is the one which Burton most hesitantly describes as digression.

Because in the precedent section I have made mention of good counsel, comfortable speeches, persuasion, how necessarily they are required to the cure of a discontented or troubled mind, how present a remedy they yield, and many times a sole sufficient cure of themselves; I have thought fit, in this following section, a little to digress (if at least it be to digress in this subject), to collect and glean a few remedies and comfortable speeches out of our best orators, philosophers, divines, and Fathers of the Church, tending to this purpose. (II.3.1.1;126)

The Consolatory Digression, containing the Remedies of all manner of Discontents, is one of the primary structural units of its partition. As an entire section, it is essential to the construction of the partition; but by the same token it is also more independent of the surrounding subject matter than are the other digressions, an entity of its own with a completeness approached only by that of the Digression of Anatomy. It has been noticed that the digression is Burton's rendition of a philosophical *consolatio*, and that its very pattern in an established tradition sets it apart (Lievsay, passim). A consolation of philosophy within a medical treatise, it is genre within genre, and so separate. But Burton's parenthetical doubt, in the apology quoted above, only emphasizes his usual insistence on the pertinence of his digressions, for this final departure on a grand scale is so relevant as perhaps not to be departure at all. It is a testimony to the place that digression holds in the substance of Burton's treatise that the greatest and longest cure of melancholy comes by way of digression from the appointed order for cures.

The digression is distilled authority, the epitome of epitomies. Many have written of consolation, "yet because these tracts are not so obvious and common, I will epitomize and briefly insert some of their divine precepts, reducing their voluminous and vast treatises to my small scale; for it were otherwise impossible to bring so great vessels into so little a creek" (II.3.1.1;126). One alone can make nothing, but all men together something, if not much. This epitome of consolation brings to Burton's scale—into the boundaries of an essential if digressive element in the form of the treatise—the things that men know about living wisely as men. The digression is learning; it is Burton's study of the doctrines of others. And if it is not new, knowledge can work though old.

To what end are such paraenetical discourses? You may as soon remove Mount Caucasus as alter some men's affections. Yet sure I think they cannot choose but do some good, and comfort and ease a little, though it be the same again, I will say it, and upon that hope I will adventure. *Non meus hic sermo*, 'tis not my speech this, but of Seneca, Plutarch, Epictetus, Austin, Bernard, Christ and His Apostles. If I make nothing, as Montaigne said in like case, I will mar nothing; 'tis not my doctrine but my study, I hope I shall do nobody wrong to speak what I think, and deserve not blame in imparting my mind.   (II.3.1.1;127)

In one consolation, Burton deplores worldly wealth by recording the doctrines of Paul and of Bernard, and then he challenges, "If I had said this of myself, rich men would have pulled me apieces; but hear who saith, and who seconds it, an Apostle" (II.3.3;148). So he both is and is not responsible for the facts of the cures of the digression, for he "makes nothing" and it is not his speech, yet he is "imparting his mind." His removal from the teachings of the consolation is multiple: by the traditional form within traditional form, by the doctrines of others, by the "ordinary" nature of the comfortable speeches. But Burton is also immediately present as the spokesman of his own mind through others' words, as the student of doctrine, above all as the one whose knowledge this is, in that all of its Christian-Stoical commonplaces are comprehended in his scale and inserted into his discourse.

The discourse in the *Anatomy* proper, on the cures of the six non-natural things, has been urging moderation, and the precepts here presented argue the reason behind the need for such moderation. Having as weapons the trivial comforts which comprise the digression, Burton is taking dead aim at the irrationality of living; the digression would help men be men by making them rationalize these discontents, the perturbations of the mind. The physician would cure by forcing us to think, as men should, about the progress of life.

We are sent as so many soldiers into this world, to strive with it, the flesh, the devil; our life is a warfare, and who knows it not? . . . Go on then merrily to heaven. If the way be troublesome, and you in misery, in many grievances, on the other side you have many pleasant sports, objects, sweet smells, delightsome tastes, music, meats, herbs, flowers, etc., to recreate your senses. Or put case thou art now forsaken of the world, dejected, contemned, yet comfort thyself; as it was said to Hagar in the wilderness, "God sees thee, he takes notice of thee": there is a God above that can vindicate thy cause, that can relieve thee.   (II.3.1.1;132)

The very hurts with which the Consolatory Digression deals injure the nature of man:

Particular discontents and grievances are either of body, mind, or fortune, which, *as they wound the soul of man*, produce this melancholy and many great inconveniences, by that antidote of good counsel and persuasion may be eased or expelled. Deformities and imperfections of our bodies, as lameness, crookedness, deafness, blindness, be they innate or accidental, torture many men; yet this may comfort them, *that those imperfections of the body do not a whit blemish the soul*, or hinder the operations of it, but rather help and much increase it.   (II.3.2;133; my italics)

Throughout the digression there is this polarization between what actually matters and what only appears to matter. A "wound hurts not the soul," Burton says (II.3.2;134), but these grievances "wound the soul of man." The essence of all remedy is in putting the correct interpretation on objects, actions, and passions: "Sickness, diseases, trouble many, but without a cause; 'It may be 'tis for the good of their souls'; . . . the flesh rebels against the spirit; that which hurts the one must needs help the other" (p. 135). And correct interpretation involves the recognition that understanding reality depends not upon sense, but reason. For metaphor and matter can equally wound the soul; it "makes no dif-

ference whether one is a slave of persons or of things:
. . . Alexander was a slave to fear, Caesar of pride,
Vespasian to his money (*nihil enim refert, rerum sis servus
an hominum*), Heliogabalus to his gut, and so of the rest.
Lovers are slaves to their mistresses, rich men to their
gold, courtiers generally to lust and ambition, and all
slaves to our affections. . . . Why then dost thou
repine?" (II.3.4;173). Right consideration of all things
and events is requisite for right living, for consideration
constantly reveals the falsity of apparent truth by
upsetting supposed equations: "money makes, but
poverty mars, etc., and all this in the world's esteem:
yet, if considered aright, it is a great blessing in itself, a
happy estate, and yields no cause of discontent"
(II.3.3;145).

The Consolatory Digression corrects our misinformation by simple substitution of reason's right for the
world's esteem. We must see fiction for what it is: we
suppose rich men happy, but they are "like painted
walls, fair without, rotten within: diseased, filthy,
crazy, full of intemperance's effects" (p. 146); and to
see, all that is necessary is that we reason: "Why should
. . . one have all, another nothing? . . . Thus they
grumble, mutter, and repine: not considering that
inconstancy of human affairs, judicially conferring one
condition with another, or well weighing their own
present estate. What they are now, thou mayest shortly
be; and what thou art, they shall likely be" (p. 154).
Reason overrules false information and correctly identi-
fies outside objects: "I will conclude with Epictetus, 'If
thou lovest a pot, remember 'tis but a pot thou lovest,
and thou wilt not be troubled when 'tis broken: if thou
lovest a son or wife, remember they were mortal, and
thou wilt not be so impatient' " (II.3.5;185).

To consider example and ponder precept is to know wisely, for in these cures, the mere proposition of reasonable statement is its own proof. One *says* cure, and cure should work: " 'Tis a patient and quiet mind (I say it again and again) gives true peace and content" (II.3.3;171). Reasonableness is a very simple way of turning *what is* into *what should be*, and he says it again and again. Burton's Q.E.D. is that of the preacher rather than that of the mathematician, for the study is one of common understanding, not of complex logic. He says again and again that low birth is not ignoble, and then concludes that he has proved it: "therefore, to conclude that which I first intended, to be base by birth, meanly born, is no such disparagement. *Et sic demonstratur, quod erat demonstrandum*" (II.3.2;144).

The cure of discontent is thus to apply reason to life, which is to "balance our hearts . . . to examine ourselves for what cause we are so much disquieted, on what ground, what occasion, is it just or feigned; and then either to pacify ourselves by reason, to divert by some other object, contrary passion, or premeditation" (II.3.6;186). To examine, to reason—Burton is asking us to remember that we are men. God, he says, "hath not made thee a monster, a beast, a base creature, as he might, but a man, a Christian, such a man" (II.3.1.1;131).

And yet from the very beginning of the *Anatomy*, he has been showing how difficult it is to know what a man is and how to be a man. Difficult, even impossible, for one; but this digression, more insistently than the *Anatomy* itself, is from many minds of many times. It is Burton's digression, but its form is not his own invention. It is a separate treatise, but it is part of his treatise. Its teaching might be a sufficient cure for melancholy, but it might also cure discontent which is not melancholy. And so the kind of knowledge, the piece of his mind which Burton imparts through the Consolatory Digression, must be the least common denominator of reasonable living; it must make such living possible, at least, by making it accessible to all men.

The discontents caused by passions of the mind disturb all order precisely because they originate in the idiosyncracies of countless men who have their individual fictions and fancies: "If every man might have what he would, we should all be deified, emperors, kings, princes; if whatsoever vain hope suggests, unsatiable appetite affects, our preposterous judgment thinks fit were granted, we should have another chaos in an instant, a mere confusion" (II.3.7;189). We tend each our own way, even though our preposterous ambitions are denied. And the *only* cure that can be begun is within each man. The melancholy of society cannot be cured, as Burton's tale of the academical scholar and the vacant prebend makes clear. It is a tale told "to your further content," and it consoles by making us see and accept the truth that such a tale could only, ever, be fiction. Never would a bishop out of "his own accord, mere motion, and bountiful nature" send a fat prebend to an unknown scholar as a present. We have to see that there's no remedy like that for social abuse: "You have heard my tale: but alas! it is but a tale, a mere fiction, 'twas never so, never like to be so, and so let it rest. Well, be it so then; they have wealth and honour, fortune and preferment, every man (there's no remedy) must scramble as he may, and shift as he can" (p. 192). If society as society were curable, offenses by and to individuals would diminish, but we work only mischief as men and as groups of men.

In fine, if princes would do justice, judges be upright, clergymen truly devout, and so live as they teach, if great men would not be so insolent, if soldiers would quietly defend us, the poor would be patient, rich men would be liberal and humble, citizens honest, magistrates meek, . . . if parents would be kind to their children, and they again obedient to their parents, brethren agree amongst themselves: . . . if we could imitate Christ and His apostles, live after God's laws, these mischiefs would not so frequently happen amongst us; but being most part so irreconcilable as we are, perverse, proud, insolent, factious, . . . so opposite to virtue, void of grace, how should it otherwise be?   (P. 202)

So the climax of the Consolatory Digression does not come with advice that will win mankind as a whole over to reasoned existence; for the world is not that way, and apparently will not soon be that way. Burton puts into his digression the knowledge that may work, that may help men to live as men and not as dogs. Through precept and example he comes to a long list of aphorisms. This is the epitome within epitome: the proverb is wisdom with all particularity distilled out of it, with only the common experience of all men left for the taking by any man: "Many other grievances there are, which happen to mortals in this life, from friends, wives, children, servants, masters, companions, neighbours, our own defaults, . . . and many good remedies to mitigate and oppose them, many divine precepts to counterpoise our hearts, special antidotes both in Scripture and human authors, which whoso will observe shall purchase much ease and quietness unto himself" (p. 203).

The proverbs set down a torrent of the most basic truths, which do not represent what King sees (pp. 71-72) as Burton's "unfocused, untamed view" of the world and his despair at being unable to comprehend experience in the aphorisms' tiny circumferences. Burton has a much vaster form and order with which he comprehends experience. But the proverbs express the quintessence of that knowledge which all men have together—and that not much—which all can feel to be fact, and which any man can use, as he needs, to turn discontent with what appears to matter into acceptance of the facts. From "Fear God, obey the prince," to "Know thyself," to "Beware of Had I wist," to "Marry not an old crone or a fool for money"—the aphorisms collected out of authors and to be supplemented at our will from cheese-trenchers and painted cloths do not pretend to represent a "way by which (supposedly) the world might finally be understood and controlled" (King, p. 78). They rather suggest reasonably truthful ways in which any man might live, at different moments of discontent, with some semblance of wisdom in a world which men neither know nor rule. They are commonplaces, bits of truth through which a man might, simply, purchase some ease and quietness unto himself.

This digression, which has drawn to Burton's scale the wisdom of many men in order to preach reasonable living, ends—following the stream of common-sense reason—by drawing Burton's treatise of cures into itself. The last member of the Consolatory Digression is concerned with remedy "Against Melancholy itself." The ordinary disease leads to discontent, and as discontent it must be remedied by reason, which says that melancholy is good when it is understood. The final member turns disease into cure by showing us that, rightly considered, this worst illness can lead to the most reasonable living. For consideration, we have seen in this digression, puts things in proper perspective. It teaches the difference between wounds that hurt the soul and those which only seem to hurt. It tells a man to look at himself and think. "Remember, O Servius, thou art a man; and with that I was much confirmed, and corrected myself" (II.3.5;182). So melancholy, when remembered for what it is and is not, can correct itself. If it is new it is pleasant; if habitual, it is more durable than dangerous (II.3.8;205). In all the extremes of passion it arouses, melancholy keeps men from worse extremes: bashfulness keeps them honest; sorrow keeps them sober; foolishness itself keeps them wise—"Wearisomeness of life makes them they are not so besotted on the transitory vain pleasures of the world. If they dote on one thing, they are wise and well understanding in most other" (p. 206).

The cure of melancholy by applied reason is "in a word." It, like all the precepts and examples, like the catch-and-use-as-you-can dashes of common wisdom, gets down to the basic understanding that misery is in the interpretation that reason puts upon it. Since our life is a warfare (and who knows it not?), a man being a man can get him merrily to heaven with melancholy as well, or better, as without: "They are no dissemblers, liars, hypocrites, for fools and madmen tell commonly truth. In a word, as they are distressed, so are they pitied, which some hold better than to be envied, better to be sad than merry, better to be foolish and quiet, *quam sapere et ringi*, [than] to be wise and still vexed; better to be miserable than happy: of the two extremes it is the best" (p. 207). Reason ends up being the cure for melancholy by making melancholy its own cure. For in the context of all that has gone before, misery is best.

Misery is best, in context. And the context is the remedy of ordinary melancholy by the remedy of non-natural things. But the cure of melancholy cures more than melancholy, and digression has taken cure into the province of reason. If you would know, you can know how to judge possibility without demanding the impossible. You can know how to keep on working with question even as you stop asking admittance where angels fear to tread. And if you would be a man and not a dog, you can look for reasonable understanding of what living means. You can take a page out of the books of men who have taught wisely, or you can get the picture from cheese-trenchers and painted cloths. And if you know and live with the expectation of reasonably far-flung curiosity and reasonably down-to-earth ease and quietness, then you are curing life, and its misery; you are getting merrily to heaven in the midst of this our warfare.

THE PERTINENCE OF KNOWLEDGE

Following the Consolatory Digression's cure by reason, the medical treatise considers in a brief span all the cures in the remaining two divisions of physic—pharmaceutica and chirurgica. Everything that has preceded this last movement in the system of cures has had to do with "diet, or living"; physic lies mainly in the kind of life a man leads. But in the last portion of Partition II, Burton brings out his medical texts, turning to the cures which more properly belong to the physician's "method, and several rules of art" (II.1.4.2;20). Now more than ever he must be dealing with the facts of this matter of melancholy; his anatomy of medicine presumably would express dependence upon the truth of the system of humoral psychology on which his treatise of ordinary disease rests. But when Burton takes up "*Pharmaceutice*, or that kind of physic which cureth by medicines" (II.4.1.1;207), he asks, by way of digression, What has medicine to do with melancholy? And he summarizes, by way of digression, what the ordinary disease and his anatomy of that disease have to do with the matter of knowledge. The three final digressions make Burton's book question the methodology by which it operates by questioning medicine's usefulness as cure for melancholy. But they also confirm the methodology by showing how medical opinion belongs to the sort of analytical book that, on the surface, the *Anatomy* is. As digression, they turn the book in on itself, and we are made to see that "anatomy," as a "proper" form for medical science, is ordered into knowledge only when it allows digression to interrupt and reorder established methodologies, for "digression" gives science a new way to see and understand itself. These last three digressions make apparent the effect which I have from the beginning been arguing as Burton's primary reason for using formal digressions: they provide him with a vantage point inside of, yet removed from, his structure which allows him to see, ponder, and re-evaluate the usefulness of that structure and, indeed, of all "perfectly" ordered, "rationally" devised books of knowledge.

Burton's last three formal digressions are not even announced as digression within the discourse. The synopsis of Partition II describes them thus: "Pharmaceutics, or Physic which cureth with medicines, with a digression of this kind of physic''; "Simples altering melancholy, with a digression of exotic simples''; "Compounds altering melancholy, with a digression of compounds." Except for the final words, "But I digress," of the final digression, these are all the notice Burton gives of his turning from the proper business of the *Anatomy*. In the subsection on medicinal physic, he introduces that topic in one sentence, and in the next is off on a digression which takes the rest of the subsection: "Many cavil at this kind of physic, and hold it unnecessary, unprofitable to this or any other disease" (II.4.1.1;207). Similarly with the subsection on simples: "I know that many are of opinion our northern simples are weak, imperfect, not so well concocted, of such force, as those in southern parts" (II.4.1.2;213). With compounds he jumps immediately into digression: "Pliny, *lib*. 24, *cap*. 1, bitterly taxeth all compound medicines" (II.4.1.5;221); but here within the subsection he picks up the discourse of ordinary disease from which, or through which, he has digressed for the last time. The three digressions are about issues of knowledge specifically connected with the matter of material melancholy, and to whatever degree Burton's pharmocopeia may prescribe medicinal cures, it stands in response to his three digressions of medicine which question the science of physic. The digressions start with opinions. People have said that medicine is unnecessary, exotic simples are better than domestic ones, compounds no good at all. And they end with opinions: that medicinal physic is useful (II.4.1.1;211), that exotic simples should be domesticated (II.4.1.2; 214), that compounds are a "most noble and profitable invention" (II.4.1.5;223). In each instance Burton argues first for one position, then concludes for the other.

In the Digression of Pharmaceutics he condemns medicine as a "corrupt trade, no science, art, no profession" and less reliable than ordinary "kitchen physic" (II.4.1.1;208). The history of medicine is one of imposture, of cures by patients' faith more than physicians' skills, of an art that is "wholly conjectural, if it be an art, uncertain, imperfect, and got by killing of men" (pp. 209-210). And then he turns, and we see why he has digressed: it is not that medicine is of no use, but that it has to be judged before it can be anatomized: "But I will urge these cavilling and contumelious arguments no farther, lest some physician should mistake me, and deny me physic when I am sick: for my part, I am well persuaded of physic: I can distinguish the abuse from the use, in this and many other arts and sciences. . . . I acknowledge it a most noble and divine science" (p. 211). Physic which was at first from the devil is now from the gods. But then he moderates his rhetoric; panegyric belongs to science no more than cavilling argument. *Judging* medicine, he allows it to be an art when the physician judges reasonably.

I have said, yet one thing I will add, that this kind of physic is very moderately and advisedly to be used, upon good occasion, when the former of diet will not take place. And 'tis no other which I say, than that which Arnoldus prescribes in his eighth Aphorism: "A discreet and godly physician doth first endeavour to expel a disease by medicinal diet, then by pure medicine. . . ." So in [his] eleventh Aphorism: "A modest and wise physician will never hasten to use medicines, but upon urgent necessity, and that sparingly too. . . ."   (P. 211)

The Digression of Exotic Simples shows medicine to be defective because, as Pliny writes to Gallus, "We are careless of that which is near us, and follow that which is afar off, to know which we will travel and sail beyond the seas, wholly neglecting that which is under our eyes" (II.4.1.2;213). Physicians are "over-curious" for the sake of curiosity instead of being devoted to know-ing for the sake of curing. The turn in Burton's argu-ment in this digression is not an about-face, but he makes a reasonable suggestion, along with "divers worthy physicians," to remedy the matter: "If our simples be not altogether of such force, or so apposite, it may be, if like industry were used, those far-fetched drugs would prosper as well with us as in those countries whence now we have them" (p. 214). And the virtue of this plan lies in improving the study of medicine itself. By questioning in digression the worth of exotic simples, Burton lets his book of pharmaceutical cures suggest improvement for the Muses' melancholy; his cure for curiosity makes medicine as a profession responsible to society, and demands likewise that society acknowledge responsibility for the state of science:

. . . amongst the rest those famous public gardens of Padua in Italy, Nuremburg in Germany, Leyden in Holland, Mont-pelier in France (and ours in Oxford now in *fiere,* at the cost and charges of the Right Honourable the Lord Danvers, Earl of Danby), are much to be commended, wherein all exotic plants almost are to be seen, and liberal allowance yearly made for their better maintenance, that young students may be the sooner informed in the knowledge of them: which as Fuchsius holds, "is most necessary for that exquisite manner of curing," and as great a shame for a physician not to observe them as for a workman not to know his axe, saw, square, or any other tool which he must of necessity use.   (P. 214)

The Digression of Compounds shows medicine to be defective because it is a matter of opinion rather than fact. The practice of making "nonsense-confused compounds" involves "no science, no school, no art, no degree, but, like a trade, every man in private is instructed by his master" (II.4.1.5;221-222). Knowing what the "most rational" authorities say about compounding medicines is knowing only what they say, not why, for none of them "gives his reader, to my judgment, that satisfaction which he ought; why such, so many simples?" (p. 222). Books of medicine are only books of opinion, and "every city, town, almost every private man hath his own mixtures, compositions, receipts, magistrals, precepts, as if he scorned antiquity, and all others, in respect of himself. But each man must correct and alter to show his skill, every opinative fellow must maintain his own paradox, be it what it will" (p. 222). That is one way of looking at the matter: without thought to condemn this knowledge as no knowledge, to take all of the contradiction among authorities as evidence of the entire worthlessness of everything they teach. But there is another way. Quite suddenly, Burton turns around: "Thus others object, thus I may conceive out of the weakness of my apprehension; but to say truth, there is no such fault, no such ambition, no novelty or ostentation, as some suppose; but as one answers, this of compound medicines 'is a most noble and profitable invention, found out and brought into physic with great judgment, wisdom, counsel, and discretion' " (p. 223).

The digression puts medicine and all of its knowledge of man's body into the framework of all the ways by which man questions and judges knowledge of outside objects. If there are about compounds many opinions which "ebb and flow with the season, and as wits vary" (p. 223), yet moderate judgment will not conclude of physicians, "they dote" (p. 222), but "so many men, so many minds; and yet all tending to good purpose, though not the same way" (p. 223). Reason answers weakness of apprehension and sets the matter straight, that this of physic is one way of knowing: "As arts and sciences, so physic is still perfected amongst the rest. *Horae Musarum nutrices*, and experience teacheth us every day many things which our predecessors knew not of" (p. 223).

Judgment is the core of the three digressions of medicine. Through questioning the validity and usefulness of the "method and several rules of art" of medicine itself, they subject the very substance of the *Anatomy* to consideration. Because he starts on one tack and ends on another, Burton in each case makes the fact of judgment, the decision itself, his topic. By way of digression, he says that physic has to do with questions of knowledge, with man knowing and judging fact and opinion in this as "in many other arts and sciences."

In the portion of the *Anatomy* digressed from, Burton does not, of course, give prescriptions like a physician, as Sir William Osler (pp. 175-176) thought. The facts are there, but very much as "facts." Authorities, opinions, analyses, catalogues, epitomies—all show Burton hard at work judging the matter of physic, collecting and sorting things that are known. The structural schemes of humoral psychology which underlie the *Anatomy*, Colie has noted, are "pulverized" by Burton's very method of description and analysis, as by his "universalization of the disease into the whole condition of humanity." And digression plays no small part in removing "the medical and spiritual problems of melancholy into a far wider area of consideration and reference" (Colie, pp. 455-456). Here in the scientific heart of Burton's medical textbook, digression shows humoral psychology itself, and the method and art of medicine dependent on it, to be possible knowledge. That is what digression has made of the melancholy spaniel's quest. For by the final digressions Burton specifically unites what he is doing—collecting and arranging the facts of an ordinary disease—with what he is talking about— knowledge itself and the reasoned life of labor and industry spent in finding things out. Medicine is a study, and a way for a man to differ from a dog.

Nature is not effete, as he saith, or so lavish to bestow all her gifts upon an age, but hath reserved some for posterity, to show her power, that she is still the same, and not old or consumed. Birds and beasts can cure themselves by nature, *naturae usu ea plerumque cognoscunt, quae homines vix longo labore et doctrina assequuntur,* but men must use much labour and industry to find it out. But I digress.

Compound medicines are inwardly taken, or outwardly applied. Inwardly taken, be either liquid or solid; liquid, are fluid or consisting. Fluid, as wines and syrups. The wines ordinarily used to this disease are wormwood wine, tamarisk. (P. 223)

The true matter and end of the *Anatomy*, and its lasting interest, do not lie simply in Burton's treatise of melancholy, nor did he intend that they should. The order proclaimed in the title is the order of a system of knowledge about matters of fact which assumes the truth of humoral psychology. And Partitions I and II, from definition through cures, describe the matter of disease in terms of humoral man. But Partitions I and II, with their traditional system for the explication of disease, cannot comprehend the whole matter of Burton's discourse unless they comprehend also his pertinent digressions. For set among the facts of the ordinary disease is another system, one which opens that order up and makes its facts pertain to a broader disease of life. The digressions speak of the definition, causes, and cures of wrong living by speaking of man the rational animal and his disordered knowledge. The tension between the medical treatise and the digressions is the tension between two views of man and disease.

The medical treatise should define man simply and the facts of his disease surely, but it does not; for digression intrudes to make question out of definition, to reveal facts not as truth but as things gathered from opinion, and to make man's nature a matter also of the nature of beings that are beyond him. The medical treatise should find causes in the extremes with which a man mistreats his body and mind; but digression finds self-abuse to rise out of defect in man's very nature which makes him rely on the reason of a brute, and to end in the disease of knowledge itself and the brutalization of man's society. The medical treatise should see cure in the rectification of the things whereby men live; but digression finds the ultimate cure for disease to lie in living by knowing the possibility of truth and by considering what living as a man means. And finally, the medical treatise should issue ordinary prescriptions for ordinary disease, but digression questions the worth of medicine itself, only to show that the medical treatise is pertinent to the disorder of knowledge because it is a way of right living, which is finding out what can be known.

The structural fabric of Burton's discourse is more complex than the simple sequence of a medical treatise. Digression and traditional form together define Partitions I and II. Digression makes the scholastic structure embrace it, impressing itself upon the form which this new treatise gives to truth: so digression is necessary to the "totality" of the *Anatomy*. When Burton digresses it is to make a statement about the very essence of his understanding of man's disease and the complex disorder of life. And that statement in turn reflects and becomes essential to the example of ordered knowledge which is the medical treatise. "I hold it not impertinent," Burton said, and in the structure made to comprehend the new science of the *Anatomy of Melancholy*, there are no impertinent digressions.

III. Love's Comment

Unlike myself thou hear'st me moralize,
Applying this to that, and so to so;
For love can comment upon every woe.
—SHAKESPEARE, *Venus and Adonis*

In the opening chapter we confronted the *Anatomy* from the outside, seeing in the apparatus which is the book's facade both Burton's directives as to the various ways the reader might enter into the meaning of his work and his concern that the *Anatomy* impart the impression of unified truth through its scholastic—even Gothic—structure. Examining Burton's use of digression, we have seen that, because his framework included within itself the possibility for expansion, turning aside becomes necessary if we are to get a right understanding of the discourse. But we have now to go back once more to look at the overall plan of the work, and in doing so we will see that Burton not only opens up the structure by digression, but contradicts it by addition. The logical order of Partitions I and II is opposed by the addition of Partition III, the treatise of Love-melancholy.[1]

---

1. For the sake of clarity throughout my discussion I shall distinguish Love-melancholy, the species which manifests itself in three forms, from love-melancholy, also called "heroical melancholy," one of the three types.

The reader who has looked at the *Anatomy*'s elaborate facade expects that the book will be one of those comprehensive works which are "organized according to a scheme of division and subdivision, condensable into a table of contents or synopsis, where all parts denoted by numbers or letters of the same class are on the same logical level" (Panofsky, p. 32). Burton declares his scholastic *manifestatio* of order by describing his "formidably logical, complex, and comprehensive" organization (Babb, p. 4) in the synoptic tables. But despite the apparent logic within the tables, there is a singular imbalance between them. Partition III is not "on the same logical level" as Partition I or Partition II, and this lapse in parallelism, it seems to me, first arouses in readers the feeling that while "on the whole Burton follows his outlines," yet the "distribution of material in the book is not quite so logical as one might expect" (Babb, p. 4).

Before discussing the structure of Partition III itself I want to clarify the specific way Partitions I and II are illogically related to Partition III, for Burton sets this Third Partition aside from his more "orderly" discourse in I and II and thereby confirms for us the kind of opening out of system we have seen achieved through digression in those first two partitions. Only by recognizing the way Partition III turns away from I and II can we ultimately see the full meaning of digression in Burton's art. For Partition III is itself a great, final digression from scholastic order, which, like the digressions of I and II, nonetheless makes use—sometimes startling, almost perverse, use—of the forms scholastic order gave the *Anatomy* at the outset. "System," we shall see, still works in Partition III, but where in I and II a proper system coexists with a digressive "system," here in III Burton makes a single progression through the kinds of Love-melancholy. Because all Love-melancholy is "indefinite," Partition III has no covert method to intermingle with or comment on the overt one, but rings all its changes within its own structure (a structure thus implicitly opposed to that of I and II, like a digression). Many readers have the vague feeling that Partition III is not like Partitions I and II (it's more "interesting," less "boring"). But I want to describe the precise structural way III is unlike I and II so that we can then be justified in looking at its singular progression, which puts man's passions—his love and hate for others and his love and lack of love for God—into the sections, members, and subsections of a system designed to describe "proper," "definite" humoral melancholy. My purpose in this chapter, then, after first suggesting some ways in which the illogicality of the relationship between Partitions I and II and Partition III might be defined, will be to explore the structure of Partition III itself in order to arrive at a description of its function in the *Anatomy* as a whole.

Love-melancholy is a species of melancholy. Now the logic of Partitions I and II would require that a species, any species, of the disease would fit into the system of analysis as a subtopic of the larger order of cause-symptom-cure. That is, the logic of the first two partitions is one of cause and effect, of action and reaction, so that Partition I states the thesis—definition, causes, symptoms, prognostics—of the disease, while Partition II—under its single topic, cure—provides the antithesis to all of the topics of I. In I and II the three kinds of "definite" melancholy are treated as subtopics of the cause-cure analysis. Thus, under causes, we find Burton treating first the general causes and then those particular to melancholy of the head, hypochondria, or whole body; and so with symptoms and cures. But in Partition III he changes the base of his analysis, using now as his major organizational scheme not the logic of thesis and antithesis, but that of division. For I and II, he advises us in the first synopsis, describe melancholy "proper to parts" while III concerns itself with "indefinite" melancholy. Like the definite disease, Love-melancholy has, as we shall see, three types. But the logic of Partition III makes the system of causes-cures subordinate to the type, so that heroical melancholy has its own statement of the cause-cure sequence, as does jealousy or religious melancholy. To put it another way, the roman numerals of the outline of the First and Second Partitions become the arabic numerals in the outline of the Third Partition, while analogous to the arabic numerals of I and II are the upper-case letters of III:

I. Causes   [thesis]
    A. General
    B. Particular
        1. Head
        2. Hypochondriacal   } types
        3. Whole Body

(followed by I' [Symptoms] and I'' [Prognostics]

II. Cures   [antithesis]
    A. General
    B. Particular
        1. Head
        2. Hypochondriacal   } types
        3. Whole Body

III.   Love-melancholy   [type]
       A.   Heroical   [type]
            1.   Causes   thesis
            2.   Symptoms   }
            3.   Cures   antithesis
       B.   Jealousy   [type]
            1.   Causes   }   thesis
            2.   Symptoms
            3.   Cures   antithesis
       c.   Religious   [type]
            1.   Causes   }   thesis
            2.   Symptoms
            3.   Cures   antithesis

So to simplify Burton's synoptic tables is, of course, to misread them; but such an abstraction is valid in order to point out the problem with Burton's tripartite structure and should not lead to a misreading of the book itself.

The Third Partition is thus a kind of distorted mirror image of Partitions I and II. As a structural unit it is not "on the same logical level" with either Partition I or Partition II, but is rather logically analogous to the First and Second Partitions taken together. They treat of definite melancholy, this of indefinite. And it is important to keep in mind that Partition III "stands out as a separate unit" (Finlay, p. 64), not just by having a preface of its own—though this announces the distinction at once—but by the very rationale of exposition which controls it. For if he fails to notice that the controlling logic of III is the reverse of that in I and II, a reader can be led to acknowledge that the "distribution of material . . . is not quite so logical as one might expect" without being forced to realize the inverted

logic which does organize Partition III and the relationships of its major topics. Babb (p. 4) describes the three
partitions in this way: "In the first volume (or 'partition')
[Burton] deals rather exhaustively with the causes,
symptoms, and prognostics of melancholy; in the second with the cure of melancholy; in the third with all
aspects of two varieties of melancholy which he sees fit
to deal with apart, love melancholy (love sickness) and
religious melancholy (melancholy which either by its
causes or its symptoms is associated with religion)."
Another critic would explain Burton's treatment of love-
melancholy while ignoring the discussion of religious
melancholy, even though he recognizes a connection
between the two.[2] My analysis of the Third Partition
will contend that both these readers must lose the
importance of Partition III, the one by not seeing that
Burton is treating not "two varieties" but three varieties
of one type of melancholy, and the other by choosing
not to discuss the final clause of the single statement
that is Partition III.

Why, then, the tripartite structure? Burton has two
organizational systems at work in the book—the logic of
thesis-antithesis and the logic of division of species—
and he sets them on top of each other without, *in the
course of the work itself,* allowing a synthesis to emerge.
Each system is a bipartite one: causes of melancholy,
cures of melancholy; definite disease, indefinite disease.
Yet by his own perverse mathematics, Burton adds two
bipartite analytical systems and comes up with neither

2. David Zesmer, "Love and Marriage in *The Anatomy of Melancholy," Dissertation Abstracts* 25 (1964), 490.

two divisions nor four, but three.[3] Because Partition III
follows Partitions I and II, the structure of the work becomes not vaguely illogical, but definitely so. The off-
balance relationship of the three partitions declares the
anomalous structure of the book as a whole even as the
digressions state it for Partitions I and II. When we turn
from the synoptic tables to Burton's distinction of the
species of melancholy in his section of definition, we see
the literal confusion which underlies the structural
anomaly:

> When the matter is diverse and confused, how should it
> otherwise be but that the species should be diverse and
> confused? . . . Some make two distinct species . . . others
> acknowledge a multitude of kinds, and leave them indefi-
> nite. . . . "As the humour is diversely adust and mixed, so are
> the species diverse"; but what these men speak of species I
> think ought to be understood of symptoms . . . infinite spe-
> cies, *id est*, symptoms; and in that sense . . . the species are
> infinite.   (I.1.3.4;174-175)

Burton's final analysis is characteristic: the "most received division" is of three kinds, melancholy of the
head, hypochondria, and whole body, but there is a
fourth which may be not one but two types of the first;
but since the fouth has several kinds he will treat of
three species in two partitions and of the fourth kind(s)
"apart by themselves in my third partition" (pp. 175-176).

"Species, *id est*, symptoms." In the Third Partition
more than in the First or Second, Burton has difficulty

3. With this contortion of the book's geometry, compare Joan Webber's analysis of Burton's use of imagery of ambiguity, especially her
discussion of three-sided pictures (pp. 108-109) and her conclusion
that Burton uses the ambiguities apparent in his "mixed scene" to
"solve his own dilemma of how to respond to man's follies," because
changing response is always possible when the proportions and aspects of the world are always changing.

distinguishing the very categories which organize his discourse. When symptoms and species become equivalent terms, discourse threatens to topple into nonsense. But Love-melancholy, or indefinite melancholy, we have seen, is more than a literal anomaly; it is structural as well when kind takes over logical precedence. And seeing this we are ready to ask how Burton makes Partition III fit onto his other structure of Partitions I and II. His method can best be called by the term he uses so often: "equivocation": say one word, "melancholy," and mean numberless disorders by it. Partition III itself is the biggest equivocation of the book, for it makes the *Anatomy* say, "melancholy, definite disease of the body (Partitions I and II), *id est,* melancholy, indefinite 'disease' of the soul (Partition III)." It equivocates by being a new definition and way of seeing melancholy that is opposed to, not merely added to the First and Second Partitions, a contrary linked illogically with a work of another logical order. "Rational" discourse could not say, "Species, *id est,* symptoms," or "definite, that is, indefinite." But Burton can so equivocate without becoming nonsensical because his logic is constrained not by rules of mathematics but by those of art, and he can always say, "in that sense" it is so.

Art, not logic. Of course we have been seeing Burton use art to open up his schoolman's order in Partitions I and II. Now the opened-up structure becomes the whole structure, and Burton is free in Partition III to rove at will, to mold and remake his sections and subsections, to cast a set of subjects (passionate love; jealousy; religious love) into three equivalent forms, only then to recast them again as it suits his developing purpose into two equivalent forms (love of men; love of

God). Partition III, we shall discover, is art liberating science, while science, or knowledge, keeps art within bounds (human, "rational" bounds, though not at all necessarily *logical* bounds). Partition III makes the *Anatomy* equivocate in the matter of melancholy's definition, and it does so by equivocating endlessly on the meaning of love. For love is man's indefinite, universal madness; passion is that disorder which most of all demands cure (or order) and which most resists it. Heroical melancholy, jealousy, and religious melancholy will all, by Burton's art, be made equal parts of his discourse, equally essential to the physician-divine's attempts to order passion into rational life. But then also by Burton's art, human love and hate for others and for God will be made chaotically unequal, or equal in different ways; for his book is about human life, and in this life man's love cannot finally be structured into three simplistically equivalent sections. Artifice, as we have been seeing from the beginning of our discussion, is in the *Anatomy* that gift whereby the artist, like God, "reveals and conceals to whom and when he will."

But whether, or how, one defines and redefines love, all definition of his indefinite disease is—has to be, Partition III shows us—equivocation. Love is passion. Love is jealous hatred. Love is religion. Ultimately, as at the outset, love is charity. All through Partition III Burton makes *kind* the primary subject matter because all that disordered melancholy man can be is involved finally in the kinds of love he allows to rule his life. In elucidating the way Burton proceeds through his equivocations of Love-melancholy, I shall hope to show a second major structural tension of the book. We discovered the first in the interplay between discourse and digression in Partitions I and II. The second exists because of the distinction between definitions, causes, and cures in I and II and those in Partition III. Only having looked closely at Partition III's definition of man's disease can we then turn to Democritus Junior's Preface and discover the keystone of Burton's structure which holds all tension in equilibrium, which makes Partitions I and II pertinent to Partition III, Partition III pertinent to Partitions I and II, and all partitions on melancholy, definite and indefinite, pertinent to man's knowledge of his tangled but ultimately ordered essence. And there is tension within Partition III, also, as will become clear, because Burton equivocates in the matter of how many species of Love-melancholy really exist as species. Heroical melancholy, jealousy, religious melancholy are all given equal structural treatment in equivalent sections, but then all Love-melancholy leads to and from man's soul, so all three sections evolve toward religious melancholy. Or to put it as Burton finally will, melancholy—indefinite, immaterial, universal melancholy—is indivisible, singular madness. Two plus two equals three, but three (sections or types) also equals one (partition), and, as one, leads us back to the beginning of the book, the Preface, where melancholy is everything that man appears to be: disordered, looking very like—though not finally becoming—an impaired version of the God of love's creation.

EQUIVOCATION: LOVE IS CHARITY

Partition III is a restatement of all that Burton has said in I and II. When he comes to write of indefinite melan-

choly, he begins the book all over again with a new
preface and a new narration. Without belaboring the
point, we should note that the "Preface or Introduction"
to the Third Partition (III.1.1.1) would itself qualify as an
illogical intrusion into the midst of a discourse controlled by the kind of scholastic form represented by the
synopses. It is, as I have suggested, a warning to the
reader that he must look closely at the structure of what
follows, and a notice that here, two-thirds of the way
through the *Anatomy*, something new is happening to
the comprehensive treatise of melancholy. Whether or
not it is accurate to say that the preface "repeats on a
very small scale the function of the one at the beginning" (Finlay, p. 64), it is at least true that it repeats
some of the topics of Democritus Junior's Preface. There
are the imagined objections to the work and Burton's
answers, mostly in the listing of authorities whose
example he follows; there is the question of levity in the
persons of grave philosophers; there are defenses of the
treatise along with a pleasant dismissal, "I will not press
you with my pamphlets, or beg attention, but if you like
them you may" (p. 7); and of course apology is followed
by the self-confident "I need no such apologies" (p. 8).
By giving Partition III a preface, Burton announces that
even as he conforms to the necessities of his book—
"love is a species of melancholy, and a necessary part of
this my treatise" (p. 4)—he is giving himself a new
beginning, another way of writing about the melancholy he has already taken from definition through
causes and symptoms to cure.

Furthermore, he indicates through the preface that he
has not simply chosen to write of Love-melancholy
"apart" because he has too many stories and anecdotes

exemplifying indefinite melancholy to enable him to treat of it in its logical position relative to the other species (whatever that might be). Rather, his preface declares, the subject matter of Partition III compels him to a different kind of discourse, which is not like the medical treatise but like the digressions. Partition III has no digressions of the formal sort we have analyzed in Chapter II. It is instead itself a digression, pulling the book as a whole in a new direction as the digressions of I and II pulled the meaning of those partitions away from exposition of knowledge toward understanding of the limits of knowledge. In I and II Burton used digressions occupying various portions of the structure from part of a subsection to a complete section, and now he carries the process of necessary digression to conclusion: an entire partition, the final major division of the *Anatomy,* digresses and takes the book out of itself.

At several points in the *Anatomy,* Burton employs metaphorical language relating to man's recreation in nature to describe himself and his writing. In order to see how he uses it here in this preface to proclaim that the Third Partition is in fact Digression, it will be well to look back at two instances of this imagery which occur in the context of Partitions I and II. At the opening of the subsection in Partition I labelled "Continent, inward, antecedent, next Causes, and how the Body works on the Mind," a section very proper to the medical treatise and having nothing digressive about it, Burton enters into his topic: "As a purly hunter, I have hitherto beaten about the circuit of the forest of his microcosm, and followed only those outward adventitious causes. I will now break into the inner rooms, and rip up the antecedent immediate causes which are there to be found"

(I.2.5.1;371). First, it should be noted that the figure
used is simile; Burton makes a comparison between
himself as writer or scientific investigator and a hunter
after game. Further, he does not carry his figurative
language very far or use it to any great purpose. The
book's subject matter becomes momentarily and metaphorically a forest, but the metaphor is vague because
the treatise is already a "microcosm," itself a figurative
comparison, and Burton's language does not make clear
how a microcosm is or is like a forest. (Put the other way
around—this forest is a microcosm—the metaphor
would make sense, but it would also not be to Burton's
point; he is not talking about forests, but melancholy,
and he only needs a forest because he is at present "like
a hunter.") And in the second sentence the simile
breaks down altogether as the undelimited space of
forests and the expansive action of beating around the
bush lead not to action consistent with the simile—for
example, to grounding a quarry or zeroing in on a
target—but to the constricted, artificially limited space
of walled rooms to be broken into. Nor does Burton hint
at what the causes are to be compared to so that they
might be metaphorically "ripped up" (game is not
ripped up, but bodies—or scholarly subjects—being
anatomized are). The simile here in the body of the
medical treatise is a pleasant transition from one section
into another section (or "room," the term is properly
used of a unit of a formal treatise) of the *Anatomy*; it does
not take hold of the discourse or tempt Burton into
expanding metaphor. The discourse, the artificial construct, instead holds the image down and constrains it
to its own terms, so that the sentence is a satisfactory

introduction to examination of immediate causes of melancholy even though it cannot be particularly satisfying as a figure of speech.

The second use of this kind of figure has already been quoted at length—the long-winged hawk at the opening of the Digression of the Air (see above, page 89). Once again the comparison takes the form of explicit simile: "As a long-winged hawk . . . so will I . . . awhile rove . . . mount aloft . . . and so descend." But here Burton uses the simile to get into his discourse and to get out of it. The topic is air, but Burton turns it into an implicit metaphor: real, breathable air to be rectified is set aside until the airy reaches of the mind have been explored. And because the writer is "like a hawk," he can fly up "into these ample fields of air, wherein I may freely expatiate and exercise myself for my recreation." The simile controls the digression by translating the medical treatise into metaphor, and it remains consistent with itself until at the end of the digression Burton, still like a hawk, stoops to follow "my melancholy spaniel's quest, my game" (II.2.3;61). Unlike the purly hunter, Burton's hawk is not an adventitious figure of speech to be dropped before it is complete, but a conscious means of turning the discourse away from its "proper" limits in the direction of metaphor.

Returning to the preface of Partition III, we find Burton once more using a similar figure as the springboard into his subject. But this time he has no simile, for he is now recreating himself in the fields of the treatise itself.

"Being to speak of his admirable affection of love" (saith Valleriola), "there lies open a vast and philosophical field to

my discourse, by which many lovers become mad: let me
leave my more serious meditations, wander in these philosophical fields, and look into those pleasant groves of the
Muses, where with unspeakable variety of flowers we may
make garlands to ourselves, not to adorn us only, but with
their pleasant smell and juice to nourish our souls, and fill our
minds desirous of knowledge," etc. After a harsh and un-
pleasing discourse of melancholy, which hath hitherto mo-
lested your patience and tired the author, give him leave with
Godefridus the lawyer, and Laurentius (*cap.* 5), to recreate
himself in this kind after his laborious studies.   (III.1.1.1;6)

Note that the only thing Burton is implicitly or explicitly
"like" is Valleriola or Laurentius or another author, all
of whom, as it were, give him the cue to his own speech:
"Give me leave then to refresh my Muse a little, and my
weary readers, to expatiate in this delightsome field,
hoc deliciarum campo, as Fonseca terms it, to season a
surly discourse with a more pleasing aspersion of love
matters" (p. 6). Where as the hawk, Burton wandered
from the discourse into the pleasant world, now the
subject matter before him is the metaphorical field to be
escaped into; it is "vast and philosophical," with room
for expatiation, lots of roving (of which, more later), and
pleasure spiced with teaching. Where as a writer of the
medical treatise, Burton could make himself like a
hunter without committing himself or the treatise to the
working out of the simile, now he is a writer of a different sort—a poet, devotee of the Muses—who turns
himself loose in a delightful world of his own making
without promising to return, to follow any other game,
or to bring himself back to a more surly discourse. Burton
thus uses the freedom which the Digression of the Air
lent to the *Anatomy* to extend the image of escape into an
expansive world so that it describes not a momentary
"digression" but the rest of the book—everything to

which this metaphor of the delightsome field is a preface.

Partition III is thus a discourse of the same sort as the digressions. It is beside the point of Partitions I and II, but to the point of the book. Love, passions and "humours" of all sorts, equivocations Partitions I and II were not supposed to treat (what Burton in the Preface calls "metaphorical melancholy")—all *kinds* of seeming madness are proper to Partition III because it is a metaphorical field and indefinite melancholy is in itself "metaphorical madness." Any equivocation of melancholy is now Burton's proper subject, and he never wanders from *"hoc deliciarum campo,"* only in it. To confirm the nature of Partition III, to reaffirm in all its parts that he is still expatiating in the world of melancholy which is no longer "definite" or "proper to parts," Burton allows the partition to grow by means of digression within itself. Not only did the Third Partition increase in volume through successive editions more consistently than did the other partitions,[4] but it is the setting for most of those slight and informal divergences from the "method" which Burton calls attention to when he catches himself up: "But I rove" (p. 329); "But this is not the matter in hand" (p. 76); "But to my purpose" (p. 216); "But I rove, I confess" (p. 261); "But I proceed" (p. 121); "But to my former task" (p. 424).[5] Whether he is speaking of the objects of love, the power

4. See Babb, pp. 18, 21 ff.; and Hallwachs, p. 110 ff.
5. Noting Burton's tendency to stray, Simon (p. 425) gives a shorter but similar list, but leaves the impression that "our Democritus" makes such "frequent confessions" throughout the book. In point of fact, only one "But I digress" in his list is from outside the third partition, and it is that notice at the end of the last digression which I have described as Burton's farewell to formal digression (see above, page 114).

of beauty, the types of jealousy, or the cure of despair, Burton by such iterations reminds us that he is still in the "delightsome field" of love matters, roving as one can only if he has turned wholly aside from the surly discourse.

The preface to Partition III further introduces Love-melancholy as a new and "metaphorical" view of the disease by attesting to melancholy as a literary phenomenon, a poetic invention. "A large part of the difficulty" of pinning down a definition of love-melancholy, one critic has noticed, "comes from the origins of the concept of heroical melancholy, which are literary rather than medical. This helps account for its status as an 'indefinite species' " (Finlay, pp. 64-65). We have already encountered Burton's appeals to the Muses as the sources of his inspiration in this partition. We shall see further that indefinite melancholy (in all its manifestations, though Finlay is right in citing heroical melancholy as most obvious) is a matter of story, of the written and spoken word, and of the Word; for the Logos, God's word in Christ and in Scripture provides much of the "matter" in the section of religious melancholy, just as Ovid, Spenser, and all writers on love provide the matter of the sections on heroical melancholy and jealousy. So in the preface Burton alerts us to the literary nature of his topic and to the fact that the book is switching from medical treatise to a kind of poetry, by his insistence that this partition meets the Horatian qualifications of a good poem: it teaches and delights.

In its apologetics the preface to Partition III focuses on the dichotomy between serious works and the pleasant fields of love stories: "And how many superintendents of learning could I reckon up, that have written of light phantastical subjects" (III.1.1.1;6). But Valleriola's—and Burton's—field is at once pleasant and philosophical, and our analysis of the partition should elucidate the extent to which this most delightful partition rests on philosophy, love of wisdom. So Burton defends the partition: "but mine earnest intent is as much to profit as to please, *non tam ut populo placerem, quam ut populum juvarem*; and these my writings, I hope, shall take like gilded pills, which are so composed as well to tempt the appetite and deceive the palate, as to help and medicinally work upon the whole body; my lines shall not only recreate but rectify the mind" (p. 7). Though he will continue to use the method of definition-cause-cure to describe indefinite melancholy, Burton employs the poetic nature of the Third Partition to emphasize here that the literary work itself is the cure. In the Preface, Democritus Junior has promised to cure the melancholy world through his book, and in this preface Burton proclaims that the partition itself is cure regardless of whether it is defining symptoms or causes or prognostics or cures. Instead of finding cures or "proper remedies" for definite ailments in the book, the reader is being cured by being a reader, and the author, just by being an author of delightful and philosophical writings, is supplying physic for the indefinite disease.

Thus the partition can both "adorn" and "nourish" because it is the artistic reflection of illness. The Third Partition is not medical treatise, but it uses the formal "rooms" of the medical treatise to construct a stage for tragicomedy: "I am resolved howsoever, *velis, nolis, audacter stadium intrare*, in the Olympics, with those Eliensian wrestlers in Philostratus, boldly to show myself in this common stage, and in this tragicomedy of love to act several parts, some satirically, some comically, some in a mixed tone, as the subject I have in hand gives occasion, and present scene shall require or offer itself" (p. 10). Finally, then, through the preface, Burton commits his Third Partition to the kind of melancholy which is seen on the world's "common stage." "Love's comment" on the two partitions of the medical treatise is that melancholy is not the woe of some sick people, but universal woe. For where in Partitions I and II he had proposed not to treat of either madness and frenzy (I.1.1.4) or those "equivocations" of melancholy—moodiness, bad temper, prolonged sadness—in every man (I.1.1.5), in Partition III he sets aside the limits, which in any case he had had difficulty obeying, and redefines the disease as the ubiquitous passion of all men.[6]

In this preface, Burton strikes the pose not of actor or critic or "superintendent of learning" but of man. "I am a man; I count nothing human foreign to me" is the declaration of the writer of the Third Partition (the statement is not, as critics often loosely imply, one used throughout the *Anatomy*). This generic man, Burton, defines the indefinite disease by the ultimate equivoca-

6. Finlay (pp. 61-63), who lays great stress on the ineffectiveness of Burton's method, notes that Burton does not "restrict himself to the limits he has set" in I and II (p. 62) and that in III Burton obviously "chose not to adhere to the limits of his definition, not to be rigorous in his method" (p. 63). The point might be made that it is digression in I and II that is responsible for Burton not sticking to the material discourse, and that a new method intrudes in III where cause (material humors, and so on) is no longer the prime determinant of definition, but effect, that is, the peculiar manifestation of passion which classifies Love-melancholy as heroical melancholy, jealousy, or religious melancholy.

tion of the human condition: madness, that is to say, not madness, that is to say, only man:

I am of Catullus' opinion, and make the same apology in mine own behalf: . . . [I write for the most part to satisfy the taste and judgment of others; I am not mad myself, but I follow those who are. Yet grant that this shows me mad; we have all raved once, and you yourself, I think, dote sometimes, and he, and he, and of course I too]. *Homo sum, humani a me nihil alienum puto.* (III.1.1.1;8)

The remainder of the first section of Partition III following the preface is devoted not to Love-melancholy, but to love. I am going to dwell briefly on Burton's discourse on love, and at some more length on its closing sermon on charity, because my thesis in this chapter depends on the reader's understanding that the Third Partition describes the universe men live in as a universe compounded of love, and the lives men lead as lives which should be governed by charity, that special love for others that has reference to God. Charity is order: men in right relationship to each other and to all else, including God, that exists. All my explication of Burton's Third Partition is intended to show his concern with diseased love (indefinite melancholy) in the light ultimately not so much of God's—or original sinless man's—perfect love, but of man's possible love, charity that can work in a melancholy world if men will let it work. I shall attempt to show that Burton forms and reforms, sections and resections, anatomizes and re-anatomizes Love-melancholy in order not to end with despair (though that is his final topic) but to end with a book, an artificially constructed reassessment and re-alignment of all man's disordered loves into the shape of comprehensible order. To spend time on love-melancholy, Burton tells us at the end of this partition, is to deny ourselves that time to spend *being* melancholy; that is what he and we do together in this partition. We spend time learning of all the men and women who misuse love; we spend time looking for cures. And that time spent *is* cure, for it is time spent in charity, in thinking on, defining and redefining, parcelling out loves, laughing and weeping at inane human behavior, seeing ourselves in light of others' stories. It is also seeing others in light of what mankind can make of itself on earth: loving, hoping, and fearing humanity which is busy with life and its cures and so not finally impaired eternally though disordered temporally.

The discourse on love which follows the Third Partition's preface is Burton's narration for his discourse on Love-melancholy. In it he describes "all the kinds of love, his nature, beginning, difference, objects, how it is honest or dishonest, a virtue or vice, a natural passion or a disease, his power and effects, how far it extends" (III.1.1.2;10). As narration, in fact, it is eminently more satisfying than was the Digression of Anatomy for Partitions I and II. For in it Burton outlines the scope of his Third Partition by tracing love through stones and beasts to God and angels and back to man, and he defines at the end of the section the kind of love which is the wisdom that all men, being sick of Love-melancholy, lack, but which all could, if they think about it, attain.

Before turning to the loves of men, Burton extends the significance of the preface by emphasizing the truly universal nature of love. The delightsome field is broad indeed, for love "universally taken" is desire; things desire other things thought to be good and beautiful, and desire always leads to the attempt to obtain the thing beloved: "for good, fair, and unity cannot be separated" (III.1.1.2;11−12). Thus love is not only man's "*primum mobile*" (p. 11), but the principle moving all creation, including inanimate objects and beasts (pp. 15−16). Yet while "love proper to mortal men" will be Burton's real subject in the narration, he puts human love in its place among rational loves, for God and angels love also. And the love that holds man's civilization together is the same love that holds God's universe together, that is, God; for "God is love itself."

Amor mundum facit, love built cities, *mundi anima,* invented arts, sciences, and all good things, incites us to virtue and humanity, combines and quickens; keeps peace on earth, quietness by sea, mirth in the winds and elements, expels all fear, anger and rusticity; . . . a round circle still from good to good; for love is the beginner and end of all our actions, the efficient and instrumental cause, as our poets in their symbols, impresses, emblems of rings, squares, etc., shadow unto us. . . . And this is that Homer's golden chain, which reacheth down from heaven to earth, by which every creature is annexed, and depends on his Creator. He made all, saith Moses," and it was good," and He loves it as good. (Pp. 16-17)

Human love is given a context of divine love, then, as Burton moves into the second member where he talks of men's loves, profitable, pleasant, or honest, and illustrates them by a sort of helter-skelter citation of Old and New Testament, pagan poets, and more recent history. "In all ages" human love is the same: the graceful speech of a Jesus or an Orpheus attracts devotion (III.1.2.3;25); true friendship, "as between David and Jonathan, Damon and Pythias, Pylades and Orestes" (p. 28), unites the minds of men. Yet the universal context of human love which Burton develops as the thematic setting for the Third Partition is not "Homer's golden chain," or God's creative love, but Christ's chain of love, the commandment to "love God above all, and our neighbour as ourself" (III.1.3;30). Understanding the discourse of Love-melancholy depends on our understanding that the partition begins as it ends with religious love. All the melancholies of love are seen through the narration, which closes with Burton's eloquent sermon on charity.

The sermon cannot be considered fortuitous or merely the proper conclusion for a physician-divine to put to an explanation of the kinds of love. The human rational love which is Burton's topic of consideration has already been shown to us in its proper context of the divine chain of love. Discourse which is to teach and delight need go no further. But the section on charity redefines human love so that the universal chain is seen to *begin* with man, a point of view possible only through Christian eyes:

> . . . there is yet another love compounded of all these three, which is charity, and includes piety, dilection, benevolence, friendship, even all those virtuous habits; for love is the circle equant of all other affections, of which Aristotle dilates at large in his Ethics, and is commanded by God, which no man can well perform, but he that is a Christian, and a true regenerate man. This is "to love God above all, and our neighbour as ourself"; for this love is *lychnus accendens et accensus*, a communicating light.   (P. 30)

Charity is the chain linking man to other men through God. It is the message of the New Testament, of the God-man; it surpasses the merely moral and natural loves which make and perfect man *qua* man because it constrains him to see the fair objects of the world reflected from its creator and sustainer: "a man is beloved of a man, in that he is a man; but all these [loves] are far more eminent and great, when they shall proceed from a sanctified spirit, that hath a true touch of religion and a reference to God" (p. 31). The "glue" which must hold together the world he is talking about, Burton thus insists, is not divine love, but human love rooted in love of the divine. For as always Burton is concerned with the universe of men.[7] But charity declares that human love is only truly perfected when referred to God: the morality of Aristotle, the friendship of Tully, are of "little worth" unless they be translated through Christian love into a "happy union of love" which governs families, cities, and the heavens themselves (pp. 32-33).

Each subsection setting forth the kinds of love (III. 1.2.1-3) ended with a view of men transformed into something inhuman—Harpies, monsters, beasts—by the excess or defect in them of pleasant, profitable, or honest love. And the sermon on charity must so end, because unless we "be truly linked and touched with this charity," we cannot be Christian men (III.1.3;33).[8] Of

---

7. See Webber, p. 113. My discussion of religious melancholy will indicate the extent to which I feel it is inexact to say that the book does not place man's vision of his world in the context of God's eternal vision.

8. The theme of metamorphosis is ubiquitous in this partition, and I shall touch on some of its appearances in the course of my study. Joan Webber has suggested to me that in describing in terms of transformation a world created and moved by loves human and divine, Burton is doing what Ovid had done in the *Metamorphoses.* That Ovid's philosopher (bk. xv) should so clearly elucidate the constant flux of life ("A universe where nothing ever stays the same, / Time like a river in its ceaseless motion") only to have the poet declare the eternality of his poem, might provide the springboard for an interesting comparison between the poet of fading Eternal Rome and the seventeenth-century Anglican author of a book that managed to reappear, in the same form yet not the same, five times in the author's lifetime and once eleven years posthumously. See also Webber, pp. 111-114.

course we are not so linked, the world falls apart, and "want of this charity" causes "all our woes, miseries, discontent, melancholy" (p. 34). We are melancholy, that is we are not men, but inhuman: "Monsters of men as we are, dogs, wolves, tigers, fiends, incarnate devils, we do not only contend, oppress, and tyrannize ourselves, but as so many firebrands we set on and animate others: our whole life is a perpetual combat, a conflict, a set battle, snarling fit" (p. 35). Instead of loving our neighbors as ourselves, we hate them as we hate ourselves, and they us.

The narration of the medical treatise asked us to consider how a man differs from a dog; this narration asks us to consider where there are Christians whose charity differentiates them from other men: "He that shall see men swear and forswear, lie and bear false witness, to advantage themselves, prejudice others, hazard goods, lives, fortunes, credit, all, to be revenged on their enemies, men so unspeakable in their lusts, unnatural in malice, such bloody designments, Italian blaspheming, Spanish renouncing, etc., may well ask where is charity? . . . Are these Christians? I beseech you, tell me" (p. 38). The point of the first narration was that men do not know as much as they think they know. The point of this narration, concluding as it does with the appeal to charity, is that men know, but are not wise. The narration prepares for the discourse by leaving the reader with the knowledge that all of his love should have something to do with charity, that because it does not, his love is hate, and that if he will see the universal sickness and consider its origins, he will regain charity, which is wisdom:

If we had any sense or feeling of these things, surely we should not go on as we do, in such irregular courses, practise all manner of impieties; our whole carriage would not be so averse from God. If a man would but consider, when he is in the midst and full career of such prodigious and uncharitable actions, how displeasing they are in God's sight, how noxious to himself, . . . surely they would check their desires, curb in their unnatural, inordinate affections, agree amongst themselves, abstain from doing evil, amend their lives, and learn to do well. . . . Why do we contend and vex one another? behold, death is over our heads, and we must shortly give an account of all our uncharitable words and actions; *think upon it, and be wise*. (Pp. 39-40; my italics)

The narration tells the reader the facts he has to know about the following discourse: that love is universal, that his universe depends on charity, that lack of charity is universal woe, and that if he would be wise, if he would think about the disordered chain of love, he will consider all the stories of love and hate that follow in the light of the supposed end of human love, man linked to man through God. In being the narration it also tells us that the universal woes and the necessary reference of man's woes to God appear in Partition III in different ways than they do in I and II: at the end of the subsection in Partition I listing the general symptoms of melancholy, for example, Burton pleads eloquently the need for all men to examine their consciences and return to God (I.3.2.1; 408-409). He there suggests the kind of equivocation or redefinition of disorder that will be made when I and II are joined to Partition III; the introductory section of III, including preface and narration, proclaims that this kind of discourse is properly *the* topic of the Third Partition. "Think upon it—upon mortality and upon the charity that should govern mortal life—and be wise" is the author's dictum that always must be borne in mind as we wander in the pleasant fields of the succeeding partition.

EQUIVOCATION: LOVE IS PASSION

The first two kinds of Love-melancholy are closely related, being the reactions of love (heroical melancholy) and hate (jealousy) called up in man by the inordinate love of woman. By treating Burton's progression from the cause of heroical melancholy to the cure for jealousy in a single section of this chapter, I shall be following Burton, whose running headlines describe both heroical love and jealousy as "love-melancholy," while "religious melancholy" is distinguished by a separate headline. As will be seen, the three varieties of Love-melancholy are also two.

Burton opens the section of love-melancholy by promising to treat his subject with the same precision that governed the non-digressive portions of Partitions I and II: "to discuss it in all his kinds, to examine his several causes, to show his symptoms, indications, prognostics, effects, that so it may be with more facility cured" (III.2.1.2;57). The section in fact follows the intended order, as does the next section on jealousy. But after his initial attack on causes, where paragraph follows paragraph with as close order as ever he achieved with bones and sinews—"Of all causes the remotest are stars"; "The place itself makes much"; "Idleness overthrows all"; "Diet alone is able to cause it" (III.2.2.1;58-63)—Burton begins to expatiate, stories and anecdotes multiply, and the precision of the treatise is lost to immediate view. Burton is sallying forth against, rather than charging in closed ranks, the walled rooms of his treatise of indefinite melancholy. His remarks indicating his wanderings, in fact, serve to remind the reader, who may very well have forgotten, with what portion of the subject of love-melancholy he is supposed to be concerned: "But this is not the matter in hand; . . . no man doubts of these matters; the question is, how and by what means beauty produceth this effect?" (III.2.2.2;76).

Love is not easily ordered or categorized, and the problem of differentiating it arises directly from the nature of the subject, universal passion. As "honest love," passionate love is so much a part of man's nature that it gives man and woman united their human essence (woman seeks man as matter seeks form), and from the beginning of the partition, Burton makes clear that "honest" love is married love: "But this nuptial love is a common passion, an honest, for men to love in the way of marriage; *ut materia appetit formam, sic mulier virum*" (III.2.1.2;52). The relationship of woman to man is that of the passions to reason in mankind, so that in this way also man and woman are made a single human soul by their love: "The husband rules her as head, but she again commands his heart" (p. 53). But the traditional reason-passion hierarchy in man is a notably unstable relationship, and honest love explodes its boundaries to become the kind of "wandering, extravagant, domineering, boundless" passion which is the subject of Burton's treatise. Passion, after all, takes two forms, and in defining love in the narration, Burton reminded us that love and hate are one, for together they are the prime mover of man the passionate animal: " 'love and hatred are the first and most common passions, from which all the rest arise, and are attendant,' as Piccolomineus holds, or, as Nich. Caussinus, the *primum mobile* of all other affections, which carry them all about with them" (III.1.1.2;11). Thus while heroical love defines man—"He is not a man but a block . . . that hath not felt the power of it" (III.2.1.2;52)—it defines his life as tragicomedy because the actions of love are liable to take the form of the actions of hate: "Laodice, the sister of Mithridates, provoked her husband, to give content to a base fellow whom she loved. Alexander, to please Thais, a concubine of his, set Persepolis on fire." So did Constantine Despota, Leucophrye, Pisidice, Diognetus, and Medea express love through passionate, destructive hate, for "Such acts and scenes hath this tragi-comedy of love" (III.2.5.1;188-189).

Boundlessness, a kind of chaotic resistance to definition, is thus the state of man's passion and of the sections that would describe the passion. But *homo sum*. Burton does fit his wandering in pleasant fields into the rooms of the discourse, thus rationalizing the insanity of love; and the very rationalizing or making logical by "art and engine" gives *him* a place in the universal indefiniteness.

But I conclude there is no end of love's symptoms, 'tis a bottomless pit. Love is subject to no dimensions; not to be surveyed by any art or engine; and besides, I am of Haedus' mind, "no man can discourse of love matters, or judge of them aright, that hath not made trial in his own person. . . ." I confess I am but a novice, a contemplator only, . . . [I know not what love is nor am I in love], . . . yet *homo sum*, etc., not altogether inexpert in this subject, . . . and what I say is merely reading . . . by mine own observation and others' relation. (III.2.3;184)

The "engine" Burton eventually will use to encompass love-melancholy is the invention of jealousy as a type of Love-melancholy on the same logical level as heroical melancholy, an invention which contradicts the cure of heroical love and prepares for the treatise to refer men's loves to God's love in the section on religious melancholy.

Immoderate, inordinate love is folly, the opposite of that wisdom which is our end as rational animals differing from dogs, and our goal as readers of Burton's Third Partition. And it is precisely that kind of folly for which Burton tried to give the cures of common-sense wisdom in the Consolatory Digression. Common sense, for example, tells a man, "Keep thine own counsel, reveal not thy secrets, be silent in thine intentions" (II.3.7;204), but men in love "fly to bawds, panders, . . . rather than fail, to the devil himself," and are caught in the machinations of the "art, or a liberal science, as Lucian calls it" of bawdry (III.2.2.5;126-127). Common sense tells a man, "Marry not an old crone or a fool for money" (II.3.7;205), but the passion for money lures men to folly and turns truth inside out: "If she be rich, then she is fair, fine, absolute and perfect, then they burn like fire. . . . If he be rich, he is a man, a fine man, and a proper man, she will go to Jacaktres or Tidore with him" (III.2.2.3;100-101). Passion even has its own kind of perverse wisdom which captures the essence of its folly: a lover picks a quarrel with her sweetheart in order to be reconciled, "*Amantium irae amoris redintegratio,* as the old saying is, the falling out of lovers is the renewing of love. . . . And surely this aphorism is most true; . . . 'If a lover be not jealous, angry, waspish, apt to fall out, sigh and swear, he is no true lover' " (III.2.2.4;114-115). Folly is the only wisdom of men—the very best men—ruled by the *primum mobile* of the passions, and the result of folly is that they cannot govern themselves (a result to which we shall see Burton address himself in the cures): "the very best of them, if once they be overtaken with this passion, the most staid, discreet, generous and wise, otherwise able to govern themselves, in this commit many absurdities, many indecorums, unbefitting their gravity and persons" (III.2.3;153).

The inverted world of wisdom that is folly is a fictional one where artifice is not only the cause and effect of men's illness, but also the method used to define it. Artificiality is the greatest "provocation to lust," and Burton spends no little space describing the unnatural metamorphoses of women which lure men into passion, for "beauty is more beholding to art than nature" (III. 2.2.3;89). And if the effect of love as well is to "bewitch and strangely change us" (III.2.2.2;85), so does Burton construct the very arguments as to the causes and symptoms of love-melancholy by means of fictions. He describes bawds and panders as practicing an "art or liberal science," and this is exactly what he does in shaping love-melancholy to the form of a medical treatise. He "liberates" himself from the rules and subject matter of science, but keeps the form of the medical treatise; the "rooms" of the surly discourse house the delightful fictions of love-melancholy. So both discourse and fictions are liberated—fiction is given the shape of "Truth" (and stories do tell truths), while the scientific form is allowed to reach out and envelop truths about melancholy disguised as fable. Burton thus achieves science liberated, or art.

As a liberal scientist, Burton in the Third Partition uses fiction, the pleasant stories that make up the body of this discourse, to prove his points and yet be proved by them. Love-melancholy is both the subject matter of poetry and poetry's inspiration, so "art or liberal science" allows tautology and circular reasoning, for these illogical methods can illuminate truths. Man lusting, for example, is inhuman because passion rules reason; he is a "brute"; myths tell us that men become beasts; the poets who made the myths meant to say what I am saying, that man is brutish:

The major part of lovers are carried headlong like so many brute beasts; reason counsels one way, thy friends, fortunes, shame, disgrace, danger, and an ocean of cares that will certainly follow; yet this furious lust precipitates, counterpoiseth, weighs down on the other; though it be their utter undoing, perpetual infamy, loss, yet they will do it, and become at last *insensati,* void of sense; degenerate into dogs, hogs, asses, brutes; as Jupiter into a bull, Apuleius an ass, Lycaon a wolf, Tereus a lapwing, Callisto a bear, Elpenor and Gryllus into swine by Circe. For what else may we think those ingenious poets to have shadowed in their witty fictions and poems, but that a man once given over to lust (as Fulgentius interprets that of Apuleius, Alciat of Tereus) is no better than a beast.   (III.2.1;154-155)

That would be a strange kind of reasoning for a scientific discourse, since the proof seems to be of the poetry, not of the premise, which is assumed. As logical statement it is about as rational as Burton's Q.E.D. was in the Consolatory Digression (see above, page 107), but, as that Q.E.D. showed digression's ability to open up "proper" boundaries, so this "reasoning" is indicative of the way poetic fiction is used to liberate the treatise and expand our understanding of human actions and of the way poetry proves truth about life if not about scientific facts: lovers, Burton will finally show us, *act* like characters out of fiction; they poeticize life.

Burton, of course, is not pretending to be a poet creating the pleasant fields of love: he is the poetic scholar wandering in them. His method is to collect and dilate, so that even as the scholar constructing a treatise of the causes of love-melancholy disappears behind a mass of stories, figures of speech, and poetic topics, so the poetry that supplies the proof of the diverse causes disappears into the scholarly exhaustiveness. Thus Burton must delineate the ways in which woman's beauty "ariseth from the due proportion of the whole, or from each several part." A poet would make an *effictio*, but Burton not only refers us to a whole list of "poets, historiographers, and those amorous writers" who have "most accurately described a perfect beauty, an absolute feature, and that through every member," he also takes their descriptions of eyes, teeth, neck, etc., and collects under each "absolute feature" several or many examples of poetic tributes. Thus he achieves not a generalized portrait of beautiful woman, cause of love-melancholy, but a greatly expanded scholar's *effictio* which seems to say more about poetic inventiveness than about woman's beauty as cause of passionate love. The three-page passage becomes almost a parody of itself as it climaxes with a long section headed by a single trait, "A flaxen hair," which draws in everyone from Castor and Pollux to King Arthur's wife, to "effeminate fellows" (something of an anomaly) and "Venetian ladies at this day" in order to establish flaxen hair as a legitimate characteristic of beauty (III.2.2.2; 79-82).

The point of Burton's use of his many pleasant stories is that they are fiction. Truth about heroical melancholy comes through the cause-sympton-cure sequence which says scientifically that love-melancholy exists everywhere as man's universal ill. Scientifically ordered rooms of the treatise disclose this truth, but to prove it, Burton relies on fiction that proves itself, as it were, to be fiction ("For what else may we think those ingenious poets to have shadowed"). He can prove a fact about love-melancholy by relating a story: "This story I do therefore repeat, that you may see of what force these enticements are"; but such a story is its own truth, and "Whether this be a true story, or a tale, I will not much contend; it serves to illustrate this which I have said" (III.2.2.4;117). The member concerned with symptoms of love-melancholy establishes that the textbooks of the liberal scientist are not those of the medical man. Poet follows poet, myth follows myth, and the rooms of the liberated treatise house endless citations of literary authority. So on one page: "These be the companions of lovers, and the ordinary symptoms, as the poet repeats them"; "Every poet is full of such catalogues of love-symptoms"; "The comical poet hath prettily painted out this passage amongst the rest" (III.2.3;142).

The tragicomic world of love-melancholy allows man to see himself in a storybook existence where life is pleasant fiction; for even love's raging fire is expressed by "amorous emblems," and "continual pain and torture" is testified to in the case histories of poets, not of madhouse physicians (pp. 150-151). Effects in life are made dependent on the causes in art. A story is told; it is amplified by poetry and proved by the logic of mythology; and from it we conclude a truth about life: Paulus Jovius taxes an "old gouty fellow" for loving a young girl and wishing to dance:

Many laughed him to scorn for it, but this omnipotent love would have it so. . . .
      Love hasty with his purple staff did make
      Me follow and the dance to undertake.

And 'tis no news this, no indecorum; for why? a good reason
may be given of it. Cupid and Death met both in an inn; and
being merrily disposed, they did exchange some arrows from
either quiver; ever since young men die, and oftentimes old
men dote.   (Pp. 178-179)

The final truth about life ruled by inordinate passion is
that fiction is truth, that action in life is reduced by lovers
to the plane of *mere* fiction so that the poetical truth of
mythological metaphors is translated into the poeticizing
of life by hyperbole:

Our knights errant, and Sir Lancelots of these days, I hope will
adventure as much for ladies' favours, as the Squire of Dames,
Knight of the Sun, Sir Bevis of Southampton, or that renowned
peer, [Orlando]; . . . he is a very coward, a block and a beast,
that will not do as much, but they will sure, they will. . . . If
she bed them they will go barefoot to Jerusalem, to the Great
Cham's court, to the East Indies, to fetch her a bird to wear in
her hat, . . . serve twice seven years as Jacob did for Rachel.
. . . Her dog, picture, and everything she wears, they adore it
as a relic.   (Pp. 166-167)

And so the final symptom of love-melancholy: as fictions
make men love, men in love make fictions: "But above all
the other symptoms of lovers, this is not lightly to be
overpassed, that likely of what condition soever, if once
they be in love, they turn to their ability, rhymers,
ballet-makers, and poets" (p. 179). Burton's treatise of
heroical melancholy, then, defines lovesickness as logical tautology, for it begins in artifice which inverts man's
nature, it is described through fiction which alone can
express it truly, and it ends in the production of artifact:
"This love is that salt that seasoneth our harsh and dull
labours, and gives a pleasant relish to our other un-
savoury proceedings. . . . All our feasts almost, mas-
ques, mummings, banquets, merry meetings, weddings,

pleasing songs, fine tunes, poems, love stories, plays, comedies, Atellanes, jigs, Fescennines, elegies, odes, etc., proceed hence" (p. 181).

The tragicomedy of love thus threatens to be a self-perpetuating, self-contained world of pleasant fiction made unpleasant by the fact that its causes and its prognostics center in folly which takes the form not only of harmless fictions but of distinctly uncharitable "acts and scenes." Lovers kill themselves or burn cities or kill their children for the sake of love: "Such acts and scenes hath this tragicomedy of love" (pp. 188-189). But art's improvements on nature can represent truth about wisdom as well as truth about folly. Dancing as cause of love-melancholy is a "great allurement," and yet, its very artificiality, which can (the story goes) be so suggestive as to lead dancers and spectators, too, posthaste to bed (III.2.2.4;118-119), also expresses metaphorical truths about physics and political science, for sun, moon, stars, "our greatest counsellors, and staid senators," all dance (pp. 120-121). That kind of truth can only be seen of course when art is ruled by moderation (p. 121), which is to say that it reflects the rule of law, natural or political. And the cures of love-melancholy are through artifice, but also of artifice and by law. Heroical love has to be seen in light of rules that restate passion as ordered love, a reasonable kind of existence that makes evident the relationships charity (which is what we are still "thinking on") defines in life.

To begin his cures Burton starts with the authority of the surly discourse and gives rules of "Labour, Diet, Physic, Fasting, etc.," and yet he does not leave the pleasant fields but roams amid poets, philosophers, and Church Fathers somewhat whimsically: try imprisonment, and a diet of bread and water to punish lovers out of loving, "But this, you will say, is comically spoken" (III.2.5.1;191). "Witty invention" then offers cures, and takes the form of tale-telling to bolster the counsels given: Petrarch would not take Laura once she was offered him, for "great discretion it argues in such a man that he can so contain himself; but when thou art once in love, to moderate thyself . . . is a singular point of wisdom" (III.2.5.2;198). But invention goes further to include lies, for what is more appropriate than that the disease contracted through fiction should be cured by fiction: "other remedies are to be annexed, fair and foul means, as to persuade, promise, threaten, terrify, or to divert by some contrary passion, rumour, tales, news, or some witty invention to alter his affection" (p. 200). "Artificial allurements," after all, have made the beloved what she is, so that foul means become fair and you tell the truth while lying if you tell a lover his beloved is bald or her breath stinks, or tell her that he is an eunuch or common drunkard (p. 201).

Burton next cures by suggesting "good counsels and persuasion," which, be it noted, "I should have handled in the first place" (III.2.5.3;204). But he did *not* handle them first, allowing the advice which is offered for all situations (if she be honest or a whore; if they be of equal or unequal ages; if she be beautiful or ugly, rich or poor, and so on) to follow the witty inventions of deception. "Counsel" is here the interpretation put upon a fiction, the explanation that enlightens and makes a pleasant tale didactic. But interpretation is a chancy business, for stories can mean folly (dancing is seduction) or wisdom (dancing is the order of the universe). So as we read the counsels which can fit either side of any coin of love and see wisdom extracted from any appearance of foolishness, we are compelled to realize that all advice is deception of a kind, for truths are contradicted by opposite truths, which is to say again that foul means are fair and that truth is only a lie told from a different point of view: "Take heed; if she be a slut, thou wilt loathe her; if proud, she'll beggar thee, . . . if fair and wanton, she'll make thee a cornuto; if deformed, she will paint. . . . If she do not paint, she will look so filthy, thou canst not love her, and that peradventure will make thee unhonest" (p. 222).

Burton's final cures appear in answer to the stalemate that wisdom has got itself into, and they suggest opposite means of correcting the storybook artificiality of the universe of love-melancholy. The first is prelude: "Philters, Magical, and Poetical Cures." The world of poetical fiction is momentarily joined to and read as part of the world of the supernatural, and a single judgment is made of the physic offered by both—that it is unlawful: "Where persuasions and other remedies will not take place, many fly to unlawful means, philters, amulets, magic spells, ligatures, characters, charms, which as a wound with the spear of Achilles, if so made must be so cured" (III.2.5.4;226). The "fabulous remedies" of "old poets and phantastical writers"—leaping from charmed rocks or bathing in charmed rivers—are juxtaposed with the "characteristical images" of astrologers and "magnetical medicines" of the magicians. To none of these cures does Burton in any way subscribe; in none of them does he indicate interest. They are listed and tales told without comment except for the non-committal " 'Tis not permitted to be done, I confess; yet often attempted" and except for a single reference to "absurd remedies" (pp. 226-227). The subsection stands as almost toneless reportage in the midst of the partition in which Burton can always be detected roaming and delighting.

"Fantastic" remedies for love's fantasies make no effort toward wisdom, and being as foolish as heroical melancholy itself, they are simply "unlawful." By dispatching them so quickly Burton seems to suggest that the wounds of love are not after all to be cured by the same instruments that inflicted them. The last cure reacts against these; it is the cure of rebellion, but rebellion against love which is fantasy: "Where none of all these remedies will take place, I know no other but that all lovers must make an head and rebel, as they did in Ausonius, and crucify Cupid till he grant their request, or satisfy their desires" (III.2.5.4;228). The "last refuge and earnest remedy" for lovers is startling: "When no other means will take effect . . . let them go together, and enjoy one another" (III.2.5.5;228). But of course simple satisfaction is not meant, for Burton's wanderings in pleasant fields lead him not into an euphoric world of promiscuous anarchy, but to the rule of law and "honest" love. The strongest cure for the illness of man the passionate animal is legality. Burton's final prescription for the artificiality of heroical love contrasts sharply with the foolish, unthinking, and blasphemous plundering of Love's castle represented, for example, by the fiction of the *Romance of the Rose*. For Burton is seeking not romance but wisdom, and somehow his wanderings have to bring him out on the road to charity.

Thinking about charity's wisdom, Burton gives a definite alternative to, rather than ameliorative for, heroical melancholy that goes past diet, deception, good counsel, and unlawful means to "the custom and form of law," which is a man and a woman united as husband and wife. Magical philters and poetical cures are unlawful in being unnatural, but this custom of marriage is the law of nature:

When you have all done, saith Avicenna, "there is no speedier or safer course than to join the parties together *according to their desires and wishes, the custom and form of law;* and so we have seen him quickly restored to his former health, that was languished away to skin and bones; after his desire was satisfied, his discontent ceased, and we thought it strange; our opinion is therefore that in such cases *nature is to be obeyed."* What remains then but to join them in marriage? (P. 229; my italics)

As sections and subsections in Partitions I and II always gave Burton an alternative to the chaos of too many authorities and too much indecision, so Partition III gives life its rule of law. Not only does the form of the scientific discourse enclose and distinguish Burton's explorations of human loves, the form reflects the answers, for with all kinds of Love-melancholy, the ultimate human cures will be "custom and *form"*—of law, of words (even God's Word) spoken in context, of human thought in language subjected to formal rationalizing limits, as life is made reasonable by love that is formed and ordered. So "following nature" here implies a context of law to restrain love. For the purposes of this section Burton insists on marriage, even to the point of converting all the stories of difficult courtships he can muster, including those of Echo and Narcissus and Dido and Aeneas, into ones which assume marriage to be the goal (III.2.5.5). Nor is he using "marriage" as mere euphemism for doing what comes naturally; he worries out all the impediments to marriage and ways to get around them, and he is speaking always of the "custom and form of law": " 'Tis *cornutum sophisma,* hard to resolve: if they marry they forfeit estates, they are undone, and starve themselves through beggary and want; if they do not marry, in this heroical passion they furiously rage, are tormented, and torn in pieces by their predominate affections" (p. 243). To follow nature in this sense is to follow also St. Paul—"Better marry than burn" (p. 245)—so that "rash vows" of chastity and popish pronouncements—"a greater sin for a priest to marry, than to keep a concubine at home" (pp. 244-245)—like false servitude to the supposedly necessary influence of the stars (p. 243) are as unlawful as magic potions. They are man-made misconceptions of the ordinances of God: "it is abominable, impious, adulterous, and sacrilegious, what men make and ordain after their own furies to cross God's laws" (p. 245).

In contrast to the preceding section, Burton is full of interest in his subject. Didacticism and entertainment merge as the author greets his characters jovially. He is especially enthusiastic when he considers tales of those who ignored artificial allurements and married for love only; the king of Egypt married a virgin for love: "I say this was heroically done, and like a prince; I commend him for it, and all such as have means, that will either do (as he did) themselves, or so for love, etc., marry their children" (p. 241). And so of others: " 'Tis well done, methinks"; "If thou lovest the party, do as much"; " 'twas nobly done of Theodosius": the tragicomedy of love becomes unalloyed comedy. Passion, indeed, is cured and order restored not only in the heirarchy of the reasonable marriage but in society as well when unselfish love seeks a wife without regard for dowries: "If they would care less for wealth, we should have much more content and quietness in a commonwealth" (p. 239).

Married love has another unselfish end, of course, when Nature's law and God's law join forces to define heroical love without those unnatural excesses which dehumanize man. In the context of legal and customary restraint, love—even the physical union itself—converts man from passionate animal to political animal, builder of cities. Burton barely mentioned this end of "honest love," the propagation of the race, when he acknowledged the ideal conjugal love in the subsection of love's power and extent (a single untranslated Latin phrase serves, *"et quae generi humano immortalitatem parat"* [III. 2.1.2;52]). Coming instead after all the fictions and delight in artifice of the preceding section, the discussion here, with its citations of Tacitus, Trismegistus, and the others, has the force of a reply to the merely literary, delightful, character of the world of heroical love. Honest love is not a self-perpetuating fiction, but a self-perpetuating world of empires. For when he submits his passions to the rule of law, man creates the basis of social and political order:

And howsoever, though it were all troubles, . . . it must willingly be undergone for public good's sake. . . . *Malum est mulier, sed necessarium malum,* they are necessary evils, and for our own ends we must make use of them to have issue, *Supplet Venus ac restituit humanum genus,* and to propagate the Church. For to what end is a man born? why lives he, but to increase the world? and how shall he do that well, if he do not marry? *Matrimonium humano generi immortalitatem tribuit,* saith Nevisanus, matrimony makes us immortal, and, according to Tacitus, 'tis . . . the sole and chief prop of an empire, . . . which Pelopidas objected to Epaminondas, he was an unworthy member of a commonwealth that left not a child after him to defend it.   (III.2.5.5;251)

But love under the custom and form of law, being the best available cure for heroical love, cures the pain of love

without necessarily curing its folly. Burton brings out his
two briefs for and against marriage. He epitomizes the
wisdom that counsels the good of marriage only, in his
"antiparodia," to epitomize the wisdom that advises
against it. The stalemate of wisdom's interpretations of
the acts and scenes of love has not been broken, for good
counsel can still interpret any situation as good or evil:
"Hast thou means?—thou hast one to keep and increase
it"; but then, "thou hast one to spend it." "Thou art
made a father by a fair and happy issue"; but then "Thou
art made a cornuto by an unchaste wife, and shalt bring
up other folks' children instead of thine own." "If nature
escape not punishment, surely thy will shall not avoid
it"; but then, "Is marriage honourable? What an immortal crown belongs to virginity!" (pp. 252-253). Marriage is not the final answer, but *an* answer to be put to
the test. Art and reason equally can argue about the effectiveness of the restraint imposed on man by custom
and law, so the thing to do is, with common man, to try it;
"so doth every philosopher plead pro and con, every
poet thus argues the case (though what cares *vulgus
hominum* what they say?); . . . when all is said, yet since
some be good, some bad, let's put to the venture"
(p. 253).

Burton closes the section with epithalamia and with
best wishes for those who join the experiment: "God
send us all good wives, every man his wish in this kind,
and me mine!" (pp. 255-256), but he does not close the
question of love-melancholy. For the last lines of the
section find him looking back to his earlier—his "rather"—speech (which includes all the pleasant fields of
love and the suggested cures for love-melancholy) as he
looks forward to his new topic. Having said "sufficient"

of love-melancholy he turns to jealousy, but only in saying with Chaucer that is he going forward in order to answer the purpose of what has gone before.

[We have now said sufficient on the subject of love, under correction, as he saith, of any one who knoweth better. He who would know more of the remedies for love may consult Jason Pratensis, etc.; among the poets, Ovid, our own Chaucer], etc., with whom I conclude.

> For my words here and every part,
> I speak hem all under correction,
> Of you that feeling have in love's art,
> And put it all in your discretion,
> To entreat or make diminution,
> Of my language, that I you beseech:
> But now to purpose of my rather speech.   (P. 257)

Burton's treatment of jealousy shows clearly why the answer of customs and law to heroical melancholy does not work, for in it he takes the other view of man the passionate animal and finds in him the equivocation of "love, that is, hate." By separating jealousy from his other subjects, he specifically invents an order for treating Love-melancholy which proves heroical passion and jealously to be opposite ways of looking at universal malaise from the single point of view of honest married love. Given its own section, jealousy takes on the property of a major equivalent topic to heroical melancholy, while marriage, as the cure for passion, becomes structurally the fulcrum on which are balanced the two discussions of the passionate melancholy (love) which precedes it and the passionate melancholy (jealous hatred) which occurs after it. Burton has told us before that the illnesses which precede and follow matrimony are a *single* disease, "this burning lust" (III.2.1.2;54). But having understood that marriage means a reinstatement of the rule of law into the chaotic and less than productive situations of love, we now see jealousy as not simply post-married love-melancholy, but counterstatement to the "venture" of married love. Having an equivalent room invented for it in Burton's discourse, jealousy replies to the cure given at the end of the earlier section:

[Some] put jealousy for a cause of melancholy, others for a symptom; because melancholy persons, amongst these passions and perturbations of the mind, are most obnoxious to it. *But methinks* for the latitude it hath, and that prerogative above other ordinary symptoms, *it ought to be treated of as a species apart,* being of so great and eminent note, so furious a passion, and almost of as great extent as love itself, as Benedetto Varchi holds, "no love without a mixture of jealousy. . . ." For these causes *I will dilate and treat of it by itself, as a bastard branch or kind of love-melancholy, which, as heroical love goeth commonly before marriage, doth usually follow,* torture, and crucify in like sort, deserves therefore to be rectified alike, requires as much care and industry in setting out the several causes of it, prognostics and cures.   (III.3.1.1;257; my italics)

Jealousy is an equivocation of love, and to describe the relation between the two kinds of passion, love as love and love as hate, Burton makes his structure equivocate. In Partition I he had been able to sort Love-melancholy from the other types partly by reducing other men's infinite species to infinite symptoms (see above, page 128). Here he provides a special room in his treatise for the "bastard branch or kind of love-melancholy" by inverting his previous formula and saying, "symptom, *id est,* species." Jealousy could be thought of as a subtype of heroical melancholy, but the structure of corresponding sections says that it is a species equivalent to the preceding species, and so verifies the wisdom and usefulness of Burton's shift in the Third Partition to the dominant logical order of *kind*.

Burton defines jealousy first in terms of love: it is a " 'certain suspicion which the lover hath of the party he chiefly loveth, lest he or she should be enamoured of another'; or any eager desire to enjoy some beauty alone, to have it proper to himself only, a fear or doubt lest any foreigner should participate or share with him in his love" (p. 258). But he then discards as equivocations those "jealousies" which focus on the beloved as object—parents' jealousy over their children, Paul's over the Church, God's over his people—for these are metaphors, "to show the care and solicitude they have of them" (p. 258). Only the metaphorical meaning of jealousy is love—"care and solicitude"—for "proper" jealousy is "bastard" love, illegitimate love which focuses not on the fair object but on the concern of the lover for himself, and manifests itself as "fear, sorrow, anguish, suspicion, hatred, etc." (p. 259).

Jealousy, in all the equivocations Burton mentions, represents the opposite of that charity we as Burton's readers are supposed to be "thinking on," for it restates love's actions as tyranny over one's fellow men (pp. 259-261). The true topic of his discourse, jealousy in marriage, especially proves the truth of "love, *id est*, hate" because it destroys the delight of the best possible occasion of love and substitutes for conjugal love

". . . a fury, a continual fever, . . . a martyrdom, a mirth-marring monster: . . . This jealousy which I am to treat of, is that which belongs to married men, in respect of their own wives; to whose estate, as no sweetness, pleasure, happiness can be compared in the world, if they live quietly and lovingly together; so if they disagree or be jealous, those bitter pills of sorrow and grief, disastrous mischiefs, mischances, tortures, gripings, discontents, are not to be separated from them. (Pp. 263-264)

By inventing an equivalent logical place in his treatise for jealousy, Burton tips the balance against his own cure for love-melancholy and so denies the hope given melancholy man in the last part of his earlier section (or, again to recall the transitional Chaucer quotation, of his "rather speech"). If the best we can do is the restraint of passion by the custom and form of law, we have not yet found wisdom, for legalism produces self-centered concern lest the fair object in any way be shared, and so marriage recreates itself illegitimately as jealousy. The section on jealousy confirms, momentarily at least, that Burton's "*antiparodia*" was right: married love brings forth not "fair and happy issue" but its own bastard, hatred.

Jealousy's symptoms and prognostics work out Burton's theme that the "issue" of marriage is not the comfortable reinstatement of order, not in fact the propagation of the race and of empires and the reassertion of stability in man, but tyranny—the wild tyranny of hatred over love: the jealous husband "continues off and on, as the toy takes him, the object moves him, but most part brawling, fretting, unquiet he is, accusing and suspecting not strangers only, but brothers and sisters, father and mother, nearest and dearest friends" (III.3.2;281). Furthermore, married love, reduced to the melancholy of jealousy, "reproduces" not true civilizations, but cruel, bastardized images of nations and families, for it leads to the twisting of law and custom out of the shape that human understanding should give them: the grotesque inhumane laws against jealousy and adultery, whether of the Hebrews, Egyptians,

Carthaginians, Turks, Athenians, or Italians, "wherein they are to be severely punished, cut in pieces, burned, *vivi-comburio*, buried alive, with several expurgations, etc., are they not as so many symptoms of incredible jealousy?" (p. 285). And jealousy's prognostics are its descendents, hatred, frenzy, madness, injury, murder, and despair (III.3.3;286). Thus love's acts and scenes viewed through this equivocation are not tragicomedy, but pure tragedy, and the substance of the section is in its "tragical stories" (p. 287).

The cures restore to the world of Love-melancholy its tragicomic nature, for they consider jealousy as a manifestation of folly rather than as an absolute "fountain of murders." Burton asks that for cure jealous men make the same estimation of their jealousy that the discontented are asked in Partition II to make of their discontent: "Only this I add, that if it be considered aright, which causeth this jealous passion, be it just or unjust, whether with or without cause, true or false, it ought not so heinously be taken; 'tis no such real or capital matter, that it should make so deep a wound" (III.3.4.1; 289). Burton's counsels turn men back, as it were, to the kind of wisdom possible in Partition II for rational man; passionate man is told that this wound hurts not his soul, and he is asked to consider aright—which, we remember, meant considering himself in terms of his own limited human nature and being content with life's journey as it is.

Jealousy has contradicted the proposition that the form legality gives to life is a workable cure for love's follies, so Burton is reduced to offering wisdom that can be read on either side of any coin, the same kind of wisdom that may or may not satisfy men sick of heroical

melancholy or men sick of other discontents. Once more
we are given the wisdom of common-sense philosophy:
"wise men bear their horns in their hearts, fools on their
foreheads" (III.3.4.2;296); "If a man have a lock which
every man's key will open as well as is own, why should
he think to keep it private to himself?" (III.3.4.1;290).
The world of love which is hate resumes a comical cast,
and the stories are again ironical and even laughable.
There is the cure of communal life represented in "a
new sect of Adamites" of whom it is said, "When the
priest repeated that of Genesis, 'Increase and multiply,'
out went the candles in the place where they met, 'and
without all respect of age, persons, conditions, catch
that catch may, every man took her that came next' "
(III.3.4.2;298). Or there are the ounce-of-prevention
stories of self-castration which, whether of the baker in
Basil, or the young man assigned to conduct his queen
to Syria, or of St. Francis himself, are somehow made
delightful (p. 299).

Jealousy was to have been to the purpose of Burton's
"rather speech," his earlier section on love-melancholy;
it has instead ended like the preceding parts of the book
in being not only like all the counsels for and against
love but even like the counsels of Partition II. But Burton
does not conclude the section of jealousy any more than
he concluded the section of heroical melancholy. For
Love-melancholy has a third manifestation, and the
proverbial wisdom of cheese-trenchers is not the wisdom of charity we have in mind, nor is it the final cure
for jealousy. The last and best cure for jealousy is not
even given. Instead, Burton keeps it a secret, except that
he hints, by his closing remarks, that what he will not
"publish" may yet be discovered to us if instead of
proverbial counsels we take as guide a new kind of proverb which is prayer.

One other sovereign remedy I could repeat, an especial antidote against jealousy, an excellent cure, but I am not now
disposed to tell it, not that like a covetous empiric I conceal it
for any gain, but for some other reasons, I am not willing to
publish it; if you be very desirous to know it, when I meet you
next I will peradventure tell you what it is in your ear. This is
the best counsel I can give; which he that hath need of, as occasion serves, may apply unto himself. In the meantime, *Di
talem terris avertite pestem*, as the proverb is; from heresy,
jealousy and frenzy, good Lord, deliver us. (III.3.4.2;311).

Aphorism becomes petition, and the new proverb
which we take for cure "in the meantime" between now
and when Burton next meets us, indicates that to be
cured of jealousy we have to ask delivery from *all* kinds
of Love-melancholy. If we are "very desirous to know,"
we may meet Burton next in the rooms of religious
melancholy, and the best cure for jealousy, not published abroad but whispered in our ears, may be found
there if we have taken the proverbial prayer to heart.
For the wisdom of this proverb asks us to look at
jealousy, the manifestation of love as hate, as the logical
center on which the partition hinges its discussions of
heroical melancholy or frenzy, and religious melancholy
or heresy: "as the proverb is; from heresy, jealousy and
frenzy, good Lord, deliver us."

EQUIVOCATION: LOVE IS GOD

Burton opens the final section of his book by asserting
that, as he had given jealousy a place in the structure
analogous to that of heroical melancholy, so he has
designed a similar structural innovation in this matter of
religious melancholy: "That there is such a distinct
species of love-melancholy, no man hath ever yet
doubted; but whether this subdivision of Religious

Melancholy be warrantable, it may be controverted. . . .
I have no pattern to follow as in some of the rest, no man
to imitate. No physician hath as yet distinctly written of
it as of the other; all acknowledge it a most notable
symptom, some a cause, but few a species or kind"
(III.4.1.1;311-312). As of jealousy, he is saying of religious melancholy, "symptom—or cause—*id est*, species,"
but that is not where his innovation lies, for "some do
not obscurely make a distinct species of it, dividing
love-melancholy into that whose object is women and
into the other whose object is God" (p. 312). The innovation lies instead in making a third subdivision which
completes the process of structural equivocation we
have been following.

Having first by his structure declared jealousy to be a
type equivalent to heroical and religious melancholy,
but having used that room in his treatise to make his
way from love to religion, Burton now reverts to a twofold distinction of types. His "pattern" of subdivisions is
new because it gives Love-melancholy its three types,
and yet, since religious melancholy deals with a species
opposed to "that whose object is women," the final
section is simultaneously the logical answer to or development from the single set of problems Burton has
been following throughout both sections of heroical love
and jealousy. Religious melancholy, in fact, reasserts
universal madness which is indivisible; for by making
three species of Love-melancholy where there are two,
Burton contradicts the whole rationale of division and
subdivision and recreates a picture of man gazing at
chaos:

Give me but a little leave, and I will set before your eyes in
brief a stupend, vast, infinite ocean of incredible madness and

folly: a sea full of shelves and rocks, sands, gulfs, euripes and contrary tides, full of fearful monsters, uncouth shapes, roaring waves, tempests, and siren calms, halcyonian seas, unspeakable misery, such comedies and tragedies, such absurd and ridiculous, feral and lamentable fits, that I know not whether they are more to be pitied or derided, or may be believed, but that we daily see the same still practised in our days, fresh examples, *nova novitia,* fresh objects of misery and madness in this kind that are still represented unto us, abroad, at home, in the midst of us, in our bosoms.   (P. 313)

However, liberal science, method freed by art, is equal to the occasion. Burton divides religious melancholy according to whether it manifests love of God in excess or defect, thereby emphasizing the relationship between this section and those on the love whose object is women. Now the love of God is the love of men also, and the definition of God as fair object leads us immediately to a different kind of legalism from that suggested as the "honest" cure to heroical passion. We are back to charity: the love of God is a "habit infused of God, . . . 'by which a man is inclined to love God above all, and his neighbour as himself.' . . . 'In this we know,' saith John . . . 'we love the children of God, when we love God and keep His commandments.' " The legalism of form and custom has been found unsatisfactory as a cure for passionate man's disease, and so this section presents another love which is "honest" but which depends on God's law rather than man's custom: "This is the love of God, that we keep His commandments" (pp. 318-319). And the commandment in question is that of Christ, which involves love of men in our love of God.

Furthermore, love of God demands that a distinction

between God and creation be made, so that in loving
men we have a reference point ouside the melancholic
world. We are back to the question of artificial and
natural worlds, and to the problem of the self-perpetuating world of love's tragicomedy. Religious melancholy, in excess or defect, is specifically uncharitable
and unnatural.

> We love the world too much; God too little; our neighbour
> not at all, or for our own ends. . . . The chief thing we respect is
> our commodity: and what we do is for fear of worldly punish-
> ment, for vainglory, praise of men, fashion, and such by-
> respects, not for God's sake. We neither know God aright,
> nor seek, love, or worship Him as we should. And for these
> defects, we involve ourselves into a multitude of errors, we
> swerve from this true love and worship of God: which is a
> cause unto us of unspeakable miseries; running into both
> extremes, we become fools, madmen, without sense. (P. 318)

The division of religious melancholy into excessive and
defective types is according to law and nature. Superstition is overconfidence in our ability to "satisfy the
law"—that is, man-made laws misrepresented as
God's—while atheism is the inability of "carnal-minded
men" to distinguish God from nature, resulting in a
confused and false perception of the world (p. 319).

In discussing superstition, Burton develops the theme
of legitimacy and illegitimacy we have followed through
heroical melancholy and jealousy. As heroical-melan-
choly has a "bastard branch" in jealousy, so superstition
is the bastard of true religion—"religion's ape, religion's
bastard, religion's shadow, false glass." It is as thor-
ough as it is boundless, attacking the whole man—the
"brain, heart, will, understanding, soul itself, and all
the faculties of it, *totum compositum*," and the "world

itself . . . all times have been misaffected, past, present" (III.4.1.1;321). Seeing superstition as the "quintessence of madness" (p. 320), we understand what kind of bastardy we have descended to, for superstition, in depriving us of civility, makes humanity itself counterfeit. We may differ from dogs only in being sticks and stones: "religion makes wild beasts civil, superstition makes wise men beasts and fools; and the discreetest that are, if they give way to it, are no better than dizzards; nay more, if that of Plotinus be true, . . . that's the drift of religion, to make us like him whom we worship, what shall be the end of idolaters, but to degenerate into stocks and stones?" (III.4.1.3;361). As marriage is supposed to perpetuate commonwealths and empires, so religion is supposed to give states the legitimacy of divine authority, but "human invention" reverses the order and turns divine law to human ends, which involves creating religion in the image of the state: the devil's instruments "are politicians, statesmen, priests, heretics, blind guides, imposters, pseudoprophets" who maintain, alter, and vary religion, subverting it to "mere policy, a cloak, a human invention" (III.4.1.2;328).

So when Burton is speaking of the love of God in excess he is speaking not only of sick individuals but even more of sick institutions of civilization, the bastardized chain of "love" uniting men as they are supposed to be united in Christ through the Church. The devil "doth so combine and glue together his superstitious followers in love and affection, that they will live and die together: and what an innate hatred hath he still inspired to any other superstitions opposite!" (III. 4.1.3;348). Love *and* hate are the first general symptom of superstition—"no greater concord, no greater discord than that which proceeds from religion" (p. 348)—so that collective man expresses his passion through distorted reflections of God's universe and of men's community with God. Superstition can be epitomized as the devil's counterfeiting heaven and hell (III.4.1.2;331) or as man's invention of a community of love-and-hate, for the tragicomic world of fiction becomes the tragic world of fact when religion issues in illegitimate states and bastard societies:

... that high priest of Rome, the dam of that monstrous and superstitious breed, the bull-bellowing Pope which now rageth in the West, that three-headed Cerberus, hath played his part. "Whose religion at this day is mere policy, a state wholly composed of superstition and wit, and needs nothing but wit and superstition to maintain it, that useth colleges and religious houses to as good purpose as forts and castles, and doth more at this day"—by a company of scribbling parasites, fiery-spirited friars, zealous anchorites, hypocritical confessors, and those praetorian soldiers, his janissary Jesuits, that dissociable society . . . then he ever could have done by garrisons and armies.   (P. 332)

Thus Burton's descriptions of the causes and symptoms of excessive love of God reveal repeatedly the focus on man as *political* animal. His illness is defined by political boundaries—"How many towns in every kingdom hath superstition enriched!" (p. 334); "what province is free from atheism, superstition, idolatry, schism, heresy, impiety, their factors and followers?" (p. 337); "a whole kingdom cannot contain them" (p. 341)—or by political chronology—"How many such imposters, false prophets, have lived in every king's reign! what chronicles will not afford such examples!" (p. 336)—or by political actions—"What makes them so freely venture their

lives, to leave their native countries, to go seek martyrdom in the Indies, but superstition? to be assassinates, to
meet death, murder kings, but a false persuasion of
merit, of canonical or blind obedience" (p. 335). Or it is
defined by its political consequences: superstition breeds
superstition, and the devil has as "actors in his tragedy"
false prophets, schismatics, "blind guides" who "oppose one superstition to another, one kingdom to another, commit prince and subjects, brother against
brother, father against son, to the ruin and destruction of
a commonwealth, to the disturbance of peace, and to
make a general confusion of all estates" (pp. 335-336). A
people and prince under the influence of superstition
become a bastard nation, for the head leads the body
astray—"let him be of what religion he will, they are for
him"—thus converting the many-headed beast of the
populace into a corporate state not to imitate divine order,
but only to follow the devil's goadings (p. 338).

The community of men should be a matter of religion,
for love is man's *primum mobile,* and love of God is keeping His commandments and therefore loving other men
through Him. And religion should be a political or institutional matter, for loving God is seeing other men
through Him and finding commonweal in the forms and
customs of law which unite humanity. The kind of
world we should have is one conforming to Christ's
commandments, and that would be a new kind of marriage, a union under the form of the law of charity: "We
are all brethren in Christ, servants of one Lord, members of one body and therefore are or should be at least
dearly beloved, inseparably allied in the greatest bond
of love and familiarity, united partakers not only of the
same cross, but coadjutors, comforters, helpers, at all

times, upon all occasions" (III.4.1.3;348). But as a husband loves a wife so that love becomes the tyranny of
jealousy and issues in violence rather than legitimate
perpetuation of love, so the selfish love-hate of a prince
becomes the tyranny of legalism and issues in fearful
obedience rather than legitimate perpetuation of the
common welfare: "for the most part by threats, terrors,
and affrights, [princes] tyrannize and terrify their distressed souls: knowing that fear alone is the sole and
only means to keep men in obedience" (p. 340).

Expatiation in the discouse on Love-melancholy thus
comes to involve Buton not only with fictional fairy-
lands representative of man's pleasant follies, but with
matters also of the states and nations of the world which
represent facts as harsh and displeasing as any dealt
with in the "surly discourse." The stories that fill the
rooms of the treatise of superstition are tales of Italy and
France, the Popish state, old Britain and modern England. They are stories out of histories and chronicles,
stories of inquisitions and pogroms, of Chinese and
Turkish wars. Spenser and Ovid have given ground to
Tacitus and Bede. And so at this point in his treatise
Burton stops to ask if he is still in a position to view the
world as a tragicomic one. To describe the symptomatic
manifestations of excessive love of God is to see love as
hate (p. 348) and to see love-hate reigning not just over
the soul of man but over the world: "Other fears and
sorrows, grievances of body and mind, are troublesome
for the time; but this is for ever, eternal damnation, hell
itself, a plague, a fire: an inundation hurts one province
alone, and the loss may be recovered; but this superstition involves all the world almost, and can never be
remedied" (III.4.1.3;347).

That is Burton's "passionate preface" (p. 346) to his "tale" of the symptoms, and it arises out of his inability to look on the world of history as he looked on the world of fiction. At this point he is no longer responding with tears and laughter together to a tragicomic scene, for the bastardizing of religion wrenches tragedy from comedy and causes a kind of schizophrenic reaction to the "mixed scene":

Fleat Heraclitus, an rideat Democritus? in attempting to speak of these symptoms, shall I laugh with Democritus, or weep with Heraclitus? they are so ridiculous and absurd on the one side, so lamentable and tragical on the other: a mixed scene offers itself, so full of errors and a promiscuous variety of objects, that I know not in what strain to represent it. When I think of that Turkish paradise, those Jewish fables and pontifical rites, those pagan superstitions, . . . I cannot choose but laugh with Democritus: but when I see them whip and torture themselves, grind their souls for toys and trifles, desperate, and now ready to die, I cannot choose but weep with Heraclitus. (P. 346)

Christian *homo* sees in the world's mixed scene not only love expressed as hate but love and hate fighting each other to a cataclysmic standoff. Religion is not truth but fiction; law is not God's commandment but men's contrivance. And so the cruel and the absurd, the ridiculous and the monstrous coexist in an uneasy "mixed" state which is ignorance.

In a word, this is common to all superstition, there is nothing so mad and absurd, so ridiculous, impossible, incredible, which they will not believe, observe, and diligently perform, as much as in them lies; nothing so monstrous to conceive, or intolerable to put in practice, so cruel to suffer, which they will not willingly undertake. So powerful a thing is superstition. "O Egypt" (as Trismegistus exclaims), "thy religion is fables, and such as posterity will not believe." (P. 351)

Posterity, of course, substituted its own fables, for the historical world teaches that people will believe any fable and build empires on the strength of it. Ignorance is "a cause of their superstition, a symptom, and madness itself" (III.4.1.2;338), and whether it be the learned stupidity of Roman scholastical divines (III.4.1.3;369) or the studied unlearnedness of Protestant schismatics (p. 370), superstitious religion converts men to irrationality—"their religion takes away not spirits only, but wit and judgment, and deprives them of their understanding" (p. 371). The masses of common men believe anything that "these brainsick heretics once broach, and imposters set on foot," and if that is spoken of the past, yet we have now a "new company of actors, . . . a rope of popes" whose authority has allowed them to "establish their own kingdom, sovereignty, greatness" (p. 366): the state of ignorance is, as it were, institutionalized into an ignorant state. Through superstition's ignorance and the fear that accompanies it, man creates gods out of men and recreates God in his own image: "kings, emperors, valiant men that had done any good offices for them, they did likewise canonize and adore for gods" (p. 354), and what are Jupiter's or Pan's shapes but the monstrous cariacatures of melancholy men we have repeatedly encountered?—"Those images, I say, were all out as gross as the shapes in which they did represent them: Jupiter with a ram's head, Mercury a dog's, Pan like a goat, Hecate with three heads, one with a beard, another without" (pp. 356-357).

Finally, man's ignorance allows him to create a sort of god whose monstrosity lies in his being the most in-

offensive thing man can imagine, namely a good man—
people in India "worship the devil, and allege this
reason in so doing: God is a good man and will do no
harm, but the devil is bad and must be pleased, lest he
hurt them" (p. 360). In studying the Preface, we shall
see that Burton's concern for the civilization of men lies
at the heart of his book, for civilization is the way man
regains paradise, in earthly terms, through a process of
reforming himself and his world. The Preface suggests
that the reformation is possible only poetically, not
really, and this view of the superstitious state of men
making uncivilized empires by ignorance out of unlawful laws confirms the essential barbarity of a universe
not annexed to its Creator by love, but formed into perverse imitations of the community of God and men.

So the manifestations of excessive love of God are not
resolved into a common picture. Superstition "involves
all the world" but it also splits it up into as many scenes
as there are countries and tribes, as many acts as there
are heretical brain-sick men. There is no tragicomedy;
there is the comic view: the ancients made their gods
like the silliest men, "so weak and brutish, some to
whine, lament, and roar, as Isis for her son . . . Venus
run away crying, and the like; than which what can be
more ridiculous?" and there is the tragic view: "Lamentable, tragical, and fearful those symptoms are, that they
should be so far forth affrighted with their fictitious
gods" (p. 357). But man looking on and recording the
scene continues to ask, shall I laugh or shall I weep? for
the prognostics for superstitious man are a state of folly
which is madness and despair within him and a state of
anarchy which is lawlessness and despair in his world:

"What can these signs foretell otherwise than folly, dotage, madness, gross ignorance, despair, obstinacy, a reprobate sense, a bad end? What else can superstition, heresy produce, but wars, tumults, uproars, torture of souls, and despair, a desolate land, as Jeremy teacheth" (III.4.1.4;372). Men united by love-and-hate to their mad conceptions of God live in a state of universal uncharitableness epitomized by that neither tragical nor comical story of the Jew who drowned in a privy because his own people would not pull him out on Saturday, nor would the Christians on Sunday, and so he died before Monday (p. 375).

The cure for superstition is no cure at all. With this topic, the *Anatomy* has reached its lowest ebb. The image of the universe is a fearfully tangled one: love and hate, legalism and tyranny, mad men and mad empires, religion and superstition, gods and men are heaped together in monstrous disorder that "can never be remedied." Burton's effort to cure is lame and he knows it. Universal tolerance is suggested (p. 377); toleration after all would provide a kind of "wisdom," but only the wisdom of self-perpetuating folly, which is the wisdom of a world that exists by creating and recreating its own fictions: "new gods, new lawgivers, new priests, will have new ceremonies, customs and religions, to which every wise man as a good formalist should accommodate himself" (p. 376). Burton says, in this meager room of cures, that being a good formalist may be about the best answer, for his only positive suggestion is that of Paul, "the medium is best": admonish, and if that won't work, excommunicate. "For the vulgar, restrain them by laws, mulcts, burn their books, forbid their conventicles; for when the cause is taken away, the effect will soon cease" (p. 378). But the solution is belied by all the assembled evidence of madness which precedes it, as well as by jealousy's disproving of the effectiveness of custom and form.

And Burton's complacent tone—"the effect will soon cease"—mingles discordantly with the echo of his own laughter and weeping ringing in our ears. For the first time in his treatise of liberal science, Burton closes his cure with physic, as if falling back on material things because he cannot summon enough wisdom even to attempt the cures by counsel. For the first time in his expatiation in philosophical fields he throws his hands up, confines his actors willy-nilly to the madhouse, and unceremoniously leaps into the next room with an exasperated, "that's enough of that": "We have frequently such prophets and dreamers amongst us, whom we persecute with fire and fagot; I think the most compendious cure, for some of them at least, had been in Bedlam. *Sed de his satis*" (p. 379). It is enough because it is all that a physician-divine (p. 378) can do with a world that turns love of God into tyrannical hatred of men. The only other hope is outside that world. The cure is lame because, as Burton saw when he started the attempt, only the advent of a divine physician could make any difference: "To purge the world of idolatry and superstition will require some monster-taming Hercules, a divine AEsculapius, or Christ Himself to come in His own person" (p. 375).

If the picture of the universe disordered by bastard religion gives Burton his lowest view of the world, his discussion of atheism shows this sin to be the annihilation of the world of the *Anatomy*. The discourse on atheism, like the "unlawful cures" of heroical melancholy, serves as a foil to the succeeding discussion, for Burton closes his book by finding that love cannot comment on folly if God is not in the picture, but that it can give its truest comment out of the depths of despair.

The discourse on atheism brings the book to a halt, for denial of God destroys the universe, subverts the world, and denies existence, finally, to man himself. The "grand sin" is the sin of regarding as mere fiction the truth fiction can represent. Poetical stories should say something about the universe and truth, as that atheists are rebels against the God they deny: "A company of Cyclopes or giants, that war with the gods, as the poets feigned, antipodes to Christians, that scoff at all religion, at God Himself," but atheism looks at the universe and truth and says, this is mere fiction: "That there is either heaven or hell, resurrection of the dead, pain, happiness, or world to come . . . for their parts they esteem them as so many poet's tales, bugbears; Lucian's Alexander, Moses, Mahomet, and Christ are all as one in their creed" (III.4.2.1;379). Now "loose atheistical spirits" (like the superstitious, they are defined by the boundaries of kingdoms [p. 380]) would presumably make their ways with worldly facts to worldly wisdom and possibly find the cure for the chaos of superstition which Burton has not yet found. And indeed that would appear to be the case, for "mere carnalists," not having to worry about God as a reference point for the ordering of the world, seem to do a better job of controlling factual life than religious man—"professed atheists thrive: . . . This is a prime argument: and most part your most sincere, upright, honest, and good men are depressed" (p. 383). Having dismissed the context of the world as fiction, they can concentrate on the world itself, saying, "Let them take heaven, paradise, and that future happiness that will, *bonum est esse hic,* it is good being here." But their thriving is, of course, to Burton deception, for they "are in a reprobate sense, mere carnalists, fleshly-minded men, which howsoever they may be applauded in this life by some few parasites, and held for worldly wise men, 'They seem to me' (saith Melanchton) 'to be as mad as Hercules was when he raved and killed his wife and children' " (p. 382).

As mad, that is, as jealous men or those other sufferers whose melancholy will not be controlled by the form and custom of law. The trouble with apparent, "civil" honesty (whether it begins in denial of God or in hypocritical pretense at belief), and the reason it descends to madness, is that in dismissing God as a reference for law, it dismisses the meaning of law. Without God, princes may rule, but love becomes lust and laws become tyranny: Mahomet the Second, sacker of Constantinople,

"believed neither Christ nor Mahomet; and thence it came to pass that he kept his word and promise no farther than his advantage, neither did he care to commit any offence to satisfy his lust." I could say the like of many princes, many private men (our stories are full of them) in times past, this present age, that love, fear, obey, and perform all civil duties as they shall find them expedient or behoveful to their own ends.   (Pp. 381-382)

And like outright atheists, sober men who profess religion for worldly ends are "beloved of all men" yet—God knows—they "are not sound within" (p. 390). Civil honesty, in fact, leads to uncivilized dishonesty, for it ends by "not caring at all for God's or men's laws" (p. 383).

Furthermore, "worldly wise" philosophy (pp. 384-386) which holds "all religion a fiction, opposite to reason and philosophy," also appears at first more effective in defining life than does religion, only when scrutinized to reveal itself as madness. Philosophers can "give many good moral precepts, honest, upright, and sober in their conversation" and yet "too much learning makes them mad." When they equate nature and God, they read the equation the wrong way about, and instead of saying, "Nature is God's order . . . Fortune His unrevealed will," they read heaven and earth as God, bastardizing the truth that "God is all in all, God is everywhere" to mean that everything is God. So they become mad with the madness of scholars who abuse their knowledge—they read history from "stars and such things" in the mistaken belief that they are "inevitable causes of all future accidents"—and they become mad, ironically, with the madness of the superstitious, for they make the heavens gods—"Thus the heavenly bodies build up religions for the good of mankind, and when their influence ceases, the religion also passes away" (Jackson's translation).

Atheism and its sister, hypocrisy, in deifying the world, effectively—from the point of view of Burton and his book—annihilate it. For atheism is defined in simplest terms as the denial of God's law of love: "In all ages, there have been such that either deny God in all or in part; some deride Him, they could have made a better world and rule it more orderly themselves, blaspheme Him, derogate at their pleasure from Him. 'Twas so in Plato's time, 'Some say there be no gods, others that they care not for men, a middle sort grant both' " (p. 387). "There are no gods, and they care not for men."

"Love God, and thy neighbor as thyself." The *Anatomy* is committed to a world dependent on God and His chain of love, but the denial of God and His care for men is tantamount to denying other men, for atheists and hypocrites who "fashion themselves to the world" are the supremely selfish men: "All their study is to please, and their god is their commodity, their labor to satisfy their lusts, and their endeavours to their own ends" (p. 390).

Though love is supposed to comment on all man's woes, and Burton has said *"homo sum, humani a me nihil alienum puto,"* the partition of love cannot admit not-love as it can admit love-and-hate, nor can Burton avoid counting not-love foreign to him. He is Christian man dealing with the infirmities of men, but men's life is love of God and of other men no matter how excessive or defective that love may be, and men whose only reference is self are, in fact, *nihil.* The men whom Burton is hoping to cure of definite and indefinite melancholy are those who are trying to get merrily to heaven. But atheists and their ilk are "antipodes to Christians," bent on getting merrily, if lethargically, to hell:

To these professed atheists we may well add that impious and carnal crew of worldly-minded men, impenitent sinners, that go to hell in a lethargy, or in a dream; who though they be professed Christians, yet they will . . . make a conscience of nothing they do, they have cauterized consciences, and are indeed in a reprobate sense, "past all feeling, have given themselves over to wantonness, to work all manner of uncleanness even with greediness. . . ." They do know there is a God, a day of judgment to come, and yet for all that, . . . they are as merry for all the sorrow, as if they had escaped all dangers, and were in heaven already.   (P. 389)

Mere carnalists' idea of heaven is earth("it is good being here"), and hypocritical Christians, like atheists, act is if all truth is fiction, for in this a "cauterized conscience" is as good as no conscience at all. So instead of offering cures for atheists and hypocrites, Burton excommunicates them from his book. He anathematizes worldly wise philosophy: "these are the decree of Peripatetics, which though I recite, *in obsequium Christianae fidei detestor*, as I am a Christian I detest and hate" (p. 386), and he pronounces against hypocrites: "But let them carry it as they will for the present, dissemble as they can, a time will come when they shall be called to account, their melancholy is at hand, they pull a plague and curse upon their own heads, *thesaurisant iram Dei*" (p. 391).

To those who are knowingly storing up God's wrath, Burton predicts melancholy but will not cure it. For the first and only time in the book, he refuses to follow an illness through causes and symptoms to cures. "Atheism, idolatry, heresy, hypocrisy, though they have one common root, that is indulgence to corrupt affection yet their growth is different, they have divers symptoms, occasions, and must have several cures and remedies" (p. 391): time after time in the *Anatomy* Burton has introduced his analysis of a kind of melancholy in this way, but with this statement he concludes his analysis of atheism. Often throughout the book he has referred us to other authorities who will supplement his discussion; never has he so definitely made the referral his *only* word. Of this topic he simply says, it belongs in another book: "To describe them in particular, to produce their arguments and reasons, would require a just volume; I refer them therefore that expect a more ample satisfaction to those subtle and elaborate treatises, devout

and famous tracts of our learned divines . . . that have
abundance of reasons to prove there is a God" (p. 392).
Burton has sometimes said he could offer counsel if he
had the space and then has taken the space; only
concerning atheism and hypocrisy does he implicitly
agree with those who say that cure is impossible. Some,
he says, hold it "vain to dispute with such atheistical
spirits" though many "schoolmen and casuists" have
written of it, especially Marinus Marcenaus who has
analyzed and answered all the arguments: "His colo-
phon is how to resist and repress atheism, and to that
purpose he adds four especial means or ways, which
whoso will may profitably peruse" (pp. 391-392). But it
is not my matter nor my purpose to resist it, Burton
seems to say: their world does not exist in my world,
"their melancholy is at hand." If the cure of superstition
exasperates him, the subject of atheism is the one woe
of mankind which leaves him tongue-tied. Love's comment on atheism is that there is nothing to say.

Despair, not atheism or worldly philosophy, is the
defective love of God which belongs in Burton's treatise, for the desperate man knows God's love without
understanding it. His despair is defined in terms of love;
love is desire, despair "a restraint from the thing desired, for some impossibility supposed" (III.4.2.2;393); it
is "opposite to hope," specifically hope in God (p. 394).
As if to assure his readers that defective love of God in
this form does belong in the book, Burton opens with
the much-vexed question of whether or not melancholy
and a troubled conscience are a single disease. Bright
had decided (Ch. xxxii ff.) that the body cannot work ill
to the soul of man, and while offering consolations to
the despairing, yet had insisted that despair was not
melancholy. Burton, typically, has it both ways, for he

has already been talking about metaphorical melancholy throughout the Third Partition, but he now reverts for a moment to the terms of the medical treatise and draws a strikingly direct line from the body of man to this disease of the soul, only, however, by making the matter of disease the instrument of the devil: "His ordinary engine by which he produceth [despair], is the melancholy humour itself, which is *balneum diaboli,* the devil's bath" (III.4.2.3;395). And after admitting with Perkins that "the body works upon the mind," Burton concludes that "there is much difference" between melancholy and despair, without making the difference very clear: "melancholy fears without a cause, this upon great occasion; melancholy is caused by fear and grief, but this torment procures them and all extremity of bitterness; much melancholy is without affliction of conscience, as Bright and Perkins illustrate by four reasons; and yet melancholy alone again may be sometimes a sufficient cause of this terror of conscience" (p. 396).

To admit that melancholy fears without cause is for Burton to emphasize that the Third Partition has brought him to questions of man's illnesses which no medical treatise could handle but which are of paramount importance to his health. To say that melancholy can cause despair is to say that two partitions of medical knowledge lead up to this worst form of soul-sickness. From bones and humors we have come to hope and fear, the affections that enable man to live or lead him to seek death. Superstition affects the whole man, *totum compositum.* But the target of despair is the soul, and despair is soul-sickness at its worst, since it makes the body into a metaphor of the soul, black humor into the fumes of conscience: "The part affected is the whole soul, and all the faculties of it; there is a privation of joy, hope, trust, confidence, of present and future good, and in their place succeed fear, sorrow, etc. . . . The heart is grieved, the conscience wounded, the mind eclipsed with black fumes arising from those perpetual terrors." Despairing man cannot "think on [charity] and be wise," for his passion destroys his human, rational nature.

Despair is the superlative of all disease, which is hell inside a man, the incurable pestilence of the soul.

'Tis an epitome of hell, an extract, a quintessence, a compound, a mixture of all feral maladies, tyrannical tortures, plagues, and perplexities. There is no sickness almost but physic provideth a remedy for it; to every sore chirurgery will provide a salve; friendship helps poverty; hope of liberty easeth imprisonment; suit and favour revoke banishment; authority and time wear away reproach: but what physic, what chirurgery, what wealth, favour, authority can relieve, bear out, assuage, or expel a troubled conscience? A quiet mind cureth all them, but all they cannot comfort a distressed soul: who can put to silence the voice of desperation? All that is single in other melancholy, *horribile, dirum, pestilens, atrox, ferum*, concur in this, it is more than melancholy in the highest degree; a burning fever of the soul.   (III.4.2.4;404)

This "more than melancholy" is what the *Anatomy* has been approaching through the definition and redefinition of Partition III: melancholy that is not melancholy, an incurable disease that must be cured. It is the shattering image of man helpless in his own mind, hopeless for his own soul. And it is the malady to be opposed to superstition because it is truly *defective* love of God, not non-existent love. Superstitious men hope too much in their own abilities to read God's laws and rule by their own, thus making themselves into gods and God into merely a good man. And desperate men fear too much because they put too great weight on their own ability to understand God, thus making God into what they think He must be. They try to outguess Him: "they will know more than is revealed of God in His Word, human capacity or ignorance can apprehend, and too importunate inquiry after that which is revealed" (III.4.2.3;399). And they suppose themselves to understand Him: preachers disregard St. Bernard and preach only of judgment without mercy, "But these men are wholly for judgment; of a rigid disposition themselves, there is no mercy with them, no salvation, no balsam for their distressed souls, they can speak nothing but reprobation, hell-fire, and damnation" (p. 399), and desperation ensues: "Our conscience, which is a great ledger-book, wherein are written all our offences, a register to lay them up (which those Egyptians in their hieroglyphics expressed by a mill, as well for the continuance as for the torture of it), grinds our souls with the remembrance of some precedent sins, makes us reflect upon, accuse and condemn our own selves" (p. 400).

The book that a desperate man reads is himself, his terrified conscience, and at the root of his despair is the assumption that God reads the hieroglyphics just as we write them, that He understands us only as well as we understand ourselves. Despair twists Christ's comandment of charity into man's tortured version of God's response—I shall love man My creature only as he loves himself: "this scrupulous conscience . . . which tortures so many, that either out of a deep apprehension of their unworthiness, and consideration of their own dissolute life, 'accuse themselves and aggravate every small offence, when there is no such cause, misdoubting in the meantime God's mercies, they fall into these inconveniences' " (p. 401). Despair tells the tale of a diabolically perverted chain of charity and of God's and men's creations. The stories that we read in the book of despair are those of the breakdown of all law and custom, for the violence that men work on other men returns to their consciences, and they transfer the violence to themselves. Tyrants of Sparta, Rome, Scotland, France so confound the world that they are in turn confounded by being unable to find someone to kill them (p. 402). Such stories are tales of the breakdown of all rule within men as well—"they think evil against their wills, that which they abhor themselves, they must needs think, do, and speak." A lawyer of Padua "discoursed aright" in all matters but that of his own despair: "Frisemelica, Bullovat, and other excellent physicians, could neither make him eat, drink, nor sleep, no persuasion could ease him. Never pleaded any man so well for himself as this man pleaded against himself, and so he desperately died" (III.4.2.4;407).

Thus despair is "violent, tragical, and grievous far beyond the rest" (p. 404), for its tragic acts and scenes are not of the external community but of man's internal constitution. And it is tragic because not loving himself at all, the desperate man can hardly love his neighbor and can only misconstrue God's love for him. Poets' feigning would tell atheistical, hypocritical men (if they understood that fiction speaks truth) their own kind of worldly wisdom, an eye for an eye:

Besides all such as are in *deos contumeliosi*, blaspheme, contemn, neglect God, or scoff at Him, as the poets feign of Salmoneus, that would in derision imitate Jupiter's thunder, he was precipitated for his pains, Jupiter *intonuit contra,* etc., so shall they certainly rue it in the end, (*in se spuit, qui in coelum spuit* [he spits on himself who spits at the sky]), their doom's at hand, and hell is ready to receive them.   (III.4.2.1;391)

But poets' feigning would tell desperate men (if they could read the truth of fiction with the understanding of love) the wisdom of a different legalism, that of charity: "The gods once (as the poets feign) with a gold chain would pull Jupiter out of heaven, but all they together could not stir him, and yet he could draw and turn them as he would himself; maugre all the force and fury of these infernal fiends, and crying sins, 'His grace is sufficient' " (III.4.2.6;412).

Burton says that atheists and hypocrites are curable, but he will not cure them: their melancholy "is at hand." He says that desperate men are incurable but he goes on to offer cure. The lengthy passage quoted above (" 'Tis an epitome of hell . . .") serves as a summary of the *Anatomy*'s cures against which despair is tested and found too powerful. Physic, chirurgery, and good counsel serve in some combination to ease all illnesses, but "who can put to silence the voice of desperation?" The answer of course is Christ. Despair cannot be cured by man's counsels, his customs, his physic, his law, but the judgment of mercy can turn his tragedy into a divine comedy. The cure of despair is not by human precept, but by "divine aphorism" (p. 420).

Burton's subsection of the cures of despair was originally (1621) a very short, abrupt passage. To it was added in the second edition what is now the major portion of the section, a sermon against despair; but even the first edition included the essential cure. Burton says at first what he has said of other kinds of melancholy, that physic and good counsel should be used together. Despair, we remember, is the quintessence and mixture of all disease; "all that is single in other melancholy . . . concur in this, it is more than melancholy." To the extent that it is melancholy, "the like course is to be taken with this as in other melancholy," that is, diet, rectification of passions, good counsels (p. 409). But to the extent that it is more than melancholy, a new cure is added: "by hearing, reading of Scripture, good divines, good advice and conference, applying God's Word to their distressed souls, it must be corrected and counterpoised" (p. 409). The first edition adds to this only the list of "excellent exhortations" where comfort and cure may be sought, but even so short a discourse has the single necessary answer: Scripture (the emphatic "applying God's Word to their distressed souls" is added later). The essential cure is there; Burton has not, even in 1621, refused the cure of the desperate in giving them a list of other authors. For where to atheists and hypocrites he was wordless, to the despairing he gave the Word. And the difference in his treatment of the two groups is made obvious when he adds, in the next edition, that "comfortable speech" in which he spells out what it means to have the Word of God as cure.

The word of the sermon, from beginning to end, is "mercy," the legalism of redemption which contradicts justice through forgiveness: " 'Thou liest Cain' (saith Austin), 'God's mercy is greater than thy sins' " (p. 411), and it is necessarily also "repentance," which allows the Old Testament law to be read as New Testament mercy: " 'An hawk came into the ark and went out again an hawk; a lion came in, went out a lion, a bear, a

bear, a wolf, a wolf; but if an hawk come into this sacred
temple of repentance, he will go forth a dove' (saith
Chrysostom), 'a wolf go out a sheep, a lion a lamb' "
(pp. 413-414). For all of the blasphemous, atheistical
thoughts, all of the abominable unnatural deeds of
which a conscience-stricken man can accuse himself, for
all of the fearful misconceptions of Scriptures he can
devise, Burton gives back one answer, that to be a man
in a universe of love is to be capable of receiving the love
of God: " 'Tis an universal promise, 'God sent not His
Son into the world to condemn the world, but that
through Him the world might be saved' (John iii, 17).
He that acknowledgeth himself a man in the world,
must likewise acknowledge he is of that number that is
to be saved" (p. 420).

Still, the universe of love is also a universe of melancholy to which men go to school to learn wisdom, and
so the cure for the disease—the gilded pill—cures by
giving the meaning of wisdom to the disease itself, and
to the *Anatomy:* "A small sickness; one lash of affliction,
a little misery, many times will more humiliate a man,
sooner convert, bring him home to know himself, than
all those paraenetical discourses, the whole theory of
philosophy, law, physic, and divinity, or a world of
instances and examples. . . . So that affliction is a
school or academy, wherein the best scholars are prepared to the commencement of the Deity" (p. 425). The
book that is itself almost a whole theory of philosophy,
law, physic, and divinity, not to mention a world of
instances and examples, goes to the school that is the
sickness of despair and finds that all the herbs and
amulets, compound concoctions, precious stones, and
exorcisms that are taken out of other authors (pp. 428-

430) are "fopperies and fictions" compared to the cure that lies in a single Word of God which is Christ: if any man would attempt to cure the devil's works, "let him follow . . . the example of Peter and John, that without any ambitious swelling terms cured a lame man (Acts iii): 'In the name of Christ Jesus rise and walk.' His name alone is the best and only charm against all such diabolical illusions" (p. 431). This word—a Word of God, but taken into Burton's discourse, and so his word of cure also—is not simply about grace unattainable in this world though available in the next. The "name of Christ Jesus" is that Word which can cure in the here and now, in the melancholy world: rise and walk. It is one word finally, just as all melancholy, definite and indefinite, is one finished comprehensive digression into the meanings of that other word which is, or should be, all that God and man are: love.

It should be noted that though the 1621 text ended with Burton's referring his readers to other authors, a set of epigrams was appended which in effect epitomized the sermon of later editions. After the motto which also appears in subsequent editions ("*Sperate miseri, cavete felices*") came the "Finis" and then on the verso page three Latin quotations from Augustine. The final quotation still follows the motto in subsequent editions, and both of these will be discussed in a moment. But the first two quotations were translated by Burton and used in the body of the sermon. I give them in the order in which they originally appeared, but in the translated form. The major points of the sermon are made succinctly: first—repent, God's mercy is great enough; and second—sickness is for teaching God's healing power:

Whatsoever thou shalt do, how great a sinner soever, thou art yet living; if God would not help thee, He would surely take thee away; but in sparing thy life, He gives thee leisure, and invites thee to repentance.   (P. 414)

He knoweth best what he doth; and be not so much pleased when he sustains thee, as patient when he corrects thee; He is omnipotent, and can cure all diseases when He sees his own time.   (P. 413)

As the narration at the beginning of the discourse of Love-melancholy asks us to look at man's love of men through God, the closing sermon asks us to look at God's love of men through Christ. The sermon is in many ways not like the rest of the book, but that is the point. It is a consolation of theology, not of philosophy, still less of science. The *Anatomy* ends with the wisdom of God because that is the only wisdom which can allow men in the world of tragicomedy to see that we all have an "universal invitation" (p. 424) to attend a divine comedy. But the sermon's consolation is not just for the hereafter, for knowing God is knowing cure now; it is the wisdom of charity taught by the God-man, and the wisdom that says God can cure melancholy, indeed "all diseases when He sees his own time."

The perspective of the world in the latter part of Burton's book is still a human perspective, and the *Anatomy* does not end with angel voices welcoming elect souls. Burton eases back from the theological consolation to a view of man's world more customary to the book as he closes it. The last word is oriented to the human scene where happiness and sadness are continually at war with each other and melancholy is the prognostic of any unfilled moment:

I can say no more, or give better advice to such as are anyway distressed in this kind, than what I have given and said. Only take this for a corollary and conclusion, as thou tenderest thine own welfare in this and all other melancholy, thy good health of body and mind, observe this short precept, give not way to solitariness and idleness. "Be not solitary, be not idle."

SPERATE MISERI,
CAVETE FELICES.

If unhappy men have hope and happy men beware, we will still have a life of tragicomedy, which is to say we will still have life. The universe is one of desires—of loves—to be felt, to be won, not to be won, to be lost. It is a world of equivocations and opposites where all definitions are possible except one, that there is no God who is love. But as tragicomedy it is to be lived and learned; it is to be got through, but not in ignorance of the references outside itself which make hope and fear possible to the sound of mind: "Do you wish to be freed from doubt? do you desire to escape uncertainty? Be penitent while of sound mind: by so doing I assert that you are safe, because you have devoted that time to penitence in which you might have been guilty of sin" (p. 432, Jackson's translation).

"Hope, ye unhappy ones; ye happy ones, fear" is love's comment. But it is not Venus' comment, which is "marry," nor is it God's, which is "Christ," but it is the comment of charity, for it has man's point of view. It allows to man his humanity—his love and his love-and-hate—even as it suggests the larger context of the inevitable judgment of God. It is a worldly wise saying, but one wise with the wisdom of a world bound together by charitable love. Burton has seen the folly of love undeterred by the custom and form of man's law, and so has cried out, "From heresy, jealousy and frenzy, good Lord, deliver us!" And having shown us the wisdom of God's interpretation of human hiero-glyphics, he now whispers to us the cure that gives delivery from madness, a cure which is a human apho-rism spoken in the light of divine aphorism: hope and fear, for you are men, and so both happy and sad; but God's grace is sufficient for your folly. The sermon on charity asked us to consider where there are Christians who differ from other men. Burton has answered through the Third Partition, with its structural and verbal equivocations, that they are loving and hating in the world, and through his sermon against despair that God will read their stories—and the *Anatomy* which was written in order not to be idle—in the light of the law of love. If we have thought about charity throughout the treatise of indefinite melancholy, we may understand how hope and fear, happiness and unhappiness, trag-edy and comedy, can be resolved through definition and redefinition of "love," through sections which dissolve even as they distinguish the categories of in-definite melancholy and lead at last to a single kind of vision, one of man the passionate animal who is capable of loving with a "true touch of religion and a reference to God." And understanding that, we may understand in turn how melancholy is not only there in the body, a question of knowledge, but here in the soul, a question of the wisdom we have been "thinking on."

IV. Facts of Time and Spirit

The spirit of human brotherhood and the urge to move forward and upward are not to be described in terms of chemical constitution and physical forces, but they are facts, nevertheless, just as real as the need for food, the love of comfort, or the fear of pain. As facts they differ from those of the so-called natural sciences, because they are concerned with consequences rather than being determined by antecedent causes. One could almost say that they are made not of matter, but of time and spirit because their chief constituents are memories of the past, anticipations of the future, and choice of values. But even though they arise from expectations, from visions of the mind, indeed from dreams, they are so real and powerful that they can sway human behavior and are thereby the most effective forces in changing the face of the earth. Thus it is certain that man cannot be completely understood merely by considering him as a piece of machinery to be dissected and analyzed objectively by the methods of the exact sciences. To be understood man must be "known" in the Biblical sense; he must be encountered and experienced as a dreaming and throbbing creature.   —RENÉ DUBOS, *The Torch of Life*

The view of the *Anatomy* I have been outlining is one determined by the book's highly artificial structure, which is defined by the tension created between the circumscribed form of a scholarly treatise and the anomalies of structure Burton allows to modify that form. He shows that the "newe science" of Partitions I and II grows out of old books through skeptical questioning as well as through acceptance of authority, and by formally digressing within the order of the treatise, he re-vivifies rather than buries the scholastic structure's potential for making statements of truth. Burton then establishes the equivocations of melancholy, again within the form, so that the indefinite diseases of life are made definite and coequal with the subject of the medical discourse. The nature of the scholarly treatise, we have repeatedly seen, is to be one form: within the construct described by the synoptic tables there is room for everything—including digressions and equivocations, additions and expatiations—that Burton had to say about melancholy through the course of six editions; rooms could even be added, if necessary, without affecting the structural integrity of the work. The tensions created within the form by digression or by the logic of equivocation are resolved within it as Burton makes the structure allow for his thematic complexities.

While examining the formal anomalies of Partitions I and II and Partition III, however, we have also described the tension created by the simultaneously tripartite and bipartite structure of the whole. That whole structure, we can now see, is both one of three partitions and one of two equivalent discussions: the structure of Partition I-Partition II-Partition III coexists with the structure of Partitions I and II together balanced by Partition III. But little as yet has been said concerning the way these two structures fit together; for the question of how the First and Second Partitions are united to the Third Partition is essentially the question of how the Preface operates as a structural entity to inform the *Anatomy* and make it, however encyclopedic, a single work. For a book like the *Anatomy* to have such a long, sometimes rambling preface which allows author and book to explain themselves in numerous ways, is itself an anomaly. The Preface does not belong with those bits and pieces of front and back matter which have accrued to the book over the years and which have been described as elements in its facade. It is not at all like the basic components of that facade, the synoptic tables which define and contain the scholarly treatise. The Preface stands outside the work, a major substantive portion of the book which is not in any way structurally like the discourse it precedes.[1]

The Preface of "Democritus Junior to the Reader" is undoubtedly the most read and best criticized part of Burton's book, to the extent that critics—especially those not devoted to humoral psychology and the medical phenomena associated with melancholy—have tended to base their evaluations of the *Anatomy* largely or solely on examination of the Preface.[2] There is a sense in which such criticism is right, and I hope to help clarify how in certain respects the Preface is the *Anatomy*

1. I do not mean to suggest here that prefaces were not accepted parts of the form of medieval and later scholarly treatises (Aquinas' and Ockham's prologues, among others, have been called to my attention). I am only trying to look at Burton's very extensive Preface in order to discover its operation in relation to the rest of his more "surly discourse," which uses the scholastic structure while the Preface does not.

2. For sensible evaluation of the criticism of Burton that errs through concentration on small portions of the work, see Nochimson, chs. i and ii.

because it contains all the meaning that digression and equivocation will give to the book *per se*. In a very different way from that of the synoptic tables, the Preface "contains" the whole book. But while the Preface with its mask, its authorial explanations, its satiric intent, has always seemed the most important part of the *Anatomy*, and particularly so for those interested in the explication of style by the elucidation of personality,[3] there is also the danger that the Preface will be read, by some, instead of or without reference to the book with its proper partitions and their necessary digression and equivocation.[4] So for our present interest in the discovery of the artistic implications of structure in a work like Burton's, it has seemed best to start with the work itself, with that construct which gives the book its name, and to examine the central problems of its structure before turning to the single substantive addition to the scholastic treatise in order to investigate how that Preface acts as a preface, how it modifies or "conduces to" our understanding of the book. The Preface can only, in fact, appear to be a structural anomaly or "problem" if one has accepted some such analysis of the workings of Burton's method as I have been describing, for if (as Finlay and Renaker hold) the method of division and definition does not function as the controlling means of statement (or as the means of controlling statement) in the book, then the Preface should be examined at the outset of any analysis to show how it declares formlessness to be the *Anatomy*'s essence. But

3. See especially Webber, ch. iv; and Nochimson, ch. iv.
4. The view of Burton as primarily social scientist in the various works of William Mueller is among those given thoughtful criticism in Nochimson's study.

we have seen in the three partitions of the *Anatomy* that Burton's structural control of his content allows the book to present the fundamental idea of artfully imposed order as the answer to the naturally disordered state of things. Two systems of cause and cure, formal and digressive, are intertwined in Partitions I and II so that melancholy life can be redefined as time spent finding things out, and the "melancholy spaniel's quest" as question on which knowledge depends and to which it is "annexed." And a different logical order in Partition III permits melancholy to be restated as lovesickness and cure to be found in charity, or man linked to man through God. Only now, with the previous explications in mind, can we see Burton's "Satyricall Preface Conducing to the following Discourse" as his other way (more extensive than the synopses, Table, and so forth) of "fore-possessing" his readers at the beginning of the book of the importance of reading from it and in it the notions we have been examining—the idea of structural, and through structure of thematic, order which is "tangled" without being ultimately impaired.

ARGUMENTUM

The Preface is external to the structure of anatomy; its subject matter and to an extent at least the voice which speaks in it are not those of the *Anatomy* proper. It is not even the introduction to Burton's anatomizing of melancholy, for that, we have seen, is part of the discourse: whereas Partition I, section 1, member 1, leads into the *Anatomy* with its definitions of man, disease, and melancholy, the Preface, from its first sentence, unsettles the reader by demanding that he consider all kinds of social and artistic questions not directly pertinent to melancholy. Nor does Burton say that his Preface is the introduction to the *Anatomy*. It does not "introduce" but "conduces" to the following discourse; it does not simply lead the reader into the book, but collects the discourse, contributes to, furthers, and promotes it, aids in bringing it about. The Preface cannot just be read before the treatise but must be read with it. Burton knows how to write a preface within the structure of anatomy, which uses some of the same topics as this Preface, and which leads into the following discourse by provoking the reader's attention and establishing the author's points of view on his subject matter. He writes such a preface for Partition III, and he calls it a "Preface or Introduction." But Democritus Junior's Preface *conduces* to the discourse of melancholy partly, at least, by being outside it and outside the synoptic tables which define it. As those synopses describe a certain kind of logical analysis for the book, the Preface translates them into a description of a work of art which they alone cannot define.

The fact that the Preface is an entity separate from the three partitions has made some critics wish to establish either that it was written after the body of the work or that it was substantially complete before Burton conceived of an anatomy of melancholy. Thus Lawrence Babb believes (p. 15) that Burton probably did not write the Preface until the 1621 *Anatomy* was "near completion," arguing that "Burton plays his role of Democritus Junior in the preface, not in the body of the book." James Roy King, on the other hand, in his theory of the book's composition, has determined that the main core of the Preface was written well before the rest of the *Anatomy*, for "had Burton composed the entire preface when he completed the book, he could scarcely have avoided references to the medical aspects of his problems (physical causes being, as he sees it, the root of melancholy), and he would certainly have stressed much less strongly the moral aspect" (King, pp. 87-88). Both points of view are possible, but both have their critical drawbacks. It is true that, as Babb remarks (p. 15 n.), the name "Democritus Junior" occurs only once in the *Anatomy* proper, and that in a 1638 addition; but Burton himself, as will be seen, argues that he wrote the *Anatomy* in order to finish Democritus' incomplete book. The idea of the mask, then, if not the written form of the Preface, may well precede the writing of the book, and the fact that Burton does not speak consistently or primarily with Democritus Junior's tone of voice in the book does not necessarily prove that he had not conceived of the mask, but only proves that the treatise of melancholy and the Preface are different kinds of writing. King's reasoning is even more assailable, since the Third Partition, with its literary character and its poetical and historical sources, is as noticeably independent of the medical authorities (except for the reference lists in the subsections of cure) as is the Preface, and that final part of the book stresses the "moral aspects" of melancholy rather than its "physical causes." It is quite easy, in fact, to turn from a fresh reading of the last partition back to the Preface and agree that Burton wrote the Preface after having written Partition III.

I believe, however, that it is not necessary to conclude on one side or the other, for the question of the Preface's function cannot be determined by the relative time of its

writing any more than can the function of any other
portion of the book, if, as I have been arguing, the Preface is not to be seen simply as an introduction to the
book which follows it. We do not have in the *Anatomy* a
collection of facts and observations temporally ordered
as King wants to order them: he notes, for example
(pp. 87-88), an "absence in the middle section [of the
Preface] of any reference to the medical writers who
eventually come to influence Burton so strongly." One
part of the book does not supersede or supplant another, and it is essential to our analysis of the Preface and of
the *Anatomy* not to think of the Preface either as Burton's last thought or revised opinion about what the
already written book means, or as an essay pre-existent
to, and therefore unexpressive of, the final conception
of the book. Time, it has been noted, plays strange tricks
with the *Anatomy*, for the book is created and recreated
over three decades, and each moment of creation coexists with the others (see, for example, Webber, pp.
83-84). The *Anatomy*, from the point of view of structural
analysis, is less definably a temporal construct than a
spatial one, and such analysis should show that as the
Preface is "before" the book in the reading of it, it might
equally be described as being, for the reader, "above"
the book—a kind of overall point of view for his reading
the *Anatomy*. The Preface is our vantage point for the
whole book because it sets up the scenes of human disorder as backdrop for the medical treatise so that the
reading of the scholarly discourse is preparatory for the
id est of Partition III where science is read as sapience
and health is human charity.

The synoptic tables describe the *Anatomy* as an archi-
tectural creation, and we have borrowed Panofsky's

analogy between scholastic treatise and Gothic cathedral to illustrate the purpose and function of the synopses
and the other front matter. One might bandy about possible extensions of the analogy (the three partitions of
the book, for example, and the nave, transept, and choir
of the church), but however valid the points that might
be made from such a working (or overworking) of cross-
disciplinary comparisons, the facts are that the synoptic
tables lay the book out on the space of the printed page
and that there is no way so to describe the Preface and
no satisfactory place in their plane to set it. The Preface
conduces; it is read with rather than simply before the
book, and so it is Burton's and our viewpoint from
which we see the *Anatomy*. Because we always have the
Preface in mind when we are within the *Anatomy* proper
we are able to see the whole from any given room. In a
sense we never turn from the Preface to the following
"more sober" discourse, but carry it with us instead as a
lens through which to read the *Anatomy*. And in *that*
sense, all that the *Anatomy* is is the Preface of Democritus Junior to the Reader.

Burton liked to see himself as author of the *Anatomy*
standing in a high place overseeing the turmoil of
common life (Preface, 18), or seeing farther and better
than any of his authorities because he stood on their
shoulders (p. 25). And as he looked down and out at the
world from his vantage point as Oxford scholar, so the
Preface sets us above the *Anatomy* and enables us to see
the whole work, to read of definite melancholy with its
black bile and hellebore while knowing also its equivocation, universal disorder; and to read of indefinite melancholy knowing that to speak of love matters, of control of passion and poetical fancy, is another way of

describing man's government of himself, an equivocation, perhaps, of the control of self by the right use of
the six non-natural things. The components of the
book's facade, we have said, suggest to its readers that
the book is constantly restating itself and that there are
many ways to get into the meaning of the *Anatomy of
Melancholy*. The imposition of Partition III on the finished order of Partitions I and II confirms the book's
reiterative and responsorial nature, but the reader does
not wait until he trudges through the sober discourse
and breaks into the delightful fields of love to discover
how Burton uses equivocation. Digression within the
First and Second Partitions questions even as it eluci-
dates the ability of a scholarly treatise to map out truth,
but the reader does not need to wait even for the first
Digression of Anatomy to discover that the discourse
will proceed by enveloping the impertinent and making
it pertinent. The reader does not wait for the book's
structure to unfold because the Preface has "fore-possessed" him of the way the book's form as a whole
works. It has not often been noticed, even by careful
readers of the *Anatomy*, that the digressions occur only
in the first two partitions: the whole book gives the impression of containing numerous digressions, and the
reason that the copious hesitations and self-reproaches
of Partition III—"but I digress," "but I rove"—seem
nothing new when the reader meets them there is that
the Preface has shown us Burton's roving humor and
made us familiar with the order of association. The anatomy of humoral melancholy in I and II drifts easily into
the equivocations Burton has promised not to treat, and
the reason we accept so naturally the kind of melancholy which "properly" belongs only in Partition III is

that the Preface has spoken long and eloquently of the metaphorical "bodies" of family and state which suffer from social disorder. The universe of folly which opens up to view in Partition III seems, when we enter it, familiar territory, for we have watched the digressions of Partitions I and II breaking down the discourse's sober constraints of inward or outward causes and up- ward or downward cures, and the digressions them- selves we have seen through the Preface's vision of ubiquitous, universal folly. And Burton's poses which change rapidly and often through the book seem always reducible to the *"homo sum"* announced finally in Parti- tion III, for the context of that declaration is really made the whole treatise of melancholy, which from its first sentence, "Man . . . was at first pure, divine, perfect, happy," is spoken through the voices of the Preface which include the author and his mask among the man- kind he takes as his subject: *"Nos numerus sumus,* I confess it again, I am as foolish, as mad as any one" (pp. 119-120). The *Anatomy* is, in Colie's terms, a vast rhet- orical paradox "designed to cheat the reader's expecta- tion. We are led to expect a straightforward medical treatise, like Bright's, and we get a great many utterly different things thrown in—a spiritual treatise, an atlas, a book of meteorology, a behavior book, and so forth, and so forth" (Colie, p. 454). And yet the breaking of "all limits established by any convention" *is* the reader's expectation, because in the midst of the front matter is the Preface which is designed to deny all the expecta- tions aroused by the title, the subject matter, and the logical blueprints of the synopses.

The first sentences of the Preface put the reader in the position of asking questions that had not occurred to

him: "Gentle Reader, I presume thou wilt be very inquisitive to know what antic or personate actor this is,
that so insolently intrudes upon this common theatre to
the world's view, arrogating another man's name;
whence he is, why he doth it, and what he hath to say"
(p. 15). Nothing, surely, could have been more commonplace to a seventeenth-century reader than to pick
up a book with a pseudonym, or initials, or no name at
all on the title page, but the Preface demands that he
consider this commonplace to be "arrogation," even
"usurpation," and that he claim his own right to full
disclosure of the reasons for the impersonation. But
even more, he is suddenly made to feel that that long
and quite explicit title has told him nothing, for the
author thrusts into his own mouth questions of "why"
and "what" that the title would seem to have answered.
All at once he discovers that in knowing that the book
will be anatomy, a treatise in three partitions divided
into sections, members, and subsections; in knowing
that his author will not only look at melancholy, a much
talked of disease, almost a pastime in his age, as a medical phenomenon, but will also delve into its historical
and philosophical implications; in knowing from one of
the mottoes either that the book will be a pastiche of collected knowledge ("*Omne meum, nihil meum*"—first and
second editions) or that it is designed to entertain while
informing him ("*Omne tulit punctum, qui miscuit utile
dulci*"—third and succeeding editions), and in knowing
that it has in fact passed the test of popularity in this
way ("The_____ Edition, corrected and augmented by
the Author"); in knowing even that he will be treated to
some kind of satirical preview of the matter of the
book—in knowing all these things, he finds he does not

know what the book is about, but is asking his author
what, and why, and whence. And then his author goes
on to tell him that all the explicitness of the title, all the
apparent disclosure of synoptic tables, of (in later editions) index, illustrated title page, descriptive and explanatory poems, is not an open book but a covered
basket because he does not know his author: "It was
therefore covered, because he should not know what
was in it. Seek not after that which is hid; if the contents
please thee, 'and be for thy use, suppose the Man in the
Moon, or whom thou wilt, to be the author'; I would not
willingly be known" (p. 15).

Thus the Preface begins, and so it continues. As the
mask is the essence of the Preface, so the Preface is by
nature a mask for the book and the mask through which
we look at the book. Its discussions of style and content,
its long "impertinent" discourses on metaphorical melancholy, lead us to expect, at any moment, only what
Burton gives us, which can be, as Colie observes (p.
454), both what he says he will give us and what he says
he will not.

The book, then, and the meaning of its structure, are
determined not by the definition of logical order inherent in the synoptic tables, but by the view of that
definition given us through the Preface, which is the
synopsis of the whole. The Preface does not deny the
rationality explicit in the scholarly apparatus, but establishes the apparatus' powers of comprehending "facts
of time and spirit" as well as facts of matter. The Preface
creates a synthesis of definite and indefinite melancholy
by demanding that we read the discourses of melancholy always in the light of the questions we have
been forced to ask: who and whence is the man who

speaks, what is he saying, why and how is he saying it?
I shall be attempting in the following sections to show
how Burton answers these questions in order to explain
the structure of the book to which his satirical Preface
conduces. I shall deal first with the man and the subject
matter, the question, that is, of what the Preface contains; and secondly with the way Burton works in the
Preface, the question of how he uses his Preface to present, or conduce to, the book itself by defining Democritus Junior's art of scholarship.

PERSONAE ET MATERIA

The Preface, I have suggested, may be seen as a
synopsis of the whole, that part of the book which
unites the three scattered synoptic tables by giving us a
guide to understanding all the variety of the three partitions unified through Democritus Junior's vision. But of
course the Preface will not conform to the synopses'
shape. There is no way to set up the Preface as a table
which by differentiation and division unfolds to map
out a series of logical equivalents that contain the book.
The Preface has been described as a constantly expanding vision of the melancholy world, an essay organized
by its "continual pattern of opening outward" from the
self Burton introduces as Democritus Junior through the
"panoramic view" of other men to the kingdoms of the
earth.[5] Yet this description, while in a sense true, is not
exact, for Burton starts the Preface in the distance of
history with his account of Democritus (p. 16), focuses

5. Ellen Louise Hurt, "The Prose Style of Robert Burton: The Fruits
of Knowledge," Ph.D. diss. University of Oregon, p. 250.

next on his own writing (pp. 16-38), and then turns to his "brief survey" of the general confusion in the world (pp. 39-72), a survey, however, which is centered on the historical account of Hippocrates' visit with Democritus (pp. 47-52). Next he describes the *particular* manifestations of metaphorical melancholy seen in human institutions—states, families, classes of men—(pp. 73-119), and this account is constructed around the "poetical commonwealth" realized only in Democritus Junior's mind (pp. 97-107). The Preface ends then with Burton's explanation of the relationship of himself and his mask to the scenes he has described and the book his reader is entering upon (pp. 119-120). If it opens outward, the Preface does so only in order to return constantly to the speaker, and it does so only by focusing constantly on externals through the persona's vision of self. In telling "what he hath to say," Burton is always expanding his view of men and events only by contracting his vision to the single thing he sees clearly—self, and the self that he recreates as Democritus Junior. Having read the Preface, in Hurt's words, "we know our man: we know the several aspects of his mind—comic, satiric, cooly descriptive, and so on. From then on, he can simply be 'himself.' He can treat a variety of aspects of his subject in a variety of fashions; we can trace their precedent back to the microcosm in 'Democritus Junior to the Reader' " (Hurt, p. 131).

The Preface appears unorganized if viewed in relationship to the *Anatomy*, but it is as much a whole as the book to which it conduces; for the Preface has not the artificial exactness of the shape of the book, but the organic unity of an order focused in a single idea, the idea of Democritus Junior. Logic requires that the partitions of the *Anatomy* open outward to comprehend the ever-widening effects of causes, whether these be black bile or lack of Christian charity. But the Preface opens constantly inward toward disclosure of self because its view is of present consequences seen through the focusing eye of Democritus Junior. The long passage of the "panoramic view" of mankind's folly culminates in the almost oppressively hasty turning from one scene to another (pp. 65-68) in which Democritus Junior catches glimpses, now over this shoulder, now over that, of what his predecessor would encounter "if Democritus were alive now to see . . . to see . . . to see. . . ." The rationale of the Preface, its proof that all men are melancholy, is the proof of observation and not of logic. Thus Democritus Junior is being precise if infuriating when, in concluding his transition from the generalized scenes of mankind's confusion to the particular scenes of institutionalized madness, he directs the reader to "Proceed now *a partibus ad totum,* or from the whole to the parts, and you shall find no other issue; the parts shall be sufficiently dilated in this following Preface. The whole must needs follow by a sorites or induction" (p. 78). At a later point, we shall be examining the use Burton makes of ratiocination in the pages just preceding this statement, but for now we should note that he has already given us thirty-three pages of commentary on the whole world's melancholy. Burton's Preface allows deduction to equal induction; "this following Preface" is also "this preceding Preface" (we are at a point well over halfway through the essay); the conclusion induced from the particular premises restates in effect the deductive major premise, that "all the world is mad, that it is melancholy, dotes." *A partibus ad totum* is also in fact *a toto*

ad partes, "from the whole to the parts." For all its opening outward, the Preface is at any moment focusing on
what the eye of Democritus that is in Burton sees, whatever way he may turn.

To emphasize the centrality of personality to the
meaning of the Preface is not, of course, to say anything
new. Various analyses have been made of the persona
who is both Burton and Democritus Junior, yet neither
one exclusively. Richard Nochimson has shown (Ch. iv)
how Burton's role in the Preface and in the book beyond
is that of a "split personality" which combines the
Heraclitean or Galenic melancholy with the exuberance
of a laughing Democritus. More important, Joan Webber's view of Burton as "cosmic personality" or "universal mind" explains the book in terms of the "I" at its
center who represents both Burton and Democritus and
yet is a totality distinct from either and "larger than the
sum of his parts" (Webber, pp. 84-96 passim). That both
of these analyses are able to reveal the artistry of the
Anatomy of Melancholy where less able criticism does not
is fundamentally attributable to their ability to deal with
the variety Burton has comprehended by the mask or
masks he assumes. Nochimson warns students of the
book against accepting too easily critiques which "seem
to suggest that one single view of the *Anatomy* can explain the meaning of the whole book" (Nochimson,
p. 96). I shall hope not to fall into the category of those
who define Burton too simplistically if, for my purposes
of seeing the relationship between the Preface and the
book, I turn now to another method of describing the
complexity of Burton's persona, one which may com-
plement these fuller analyses of the mask.

Democritus Junior got to be who he is by virtue of

what seems to me the most critical change of structure
the book underwent in its life through six editions. Indeed, the redistributing of most of the material originally contained in Burton's signed "Conclusion of the
Author to the Reader" is the only real change Burton
ever made in his structure, and the only thing which
makes the 1621 *Anatomy* in some way a different book
from the second and succeeding editions. All of his additions or revisions are made within the book, and even
the gradual accumulation of Table, Frontispiece, and
poems are, we have seen, completions of the facade,
clarification of its explanation of the book rather than
introduction of new definitions. The important thing to
observe—and it has often been observed—is of course
that it is a redistribution of material, so that the excision
of the concluding note does not actually change the
matter of the book. Nor is the content of the Preface
greatly altered between 1621 and 1624, for in the first
edition it already contained most of Democritus Junior's
poses, his apologies, his satirical condemnations, his
poetical commonwealth, and so forth. But to these, in
1624, Burton added most of the comments on his style
and the defenses of his book which had appeared in the
1621 Conclusion. The note as a formal entity is gone
after the first edition, and with it Burton's explicit signa-
ture, the first-person farewell of the man Robert Burton
of Christ Church, Oxford, to his readers. And one way
of finding who the persona of the Preface is and what he
has to say, is to question how Democritus and Burton
came together in the Preface of 1624 and thereafter, to
try to see how Democritus Junior as we know him is the
juncture at the artistic center of the *Anatomy* of two
historical persons. For Burton's joining of his Con-

clusion and his Preface into a single entity constitutes the writing together of his persona's first and last names.

In the discussion which follows, I shall be asking the reader to see how, by a structural change in the book, Burton becomes Democritus Junior and yet remains himself, Robert Burton. For Democritus Junior is not simply fictional, he is also factual; he is the artistically conceived persona and the artist who created that persona, both speaking at once, often repeating each other, and finally both confirming and negating each other by becoming one character who can speak with authority to all melancholy men because he is himself no mere man. The Preface, I shall ultimately argue, exists not to say things—facts—about quotidian reality, but as a preface conduces to our understanding that the book itself, with its orderly shape given to chaotically disordered life, is art's cure for life. So it becomes necessary to see that Burton, in becoming Democritus Junior, finds a voice which does not exist "really" (it is not just the voice of Robert Burton), nor does it exist merely fictionally (it is not just a make-believe voice speaking of unrealities). But the persona and the Preface that persona gives to the *Anatomy* exist absolutely, with reference to the book only, and so, insofar as the book's art repairs life's disorder, with reference to "real life" as well. Burton in the Preface finally becomes "No-one," the unmelancholy man whose existence paradoxically denies Democritus Junior's constant assertion that all the world must be melancholy. But before dealing with that final personality, we have to see by what process Burton first gave his persona both his own and another's identities.

When Democritus Junior accosts his readers in the opening of his Preface, he says that they should not expect a satire or "ridiculous treatise" of cosmology because of the name of Democritus. In fact the *Anatomy* contains these kinds of writing (see Colie, p. 454 ff.), but Burton's point seems to be that the *name* Democritus is not to be considered fraudulently attached to the book. He is not carving a statue and signing Praxiteles' name to it: "Besides, it hath been always an ordinary custom, as Gellius observes, 'for later writers and imposters to broach many absurd and insolent fictions under the name of so noble a philosopher as Democritus, to get themselves credit, and by that means the more to be respected,' as artificers do, *Novo qui marmori ascribunt Praxitelen suo*. 'Tis not so with me" (p. 15). Democritus Junior is not pretending to be Democritus, but is taking the philosopher's name as his own, his given name. Burton is "Democritus' because that name declares relationship, or claims it formally, as a child is given his father's or godfather's name. What the relationship is Democritus Junior promises to explain after he has briefly described Democritus' life, but that it is so is his first and most explicit statement: "My intent is no otherwise to use his name, than Mercurius Gallobelgius, Mercurius Britannicus, use the name of Mercury, Democritus Christianus, etc." (p. 16). To take the name of Democritus has for Burton a fairly restricted meaning. To be Democritus Junior is to be a whole complex of personalities, but in assuming the name, Burton makes clear, he has a single intention: by christening himself "Democritus," he claims kinship to Democritus the scholar.

Burton gives several views of Democritus of Abdera through the course of the Preface, but his first description (p. 16), given to disclose the "reason of the name," depicts not the satirist but Democritus the philosopher, divine, physician, politician, mathematician, student of husbandry and natural history: "In a word, he was *omnifariam doctus*, a general scholar, a great student." That Democritus was a melancholic solitary is mentioned, as is his habit of observing and laughing at "such variety of ridiculous objects" as he saw in the world outside, but the definition of what Democritus was, lies "in a word": scholar. And when Democritus Junior goes on to tell how that definition of Democritus fits him, it is again the scholar in himself which he describes as "Democritus." He says with gracious humility that he will not "presume to make any parallel" between himself and Democritus, and yet does so obliquely by making a parallel with his ancestor's younger contemporary: "Yet this much I will say of myself, and that I hope without all suspicion of pride, or self-conceit, I have lived a silent, sedentary, solitary, private life, *mihi et musis* in the university, as long almost as Xenocrates in Athens, *ad senectem fere* to learn wisdom as he did, penned up most part in my study" (p. 17). Democritus Junior then goes on to talk about his own ambitions toward universal knowledge—"I had a great desire (not able to attain to a superficial skill in any) to have some smattering in all, to be *aliquis in omnibus, nullus in singulis,*" and the parallel he is making is, despite humility, between himself and Democritus as "general scholars." The long interpolation concerning what it means to "live still a collegiate student, as Democritus in his garden" which describes the sequestered scholar as a spectator of all the world's confused fortunes (pp. 18-19) does not appear in 1621, but at the end of the passage Democritus Junior explains more briefly that sometimes he goes out to "look into the world" like Diogenes or Democritus and is moved by what he sees.

Yet the "reason of the name" when finally given does not relate to Democritus' satirical view of men, which after all the latter shared with Lucian and Menippus, but to Democritus the scholar, the writer of a book:

> I did sometime laugh and scoff with Lucian, and satirically tax with Menippus, lament with Heraclitus, . . . I was much moved to see that abuse which I could not mend. In which passion howsoever I may sympathize with him or them, *'tis for no such respect I shroud myself under his name;* but either in an unknown habit to assume a little more liberty and freedom of speech, *or if you will needs know, for that reason and only respect which Hippocrates relates* at large in his Epistle to Damagetus. (P. 19; my italics)

Hippocrates says that Democritus was writing a book about "melancholy and madness," anatomizing animal carcasses in order to find the causes and cure of melancholy, and Democritus Junior is "Democritus" specifically because he is writing Democritus' book. Instead of making a statue and signing it with Praxiteles' name, he is doing Praxiteles' work and giving it their common name: "Democritus Junior is therefore bold to imitate, and because he left it unperfect, and it is now lost, *quasi succenturiator Democriti* [as a substitute for Democritus], to revive again, prosecute, and finish in this treatise" (p. 20). It appears then that Democritus Junior is not being paradoxical, or is not only being paradoxical, in suggesting that his reader would be deceived if he were to consider "the *name* of Democritus" to imply necessarily a satirical or cosmological treatise. A child may grow to have more in common with his namesake than the relationship of blood or custom which his christening was originally meant to signify or honor. So Democritus Junior takes after his ancestor of Abdera in several respects, including his tendency to observe mundane folly and react passionately to it, but his name itself is "for no such respect."

One part of our author's name is "Democritus," and it is that because Democritus was a scholar writing a particular book. "Democritus" being the first name, a last name is implied (as in "Mercurius Britannicus," "Democritus Christianus, etc."), and in the 1621 *Anatomy* Burton takes as surname his own name, Robert Burton. He opens his signed Conclusion by announcing that he will "cut the strings of *Democritus* visor, to unmaske and shew him as he is":

> . . . *Amphora coepit*
> *Institui, currente rota cur urceus exit?*
> [The potter begins to fashion a wine jar;
>   why does it depart the turning wheel a pitcher?]

Democritus began as a Prologue in this Tragi-comedie, but why doth the Author end, and act the Epilogue in his own name? I intended at first to have concealed my selfe, but *secunda cogitationes &c.* for some reason I have altered mine intent, and am willing to subscribe.[6]

6. All quotations from the Conclusion are taken from the 1621 edition, unnumbered pages Ddd^r-Ddd3^v. I have normalized *i, j, u, v,* and long *s.*

"Democritus" is the "Prologue" or first name, while "Burton" is the "Epilogue" or last name. By signing the book, Burton indicates his understanding that an artifact discloses the artist: *amphora* and *urceus* are not generically different, but the potter's art determines the ultimate form, whether jar or pitcher, of the lump of clay. And in this case the difference between *amphora* and *urceus* is the difference between "Democritus" and "Burton," "Prologue' and "Epilogue." Burton's first thought says, I may sign this book "Democritus" because I am Democritus and this is his book. The second says, I myself am in this, a very self that is not Democritus; I made his book, but made it my way, and so my readers must direct their eyes at me also, for this work is mine: *"Me me adsum qui feci, in me convertite ocellos / Lectores, meus hic labor est."*

It is the name which is different at beginning and end of the book, the identification of the artist's self in the art, and so the signed Conclusion deals with style. It is here at the end of the book, in the pages signed "From my Studie in *Christ Church Oxon.* Decemb. 5, 1620" that Burton places the familiar descriptions of his method of writing later incorporated into the Preface of Democritus Junior. Style, he says, betrays us: "since I have now put my selfe upon the stage, I must undergoe and abide the censure of it. . . . I have laid my selfe open (I know it) in this Treatise" He defends himself (Robert Burton, not Democritus Junior) against complaints of too salty satire or light treatment of his subject; he describes the lack of leisure that led to his not licking his "confused lumpe" into shape or polishing away all its "harsh compositions"; he admits physic not to be his profession and so the "matter or method" not to be faultless. Finally he deals with those problems that bother a man when he sees himself in print: he thanks his friends, assumes responsibility for errors, worries over the printing job, explains his methods of quotation and marginal citation, and so turns himself, Robert Burton who made the book the way it is, off the potter's wheel onto the printed page.

"Democritus," then, in 1621, is *what* the book is; "Burton" is *how* it is. And Democritus Junior—Robert Burton exists as two selves, like and not-like, *amphora* and *urceus*, prologue and epilogue—one disguised by an usurped name, the other feeling himself exposed because his readers' eyes must see the self he sees in his work. Burton has then a third thought, and in 1624 and thereafter, Democritus-Burton comes together in the Preface as Burton realizes a synthesis which reveals and conceals simultaneously. In the second edition he fuses Burton the stylist with Democritus the scholar and achieves the full meaning of a Democritus who is Democritus Junior. The name Robert Burton never appears again in the book (though added biographical details relating to his brother, his patrons, his benefices reveal the identity), but instead of an epilogue supplying his "real" identity, we are given very clearly, beginning with the third edition, a graphic presentation of Burton's writing his given and surnames *in seriatim*. With the engraved title page, the name Democritus Junior is balanced at the front of the book by the portrait of Robert Burton. The picture is captioned "Democritus Junior," yet it is no stylized representation but a picture that changes with the editions as Burton grows older, possibly balder so that he appears with a hat worn, perhaps, to keep out the chill of his study.[7] The artifact signed with the name of Democritus has the face of the man Burton who has discovered himself to the world.

Democritus-Burton is suggested, then, with the second edition, stated explicitly through the title page portrait in the third, to be the author's full name. For the Preface, Burton's third thoughts tell him, can comprehend both names. The author realizes the potential of a Democritus Junior: if "Democritus" is a given name, "Junior" is not a surname; but if a surname "Burton" is understood and "Democritus Junior" is also "Democritus Burton Junior," then Democritus of Abdera must be assumed to be in some sense a member of Robert Burton's family. And that is what the book proclaims, for it is a book made by a person who is scholar-artist, written by a scholar named Democritus whose style betrays an artist named Burton. Both men, the fifth-century B.C. Greek in his garden and the seventeenth-century A.D. Englishman in his study, coexist in a person called "Democritus Junior." The name is allowed to expand its meaning, so that interpolated into the Preface's opening "parallel" of the two "general scholars" is the long passage (pp. 18-19) showing him or them "in some high place above you all," a "mere spectator of other men's fortunes and adventures"; and interpolated into the original Preface's definition of scholarship with its own stylistic faults ("barbarism, Doric dialect, extemporanean style, tautologies," and so forth) is the artisan's recognition, from the original Conclusion, of what style

7. Edward Bensly, "Some Alterations and Errors in Successive Editions of the *Anatomy of Melancholy*" in Osler, Bensly, and others, p. 201.

means: "I have assayed, put myself upon the stage, . . .
I have laid myself open (I know it) in this treatise,
turned mine inside outward: I shall be censured, I doubt
not" (pp. 26-27). To be Democritus Junior is to be in a
time that is past and present, to be in a place that is on
the stage and in the orchestra, to be masked and unmasked all at once. It is to bear a name for which there is
no simple "reason."

Burton certainly never uses the name I have recon-
structed as "Democritus Burton Junior," but allows it to
appear ambiguously, fleetingly, through the visage of
the "I" who is vaguely a student of Oxford but has, for
example, an elder brother who wrote a *Description of
Leicestershire* "printed at London by W. Jaggard for J.
White, 1622" (p. 36 and note). For ambiguity is the essence of the bond that unites Democritus and Robert
Burton. It is difficult in the extreme to try to attribute (or
not to attribute) any statement of Democritus Junior to
the author Robert Burton. Nochimson is perfectly right
that Democritus Junior's assertion that he wanted to
write the book in Latin (p. 30) is not proof that Burton
"was actually unable to have *his* book published in
Latin," and yet he is also right that, despite a necessarily
implied "distinction between created narrator and cre-
ator-author," Democritus Junior "does represent Robert
Burton in a very real way" (Nochimson, pp. 147-148).
The example is quite useful for our purposes, for in the
original edition of the *Anatomy*, Democritus Junior's
complaint against the "mercenary stationers" who will
not print a Latin treatise is in the Preface: that is, it is the
statement of a Democritus who is not the Burton who
later signs the book. It may thus appear to be a fictional
complaint. But with the 1624 edition, this passage im-

mediately precedes the inserted section from the Conclusion which explains Burton's inability or refusal to
"amend the style" by extensive revisions (pp. 30-31).
The two statements of 1621, one apparently simple and
factual—nobody would print my book in Latin—but
actually fictional since the speaker is an "actor," and the
other fairly hard to accept at face value—in writing this
massive treatise with all its erudition I simply wrote off
the top of my head "out of a confused company of
notes . . . with as small deliberation, as I doe ordinarily
speake"—but presumably factual since it is the attested
statement of one Robert Burton of Christ Church, Oxford: these two statements are made together in one
place and with one voice in the later editions. So fiction
and fact color each other, and the result is paradox.
Democritus-Burton may be stating facts, but then again
he is himself both fact and fiction, and who is to say
what's what?

The union of Democritus and Burton in the Preface of
Democritus Junior to the Reader in effect makes that
Preface a logical paradox, and Democritus Junior is a
Cretan saying, "All Cretans are liars."[8] A statement like
that about his desire to publish in Latin may in fact be
neither false nor true, but an absolute, a statement possible only with reference to itself, not to the real world.
The condemnation of the stationers and the artist's
apology for his method exist in the Preface, which in
turn exists for and conduces to the *Anatomy*, but they do
not necessarily say anything true or judgmental about
London stationers or Robert Burton of Christ Church,

8. See Colie, pp. 5-6, for the close association of logical and
rhetorical paradox.

Oxford. The nature of the persona takes an even more decidedly paradoxical turn, as we shall see. But it should be noted that the full detachment of the Preface begins, and the extent to which Burton's "actor" and "mere spectator" can be both of and not of the world is first fully realized, when the fact and the fiction, the self and the self-made mask, come together in Democritus Junior who is both Democritus and Burton.

Infinite possibilities for ambiguity are captured explicitly in the second and succeeding editions when Burton takes another name which mediates between the two historical persons he has joined into the single, yet double, even multiple personality of Democritus Junior. He takes, as it were a middle name: Nobody.[9] Toward the end of his Preface, Democritus Junior asks his readers to remember, if they feel his words to have been too satirical or comical, that " 'tis not I, but Democritus, *Democritus dixit:* you must consider what it is to speak in one's own or another's person, an assumed habit and name—a difference betwixt him that affects or acts a prince's, a philosopher's, a magistrate's, a fool's part, and him that is so indeed—and what liberty those old satirists have had; it is a cento collected from others; not I, but they that say it" (p. 121). And having stood behind the satirist's conventional shield—"I hate their vices, not their persons"—he repeats that *"Democritus dixit,* Democritus will answer it" (p. 122), and places his words in the long ago and far away of Saturnalian feasts when slaves could speak freely without fear of consequences. To speak in "an assumed habit or name," in

9. On Burton as everyone and no one, see Webber, p. 82 ff.; cf. Fish, pp. 314-322.

the first edition, when the real author waits till his epilogue to give his last name, is thus to be free to speak
harshly because all that one says was said back then in
the mists of time:

> When our Countrimen sacrificed to their goddesse Vacuna,
> and set turning an apple with a pot of ale and a toste by their
> *Vacunall* fires, I writt this and published this. The time, place,
> persons, and all circumstances apologize for me, & why may I
> not then be idle with others? speake my mind freely, If you
> deny me this liberty, upon these presumptions I will take it: I
> say againe, I will take it.   (*Anatomy*, 1621, p. 71)

He then immediately recants, confesses his faults, and
begs pardon—all of which is patently unnecessary since
he has already effectively claimed the inconsequential
nature of a satire that is fictional—and then he closes the
Preface and turns to his "more sober discourse." Robert
Burton of Christ Church in his "own person" then must
make a second apology in the 1621 Conclusion, where
he admits the sting satire may have and hopes he has
harmed no one. Burton says that though he has "apolo-
gized already" (a note points to the Preface) he will do
so again, and he quotes and translates Seneca's *Medea* to
apologize in these "last words"—in, that is, his own
name:

> And in my last words this I doe desire,
> That what in passion I have said or ire;
> May be forgotten, and a better mind,
> Be had of us hereafter as you find.

Here in the Conclusion another's speech is made his
own; here the "last words" are his signed epilogue, and
it is not Medea but Burton that says it, translating it
even into his own tongue.

Now beginning with 1624, the second apology follows immediately after the first in the context of the Preface. *"Democritus dixit"*—I wrote and published this in the time, place, person, and circumstances of Democritus—is followed by the apology of the now nameless, but more immediate voice from the Conclusion which does not ward off blows by Democritus' buckler, but acknowledges the satirist's predicament in Tacitus' words, and in those of an "honourable man" of *this* time (Bacon) as well: "They fear a satirist's wit, he their memories." The "last words" of the poem are no longer those of Robert Burton of Christ Church; they are now, like the first apology, those of a Democritus-Burton whose "I" is not his own or another's, but both and neither. Ambiguity, even duplicity of statement makes us realize that the Preface's speaker can say anything or all things—Democritus, not I, apologizes; I apologize; I need not apologize—because he is no single voice but a joining of historical voices in a place and time that are not one, but are merely the time and place of the book.

Then as if to reinforce the ambiguity of the double apology with its intervening recantation, Burton calls himself and his book nobody and nothing; he says it not in his own tongue nor in another's, but in two tongues which epitomize universal history. In Greek and Latin he explains that between Democritus and Burton, prologue and epilogue, one mask and another, stands No one. No one said it; it is nothing by nobody:

When our countrymen sacrificed to their goddess Vacuna, and sat tippling by their Vacunal fires, I writ this, and published this. Οὖτις ἔλεγεν, it is *neminis nihil*. The time, place, persons, and all circumstances apologize for me, and why may I not then be idle with others, speak my mind freely? If you deny me this liberty, upon these presumptions I will take it: I say again, I will take it. . . . If any man take exceptions, let him turn the buckle of his girdle, I care not. I owe thee nothing (reader), I look for no favour at thy hands, I am independent, I fear not.   (P. 122)

There is now no one "I"; and "I" is no single mask. "No one" mediates between an I who claims, " 'tis not I, but Democritus, . . . not I but they that say it" (p. 121) and an I who says, "If through weakness, folly, passion, discontent, ignorance, I have said amiss, let it be forgotten and forgiven" (pp. 122–123). It is Nobody who adds that he owes his readers nothing, for he is "independent" not only of them, but of the individual selves which are in him.

"Nobody" is of course the ultimate mask, for it either denies itself—one who is no one does not exist—or it denies existence to all but itself—if No one exists, then the only being is non-being. Beginning with the third edition, the same one whose title page portrays Democritus Junior as Robert Burton, the author tells us who Nobody is, thus defining through his "middle" name the paradoxical nature both of his persona and of the world that persona encounters and criticizes. Just before he concludes his overview of the metaphorically melancholy world and turns to the apologies and the book, Democritus Junior summarizes his conclusion that all the world is melancholy by asking himself whom he can possibly except from the indictment. In the first editions the exceptions run from Stoics and other philosophers to the pope, and the exceptions immediately appear to be no exceptions at all: " 'He never dotes, never mad, never sad, drunk, because virtue cannot be taken away,' as Zeno holds, but he was mad to say so" (p. 118). Or, with heavy irony: "The Pope is more than a man, as his parasites often make him, a demi-god, and besides His Holiness cannot err, *in Cathedra* belike: and yet some of them have been magicians, heretics, atheists, children" (p. 119). Thus the question, Whom shall I except? is answered by naming exceptions which are not exceptions, for "they are all mad." But in the third edition one is added to the top of the list: Nobody is *not* mad:

> Whom shall I then except? Ulricus Huttenus' *Nemo; nam, Nemo omnibus horis sapit, Nemo nascitur sine vitiis, Crimine Nemo caret, Nemo sorte sua vivit contentus, Nemo in amore sapit, Nemo bonus, Nemo sapiens, Nemo est ex omni parti beatus* [Nobody; for Nobody is sensible at all times; Nobody is born without fault; Nobody is free from blame; Nobody lives content with his own lot; Nobody is sane in love; Nobody is good, Nobody wise; Nobody is completely happy], etc., and therefore Nicholas Nemo, or Monsieur Nobody, shall go free. *Quid valeat Nemo, Nemo referre potest* [Nobody can say what Nobody is capable of].   (P. 117)

Nobody is thus made a person—Monsieur Nicholas Nemo; and he is given positive existence and the character of all that the world is not—sensible, faultless, blameless, content, sane in love, good, wise, and happy. And therefore he can repeat, write down, perhaps ("Οὔτις ἔλεγεν"; no one has said it), what he (Nemo) achieves and what no one (nemo) is capable of. This person called "Nobody" is then in our minds when within a few pages Democritus Junior confesses that his book is *neminis nihil*. The "I" who is Democritus and Burton is the existing exception, Nicholas Nemo, whose being annihilates the world of melancholy that is the subject of the Preface and of the book.

The mediator between Democritus of Abdera and Burton of Christ Church is the Democritus Junior who is also Nemo, the single exception to the world of melancholy. With the naming and elucidation of Nobody, Burton reaches the full explanation of that curious warning he gave his readers at the very beginning, that his seemingly open book is a covered basket because its writer is hidden, is, in fact, not of this world: " 'suppose the Man in the Moon, or whom thou wilt, to be the author,' I would not willingly be known" (p. 15). The nature of the Preface, as a "satyricall Preface," must lie in the nature of the mask, and to the extent that Democritus Junior is Nobody, the masks in the Preface exist independent of the time and place which gives birth to them, of the world which they survey, and of the very names which attach them to identifiable men. If Nobody—good, wise, sensible, and so on—exists, then the melancholy world does not: it is a drastic cure for a physician-divine to make, but a supremely effective one. In Partition III, Burton dismisses atheists from his book because they, in a different way, make the world nothing. Their denial of God's love and goodness, we saw, annihilates the world and men, and so they are not eligible for the cure of wisdom; and rather than being *of* the melancholy world, "their melancholy is at hand" (see above, pages 186-189). In the Preface, however, Democritus Junior becomes Nobody in order to become good and wise and so to be the positive representation of the God-given nature which man has lost, while at the same time he—*nos numerus sumus; homo sum*—is one of all melancholy men.

In being who he is Democritus Junior can cure the world by making it nothing, a satirical view of reality, a poetical fiction, and so by making it everything, a book which encompasses all that the real world is and is not. "Democritus" is Burton's mask, as the personate actor of the Preface declares, but "Burton" is equally Democritus' mask, as the title page illustrates. And neither is the other, but both are Nobody, the conjunction in the time and space of the Preface of a given and a family name, a prologue and an epilogue which comprehend the whole world and nothing. In examining Democritus Junior's method, we shall be asking how effective, in purely sociological terms, Burton intends his visionary cures of the world to be. But here we see that the persona—factual Burton, fictional Democritus, and nobody at all—who speaks in the Preface makes himself into the artifact which can speak absolutely of the world, its ills, its possible cures, because it exists absolutely, and with it the Preface and the book to which the Preface conduces. Monsieur Nobody cannot logically make statements about the real world because his existence annihilates it; but Democritus Junior can be observer and observed, physician and patient, player and audience in this universe of the book which exists because he exists: it is nothing by nobody. And so the stuff of the Preface is not medicine but metaphor, not logical discourse but satirical observation.

The subject matter this complex and paradoxical persona writes about is the whole world seen as humankind: Democritus Junior's vision of *materia mundi* is of mankind, that being who is at once the macrocosm of man and the microcosm of the universe. Humanity is a world which, like Strabo's geography of Greece, is laid out in the form of a man with all his members, a world

whose "humour" is melancholy, the anatomizing of
which is a task comparable to the astronomical description of the cosmos (pp. 38-39). What the world is
constantly implies what it is not: "you shall find that
kingdoms and provinces are melancholy, cities and
families, all creatures, vegetal, sensible, and rational,
that all sorts, sects, ages, conditions, are out of tune" (p.
39). Melancholy is disorder, disharmony; folly is not-
wisdom; chance is the negation of virtue's deserts.
Whatever Democritus Junior sees is the inversion and
negation of all reasonable definition: Democritus told
Hippocrates that the Abderites "account virtue madness":

Shall I tell you the reason of it? Fortune and Virtue, Wisdom
and Folly, their seconds, upon a time contended in the
Olympics; every man thought that Fortune and Folly would
have the worst, and pitied their cases; but it fell out otherwise.
Fortune was blind and cared not where she stroke, nor
whom, without laws. . . . Folly, rash and inconsiderate, es-
teemed as little what she said or did. Virtue and Wisdom gave
place, were hissed out and exploded by the common people,
Folly and Fortune admired, and so are all their followers ever
since.   (P. 41)

As the method of the *Anatomy* is definition by division
that excludes unlike subject matter, so the method of
the Preface is definition by the inclusion of everything
within common boundaries. To say that "all the world is
mad, that it is melancholy, dotes" is to refuse to draw
lines between the real and the metaphorical: "So that,
take melancholy in what sense you will, properly or improperly, in disposition or habit, for pleasure or for
pain, dotage, discontent, fear, sorrow, madness, for
part or all, truly or metaphorically, 'tis all one" (p. 40).

The vision of the Preface sees across the boundaries of the partitions to the common malady incubated and propagated in the universal "seminary of folly." The not-knowing which is man's definite disease makes common cause with the knowing falsely which is his indefinite penchant toward folly: "Some say there be two main defects of wit, error and ignorance, to which all others are reduced; by ignorance we know not things necessary, by error we know them falsely. Ignorance is a privation, error a positive act. From ignorance comes vice, from error heresy, etc. But make how many kinds you will, divide and subdivide, few men are free, or that do not impinge on some one kind or other" (p. 47).

The "vast confusion" which Democritus Junior sees and causes us to see is a world determined by time, governed, that is, by Fortune and defined by the rise and fall of her wheel. So whenever Democritus Junior steps out of his study, or climbs a hill, or sits atop the shoulders of his worthy predecessors, he tends to look on a milling throng below going in confused circles, repeating itself through time. His first survey (pp. 18-19) is indicative of this tendency: from "some high place above you all" he oversees "with one sweep all ages down to the present." The world of space—of things abroad, in court and country—comes to him, constricts itself to his view: "A mere spectator of other men's fortunes and adventures, and how they act their parts, which methinks are diversely presented unto me, as from a common theatre or scene." Centered on him as focal point and focusing point, the things we see are then extended in time, from today to tomorrow, from now to again.

I hear *new news every day,* and those ordinary rumours of war, plagues, fires, inundations, thefts, murders, massacres, meteors, comets, spectrums, prodigies, apparitions, of towns taken, cities besieged in France, Germany, Turkey, Persia, Poland, etc., *daily* musters and preparations, and such-like, which *these tempestuous times* afford, battles fought, so many men slain, monomachies, shipwrecks, piracies, and sea-fights, peace, leagues, stratagems, and fresh alarums. A vast confusion of vows, wishes, actions, edicts, petitions, lawsuits, pleas, laws, proclamations, complaints, grievances are *daily* brought to our ears. *New* books *every day,* pamphlets, currantoes, stories, whole catalogues of volumes of all sorts, *new* paradoxes, opinions, schisms, heresies, controversies in philosophy, religion, etc. *Now* come *tidings* of weddings, maskings, mummeries, entertainments, jubilees, embassies, tilts and tournaments, trophies, triumphs, revels, sports, plays: *then again,* as in a *new shifted scene,* treasons, cheating tricks, robberies, enormous villainies in all kinds, funerals, burials, deaths of princes, *new* discoveries, expeditions; *now* comical, *then* tragical matters. *To-day* we hear of *new* lords and officers created, *to-morrow* of some great men deposed, and *then again* of fresh honours conferred.   [Italics mine]

And so it continues, creating an apparent infinity of days and news. Space always limits itself so that a man looking out or down can see everything, but see it as himself, for the world takes the form of mankind, either of his body or of his self-delimiting institutions:

. . . and if thou shalt either conceive, or climb to see, thou shalt soon perceive that all the world is mad, that it is melancholy, dotes; that it is (which Epichthonius Cosmopolites expressed not many years since in a map) made like a fool's head (with that motto, *Caput helleboro dignum*); a crazed head, *cavea stultorum,* a fools' paradise, or as Apollonius, a common prison of gulls, cheaters, flatterers, etc., and needs to be reformed.   (P. 39)

Confusion is thus the disease defined spatially by the shape of mankind itself, but it is extended also through time. And Democritus Junior's vision of what mankind has been and is, is not, and may never be, is a vision of mutability without direction; the disease analyzed *"a partibus ad totum,* or from the whole to the parts" is the defect of human progress.

Democritus Junior's ability to play his role depends on the commonplace fact that the more things change, the more they stay the same: "now" is like "then," only more so. Thus the centrality of the "not impertinent" story (pp. 47-52) of Hippocrates' visit to Democritus. Democritus laughs at first because Hippocrates marvels that he has time to devote to his project of anatomizing melancholy, and the outburst continues against the vanities of life which set men going in circles, loving only to hate, making peace only to covet war, seeking riches only to hoard them. The actions of men have no direction, only repetition: "O wise Hippocrates, I laugh at such things being done, but much more when no good comes of them, and when they are done, to so ill purpose." Hippocrates' defense, that men cannot see the future or they would act more wisely, brings forth Democritus' definition of wisdom that recognizes the limits mortality sets to mutability:

". . . if men would govern their actions by discretion and providence, they would not declare themselves fools as now they do, and he should have no cause of laughter; but" (quoth he) "they swell in this life as if they are immortal, and demigods, for want of understanding. It were enough to make them wise, if they would but consider the mutability of this world, and how it wheels about, nothing being firm and sure.

He that is now above, to-morrow is beneath; he that sate on this side to-day, to-morrow is hurled on the other; and not considering these matters, they fall into many inconveniences and troubles, coveting things of no profit and thirsting after them, tumbling headlong into many calamities." (P. 50)

So when Democritus Junior takes over, all the much emphasized "newness" of the melancholy world only serves to underscore its oldness, for the change Democritus Junior sees is in degree; the kind is still the same.

When he calls for a "Democritus to laugh at Democritus," and muses over what Democritus would see if he were alive today, Democritus Junior is seeing the exact things Democritus saw, the disease of folly sprung from mutability which is the same in this as in other times:

For now, as Sarisburiensis said in his time . . . the whole world plays the fool; we have a new theatre, a new scene, a new Comedy of Errors, a new company of personate actors. . . . He that was a mariner today, is an apothecary to-morrow; a smith one while, a philosopher another, . . . a king now with his crown, robes, sceptre, attendants, by and by drove a loaded ass before him like a carter, etc. (P. 52)

Through all the pages of descriptions of universal folly, the vision is of man going in circles, his only stability being the constancy of his fickleness: "the world alters every day . . . we change language, habits, laws, customs, manners, but not vices, not diseases, not the symptoms of folly and madness, they are the same, and ever will be" (p. 53). To "speak of times present" (p. 54) is then to speak of all time, for everything that is seen is the insane clinging to Fortune's wheel while it turns the world inside out: "To see horses ride in a coach, men draw it; dogs devour their masters; towers build masons; children rule; old men go to school; women wear the breeches; sheep demolish towns, devour men, etc., and in a word, the world turned upside downward! *O viveret Democritus!*" (p. 68). Apparently the "golden chain" of the universe is not only disordered, but impaired: "nay, what's the world itself? A vast chaos, a confusion of manners, as fickle as the air, *domicilium insanorum*, a turbulent troop full of impurities, a mart of walking spirits," and so on (p. 64).

Time, then, is the extension of mankind that gives him existence by giving him motion, without giving his existence meaning by making that motion progress toward a perfection of himself: he goes in circles, not seeing that tomorrow will be yesterday. Being satirical, the Preface deals with Robert Burton's own time. Democritus Junior's insistent criticism is of what he sees from his study, hears in the news that comes to him daily; and the view of the melancholy world is thus necessarily a view of seventeenth-century England. But it is also the view of all the time included in all the books, ancient and modern, in his study, and as true as it is that "Burton's book not only anatomizes melancholy; it anatomizes the contemporary setting, the reign of the early Stuarts"; as true as it is that Burton was "well informed about the main issues, secular and religious, of the day" (Mueller, pp. 8-9), it is nonetheless true that the *Anatomy*, even the anatomy in the Preface—such as it is, from the parts to the whole and the whole to the parts—is not primarily an anatomy of "Robert Burton's England." The total impact of the Preface in its elucidation of past and present forces the conclusion that Burton is dealing with his time as an epitome of all time. He can be who he is—Democritus, Democritus Junior, Robert Burton, Nobody—because now is then, his England is Democritus' Greece, his world is mankind hanging onto Fortune's wheel as desperately now as when Lady Philosophy explained it all to Boethius. As he is Nobody and Democritus and Burton, the world Democritus Junior observes and analyzes exists in him—in his vision—as an absolute reflection of all reality, not as a particular "real" kingdom. The point has to be noted if we are to see what Burton is doing in the later parts of the Preface when he anatomizes the diseased institutions of mankind. The subject of Burton's book is "of man and humankind" (p. 15), not Jacobean or Caroline England. He is satirist, physician, anatomist; but he is not a social or political scientist if by those terms we mean to imply a primary interest in the description of institutions and amelioration of social ills. For Burton, through all the masks of the Preface, sees history not as progress from old times to new times but more as progress through all times.

Democritus Junior is ultimately concerned, as Dubos puts it, with the "spirit of human brotherhood and the urge to move forward and upward," but memory of the past, his wisdom—the wisdom of Democritus—tells him, must *be* anticipation of the future. Democritus Junior specifically refuses the opportunity to write *to his time*. In choosing to be a physician and write of "this medicinal subject" (p. 36), he rejects divinity *per se* because as he sees it, to have written as a divine would have involved him in self-perpetuating activities restricted in time and place and limited to immediate ends. It is a narrow view of divinity and of the art of preaching, but it is the one which Democritus Junior holds when he declines to write either "positively" or "in controversy." To write positively, he says, is to preach at the crossroads of his time, to admonish the leaders of the age:

. . . and had I been as forward and ambitious as some others, I might have haply printed a sermon at Paul's Cross, a sermon in St. Mary's Oxon, a sermon in Christ Church, or a sermon before the right worshipful, a sermon in Latin, in English, a sermon with a name, a sermon without, a sermon, a sermon, etc. But I have been ever as desirous to suppress my labours in this kind, as others have been to press and publish theirs. (P. 35)

To have written in controversy would have embroiled him in the great religious disputes of the day without hope of extricating himself ("having once begun, I should never make an end"); like the Jesuits who thrive on "unprofitable questions and disputations" he would have lost his humanity—his charity—in winning points: "Blind fury, or error, or rashness, or what it is that eggs them, I know not; I am sure many times, which Austin perceived long since, *tempestate contentionis, serenitas caritatis obnubilatur*, with this tempest of contention the serenity of charity is overclouded, and there be too many spirits conjured up already in this kind in all sciences" (p. 35).

Preaching and theology seen in this light are only words, words, words, which turn vocation into the sort of unproductive and self-degrading pursuit of the world which Burton shows us in his Digression of the Misery of Scholars. The kind of physician-divine Democritus Junior chooses to be involves him not in exhortation or debate, but in the cure of souls: instead of mere words which make divinity just another science, he elects to imitate the divine Word, to be "a spiritual physician . . . as our Saviour calls Himself" and to set himself the task of amending mankind's "common infirmity of body and soul" (p. 37). The brotherhood of man is the brotherhood of folly, and Burton's own age is but the latest chaotic example of the need for reform that has existed through all time. That Democritus Junior can devise a way of writing Democritus' book instead of preaching religion or politics at Paul's Cross or tangling with Jesuits depends on the fact that mankind has not made progress in improving his universal, his melancholy condition since the mad citizens of Abdera called in a physician to cure their local eccentric of his wisdom.

MODUS OPERANDI

Democritus Junior's explanation of the *Anatomy* addresses itself to the defect of progress inherent in Fortune's and Folly's world, which is a world needing reformation yet one that wisdom tells us will always be the same. Although his hope for progress cannot lie in changing mankind's natural state, or what has come to be his natural state, it can and does lie nonetheless in re-forming mankind. For Democritus Junior describes in the Preface a method of controlling the chaotic, apparently impaired, order of existence by reshaping it to a form which is not merely human, but civilized. The means presented in the Preface whereby Democritus Junior will return man to understanding are the means of scholarship. To make Democritus' book is his aim, and if he can make that book—which Democritus did not finish or which has been lost in some intervening turn of Fortune's wheel—then Democritus Junior will have made progress, for he will have put together the scattered pieces of bones and sinew, the mountains of knowledge, the bits of wisdom which have accumulated in mankind's study since Democritus first began anatomizing the *"rem substratum,* melancholy, madness" of the human condition. He will have "known" man fully. Burton's book, complete and ordered, held firmly in hand on the title page, is the cure for melancholy that "Nobody's" Preface conduces us to. Form—the melancholy world re-formed as art completed, not merely attempted—is the progress Democritus Junior achieves.

He expects to make that progress by no medicinal or "material" cure, but by the cure of understanding; his "chief motives" for allowing his discourse to "savour too much of humanity" are the manifestations of the spirit of human brotherhood peculiar to a man of learning, for they culminate in knowledge: "the generality of the disease, the necessity of the cure, and the commodity or common good that will arise to all men by the knowledge of it" (p. 38). Scholarship itself, we shall see, the vocation common to Democritus of Abdera and Democritus of England, to the divine Robert Burton of Christ Church and the physician Democritus Junior of the universal scene—scholarship provides the means of progress because its very method is re-formation. The scholar, as Burton represents him through Democritus Junior, takes all knowledge of man as his raw material and, I shall argue, re-presents it to the world in the form of a book that holds all diversity in order; the book must be constantly read, constantly written, but always whole, a unified vision of all the things men know shaped into an ordered discourse, given the form of a single, if infinitely varied, statement.

The first broad view of the world in the Preface, we have seen, is the extension of man's matter—the general shape of mankind, fool's head and all—in time that is cyclical. Mankind rides Fortune's wheel reciting Folly's creed, "I will do as I have done, as my predecessors have done, and as my friends now do. I will dote for company" (p. 72). But the second broad view of the world is not of what man is, his general condition, but of what he tries to make himself. For when Democritus Junior turns from his "random" description to his "more special and evident arguments" (p. 73), he is actually turning to look at the shapes mankind gives itself. The institutions of society are, of course, traditionally analogous to the body of man; Democritus Junior emphasizes the organic bonds between man, his "Kingdom, provinces, and politic bodies" (p. 79), and the family or "economical body" (p. 109); and the various classes of private men with which he concludes the survey are, by implication, the "members" of these various bodies (p. 120). This section of the Preface concerns civilization, the means whereby man—"truly or metaphorically, 'tis all one"—attempts to make progress by giving his natural condition the form of artificial, institutionalized order:

This island amongst the rest, our next neighbours the French and Germans, may be a sufficient witness, that in a short time, by that prudent policy of the Romans, was brought from barbarism; see but what Caesar reports of us, and Tacitus of those old Germans; they were once as uncivil as they in Virginia, yet by planting of colonies and good laws, they became, from barbarous outlaws, to be full of rich and populous cities, as now they are, and most flourishing kingdoms.   (P. 86)

In this part of his satirical Preface, Democritus Junior is more particularly concerned than elsewhere with the good and bad that he sees in England. He is arguing *"a partibus ad totum,"* and the defects he perceives in his immediate time and place, the contrasts he makes between that time and place and others, are striking. He is dealing with the stuff of social and political science—demographics, production and distribution of goods, city planning, the legal bases of social and economic stability—and much of his concern is directed toward his own kingdom, "our island of Great Britain." But it is directed that way as toward the object closest to hand, not as toward the object of exclusive interest. Democritus Junior is still not preaching positively; he is analyzing mankind from the parts to the whole and back again, and whenever he describes how it is "with us," he is speaking of "this island amongst the rest": "We have good laws, I deny not, to rectify such enormities, and so in all other countries, but it seems not always to good purpose. We had need of some general visitor in our age, that should reform what is amiss" (p. 96).

Civilized man, as Democritus Junior sees him, is mankind working, the builder of cities and so of nations, and so of health that is *commune bonum*, the common weal: "For where you shall see the people civil, obedient to God and princes, judicious, peaceable and quiet, rich, fortunate, and flourish, to live in peace, in unity and concord, a country well tilled, many fair-built and populous cities . . . the people are neat, polite and terse, *ubi beateque vivunt*, which our politicians make the chief end of a commonwealth . . . that country is free from melancholy" (p. 79). Paradise in this view is not unspoiled Eden, but civilization, a man-made thing: "To shut up all in brief, where good government is, prudent and wise princes, there all things thrive and prosper, peace and happiness is in that land: where it is otherwise, all things are ugly to behold, incult, barbarous, uncivil, a paradise is turned to a wilderness" (p. 86). Man works, and by working reshapes his world, reclaiming from chaos the perfection of a made thing.

Yea, and if some travellers should see (to come nearer home) those rich United Provinces of Holland, Zealand, etc., over against us; those neat cities and populous towns, full of most industrious artificers, so much land recovered from the sea, and so painfully preserved by those artificial inventions, so wonderfully approved, . . . so many navigable channels from place to place, made by men's hands, etc., and on the other side so many thousand acres of our fens lie drowned, our cities thin, and those vile, poor, and ugly to behold in respect of theirs, our trades decayed, our still running rivers stopped, and that beneficial use of transportation wholly neglected, so many havens void of ships and towns, so many parks and forests for pleasure, barren heaths, so many villages depopulated, etc., I think sure he would find some fault.   (P. 87)

The *Anatomy of Melancholy*, a massive treatise of scientific and humane learning, ends with the quiet, anticlimactic advice that its readers "be not solitary, be not idle"—an almost vapid remark to make to close out a book of these dimensions. Burton's eloquence concerning man's need to love his fellow man by loving God, the appeal to place human despair in the context of divine mercy, these end with a sort of tinkling inconsequence in a plea to "be not idle." Tinkling and inconsequential after the clarion call to charity, except that reverberating through the *Anatomy* to its very last word is the essential humanizing, civilizing force of industry that reforms the essentially inhumane, barbarous natural state of man which is idleness, *id est*, melancholy. The Preface's climactic movement, this section of the argument *a partibus ad totum,* describes man as he is by nature in contrast to what he might be by art and industry.

The first and worst thorn in the side of England's body politic is idleness. She is blessed by nature with the raw materials of a great nation, but nature is not enough; states become great not by "fertility of soil, but industry": "Idleness is the *malus genius* of our nation. For as Boterus justly argues, fertility of a country is not enough, except art and industry be joined unto it" (pp. 88-89). To be a great body politic is not just to be like man's body, for that is merely to be—like mankind itself—foolish and melancholy, slave to Fortune. When Democritus Junior counts cities (p. 88) and public works (p. 93) or describes the "new making or mending" of canals and navigable rivers (pp. 93-95) and laments in each case England's lack of achievement because of widespread idleness, riot, drunkenness, and, in short, want of industry, he is counting the ways mankind can and yet does not cure itself of the disease that keeps it from fulfilling its potential. If to be civilized is to build cities, then England is defective because it has only London that "bears the face of a city," and for the rest it is uncivilized, full of men "which had rather beg or loiter, and be ready to starve, than work" (p. 92). Idleness and industry are at the center of this Preface conducing to the book because the best possible vision of mankind is of the despiser of unwrought, unimproved "rude matter":

That prince, therefore, as Boterus adviseth, that will have a rich country and fair cities, let him get good trades, privileges, painful inhabitants, artificers, and suffer no rude matter unwrought, as tin, iron, wool, lead, etc., to be transported out of his country—a thing in part seriously attempted amongst us, but not effected. . . . We have the same means, able bodies, pliant wits, matter of all sorts, wool, flax, iron, tin, lead, wood, etc., many excellent subjects to work upon, only industry is wanting.   (Pp. 90-91)

Only industry is wanting, and that means that only humanity itself is wanting, for humanity is less than human unless it works: "we contemn this benefit of carriage by waters, and are therefore compelled in the inner parts of this island, because portage is so dear, to eat up our commodities ourselves, and live like so many boars in a sty, for want of vent and utterance" (p. 95).

Man the builder, the shaper, the industrious worker is thus capable of being more than he is, but is less than he might be because he is idle. If he builds, he can build a more perfect macrocosm of himself in a good state, or in a good family (the family in this Preface is an institution, man's "economical body," rather than an organic reflection of his internal constitution as in Partition III).

But there is more than one way to work, and out of misdirected industry rise "casualities, taxes, mulcts, chargeable offices, vain expenses, . . . and that which is the gulf of all, improvidence, ill husbandry, disorder and confusion," and the result is not a well-designed city but a trap, an "inextricable labyrinth of debts, cares, woes, want, grief, discontent, and melancholy itself" (p. 109). The hand of the builder may slip because of inexpertise, and design collapse into disorder, or the purpose behind the work may invalidate it as a civilizing force. Instead of improving nature into paradise, industry can cause decay; it can strap mankind with tighter bonds than ever to Fortune's melancholy merry-go-round. Great houses, the sign of "ancient families," are signs of idleness when "riot and prodigality" replace hospitality and instead of civility mankind displays his old natural barbarity in "fine cloths and curious buildings": when he overdoes himself in riotous living, "civilized" man ends up by having to "break up house, and creep into holes" (p. 108).

Because purpose determines the final meaning of constructs, they are open to interpretation, and industry, like so much that Democritus Junior describes in the Preface, is a matter of ambiguity. The difference between mad and sane lies in the way mankind views his objets d'art. At one end of the induction *a partibus ad totum* the tombs of the Pharaohs are admirable public works, their very inutility turned to *commune bonum* because they convert idleness into work, the rude matter of the body politic into the wrought objects of the state: "and rather than they should be idle, as those Egyptian Pharaohs, Moeris, and Sesostris did, to task their subjects to build unnecessary pyramids, obelisks, labyrinths, channels, lakes, gigantic works all, to divert them from rebellion, riot, drunkenness" (p. 93). But at the conclusion of the proof that mankind is mad even in what it makes of itself, we see the same works, finished now, as mere curiosities of the melancholy world rather than as evidence that man can overcome idleness by industry. They are symbols of the brutish regression that leads man to creep into holes or wallow in pigsties.

To insist in all particulars were an Herculean task, to reckon up . . . mad labours, mad books, endeavours, carriages, gross ignorance, ridiculous actions, absurd gestures; . . . madness of villages, stupend structures; as those Egyptian pyramids, labyrinths, and spinxes, which a company of crowned

asses . . . vainly built, when neither the architect nor king
that made them, or to what use and purpose, are yet known.
(Pp. 116-117)

Re-formation of the world is not simply, then, a matter
of making a thing and thereby possessing civilization. It
is remaking chaotic disorder into artificial order for a
purpose. And the civilizing power lies not in the thing
made, for buildings, canals, or cities which are no
longer being sustained by industry are simply ruinous
reminders of paradise (pp. 89-90). The purpose of building cities is to be civilized, which is to build cities, so
that to see the work going on is to see progress; to see a
thing finished, not working, is to see ruins. In recognizing this principle of purposive, sustained reformation,
we may recognize Robert Burton's purpose for his own
encyclopedic reworking of the rude matter of humanity's *rem substratum*, melancholy, into the wrought form
of the *Anatomy of Melancholy*. His book is a symptom,
not just of the melancholy world, but of reformed man,
for it is always being made and remade, read and re-
read. The *Anatomy* is civilized man working at being
civilized, working at ordering his disordered but as yet
not wholly impaired world.

Democritus Junior calls for a "general visitor" to
reform his age, someone with the force of an Attila or
Hercules or the character of a Crates, or someone with a
magic ability to "transport himself in an instant to what
place he desired, alter affections, cure all manner of
diseases, that he might range over the world, and
reform all distressed states and persons, as he would
himself" (p. 96). Such a reformer could shape the real
world into a perfected image of mankind.

He might root out barbarism out of America, and fully dis-

cover *Terra Australis Incognita*, find out the north-east and
north-west passages, drain those mighty Maeotian fens, cut
down those vast Hercynian woods, irrigate those barren Ara-
bian deserts, etc., cure us of our epidemical diseases, . . . end
all our idle controversies, cut off our tumultuous desires, inordinate lusts, root out atheism, impiety, heresy, schism, and
superstition, which now so crucify the world, catechize gross
ignorance.   (P. 97)

Yet of his desire to see the rude matter of the world
wrought to the form of man's civilizing self, Burton
says, "these are vain, absurd, and ridiculous wishes not
to be hoped: all must be as it is, . . . there is no remedy,
it may not be redressed" (p. 97). And yet not
impossible, for Democritus Junior has a reformer; he is
himself a general visitor to his age. Democritus-Nobody-
Burton-Junior sees in this Preface all that the world of
humanity is, and he proposes to build a book which will
cure idleness. The call for a general visitor and the realization that the wish is ridiculous precede his doing in
the Preface what cannot be done in the world: he makes
a paradise, a "poetical commonwealth." But before
turning to the Utopia, we should look again at what
Democritus Junior's job is, for it is the work he does that
must determine the meaning not only of the Utopia, but
ultimately of the *Anatomy*.

   Democritus Junior is a scholar. Now he has said that
his purpose is to finish Democritus' book, which means
to write the book as a cure for himself and others (p. 20).
And the scholar writes books by reforming chaos.
Democritus Junior's life has let him see everything, but
see it in disarray:

This roving humour (though not with like success) I have ever
had, and like a ranging spaniel, that barks at every bird he
sees, leaving his game, I have followed all saving that which I

should, and may justly complain, and truly, *qui ubique est, nusquam est*, which Gesner did in modesty, that I have read many books, but to little purpose, for want of good method; I have confusedly tumbled over divers authors in our libraries, with small profit for want of art, order, memory, judgment. (Pp. 17-18)

And to this rude matter the plan to finish Democritus' treatise gives purpose, method, order, and art. Scholarship is not just knowing: that is curiosity, a useless Pharaoh's tomb. Scholarship is doing: making a thing by working rude matter into shape, translating a "vast chaos and confusion of books" through the self into a patterned construct. And it is not the construct that determines its own meaning to be useful or useless, but the construction. For a scholar to be a scholar is for him to be a craftsman, a builder, an *artifex*, making progress by giving new form to old matter.

As a good housewife out of divers fleeces weaves one piece of cloth, a bee gathers wax and honey out of many flowers, and makes a new bundle of all, . . . I have laboriously collected this cento out of divers writers, and that *sine injuria*, I have wronged no authors, but given every man his own. . . . The matter is theirs most part, and yet mine; . . . which nature doth with the aliment of our bodies incorporate, digest, assimilate, I do *concoquere quod hausi*, dispose of what I take. I make them pay tribute to set out this my *Macaronicon*, the method only is mine own; I must usurp that of Wecker *e Ter.*, . . . we can say nothing but what hath been said, the composition and method is ours only, and shows a scholar.   (Pp. 24-25)

The composition and method show the scholar. To be what he is, Democritus Junior works in the same way Ptolemy worked to redesign a civilizing project left undone by Pharaohs before him (p. 94).

Scholars, of course, like all other men, are melancholy (pp. 110-114). As one of the classes of men whose follies Democritus Junior enumerates, learned men are soundly condemned. Authority itself—all the great men whose knowledge is compounded to make the *Anatomy*—falls under the same conviction: "they that teach wisdom, patience, meekness, are the veriest dizzards, hair-brains, and most discontent." The schoolmen, Erasmus, Vives, poets, rhetoricians, natural scientists, textual critics: these are members of humanity's body, and so afflicted. And the scholars of this book, father and son, are sentenced with the rest: "Democritus, that common flouter of folly, was ridiculous himself"; "But I dare say no more of, for, with, or against them, because I am liable to their lash as well as others." In the main, scholars whirl around with Fortune and Folly because their learning is of the useless sort that contributes to or expresses idleness rather than remedying it: "Bale, Erasmus, Hospinian, Vives, Kemnisius, explode as a vast ocean of *obs* and *sols*, school divinity. A labyrinth of intricable questions, unprofitable contentions, *incredibilem delirationem*, one calls it." Scholars' *made things*, like the completed forms of curious pyramids and obelisks, are without the saving grace of purpose, for learned men "rake over all those rubbish and dung-hills," but they "do nobody good"; they "mend old authors, but will not mend their own lives, or teach us . . . to keep our wits in order, or rectify our manners."

Scholarship is thus a kind of idleness, and so between Democritus Junior's express intention to be a scholar by "method and composition" and the condemnation of scholarship hangs the question, what view of the Pharaohs' pyramids to accept: "Is not he mad that draws lines with Archimedes, whilst his house is ransacked and his city besieged, when the whole world is in combustion, or whilst our souls are in danger *(mors sequitur, vita fugit)*, to spend our time in toys, idle questions, and things of no worth?'' (p. 114). The question hangs over the *Anatomy* as well, even to the last page where the exhortation to eternity ends in the plea to "be not solitary, be not idle." Is the *Anatomy* a mad book, a mere labyrinth, or is it the kind of wrought object which gives industry a purpose and makes progress possible? For if the art of scholarship is only madness, only *obs* and *sols* to infinity, then the very mind of civilized man must be hopelessly lost: "If school divinity be so censured . . . what shall become of humanity?" The Preface itself is the question: Who is this man and what is he doing? And that question is the thing that unites, furthers, promotes, collects, connects—conduces to—the book.

As the man, so is the method ambiguously defined, and the answer to all the questions, as might be expected, is—yes and no. Yes, scholars are mad, and the fruits of learning often smell like decaying dunghills. No, *this* book is not just a labyrinth, but a thing constantly being made, a world of knowledge always under construction, always having a purpose, and that not the mending of authors, but the mending of lives, the keeping of wits in order. For in creating the *Anatomy*, Burton has managed to make an object which even when complete would never be finished, a wrought form on which work would always be possible. With the third edition, Democritus Junior began to promise never to change or publish the book again. He "had done" (p. 34). But he had not done, and his work of composition and method went on to the extent that, as if to prove the point of sustained industry, Burton's own mortality could not set a final "finis" to the scholar's task. Democritus Junior's book was so made that he could complete Democritus' treatise without ever putting himself out of a job, but could always be civilizing himself and mankind by shaping and reshaping knowledge to the form of understanding.

The key that secures mankind in its melancholy condition is idleness, and idleness is the key that unbolts the door as well. For scholarship is idle—apparently useless—questioning, but it is also the epitome of purposeful work—method and composition. As Democritus was busied in his garden with anatomizing beasts, so Democritus Junior, in writing their book, is specifically avoiding idleness: "I write of melancholy, by being busy to avoid melancholy. There is no greater cause of melancholy than idleness, 'no better cure than business' " (p. 20). Yet the writing of the book is itself a kind of idleness, a "playing labour" with which he busies himself so as to cure "idleness with idleness, make an antidote out of that which was the prime cause of my disease" (pp. 20-21). When idleness is the work of compiling cure, then the scholar's exercise becomes true re-formation of self and of mankind because it is the constructive force which defines life, draws lines with Archimedes, makes partitions, sections, members, and subsections with schoolmen, while human nature compounds confusion, besieges cities, tears down civilization. It is thus that Democritus Junior will not be a positive or contentious preacher but a scholar whose book is "written by an idle fellow, at idle times." And it is thus that Democritus Junior makes a book with the form of a scholastic treatise but does not worship that form.

The *Anatomy*'s form is not limited to one expression, as the structural analyses of the Partitions have shown. Digression and equivocation, like Burton's constant "yet nevertheless" that allows him to shape and order the seemingly shapeless "facts" of knowledge, speak the truth that this book is no mere finished Pharaoh's tomb which destroys its form by being finished. For the *Anatomy* is never finally finished, its form is always open to new views, yet it is always made, an artifact complete and whole but never unused, never useless. So, I would argue, Burton's book does not cancel itself out by representing melancholy with all that disease's chaotic symptoms. Instead it cures melancholy constantly by being what it is, the useful structure of the scholar's cure, the apparent idleness that is never really idle but is always working to cure its author and its readers through their very busyness with it.

The *Anatomy* is so constantly and so consistently a thing in production that it can reappear "corrected and augmented by the author" eleven years after that author has given up time for eternity. Scholars have the effective means of civilization as the very tools of their trade: method and composition. So Democritus Junior indicates how method and composition can work if the means themselves are the end. His curious transition from the general view of the world to the views of institutional man ends, we have seen, in his reasonable but illogical move *"a partibus ad totum,* or from the whole to the parts."* The transition begins, moreover, with the appearance of logical argumentation that conceals a quotidian kind of argument by reiteration (pp. 73-75). The "special and more evident arguments" are lined up impressively in first, second, and third ranks, each having a primary authority and many secondary opinions, and each presumably a distinct point or premise in the argument. But the points are very hard to distinguish; the second is "grounded upon the like place of Scripture" as the first; the third not only "may be derived from the precedent" but seems to repeat it; and all can be reduced to variations on the theme, everyone thinks he is wise but is foolish. But for the scholar to say, "first argument, second argument, third argument" is for him to be getting things—a confusion of things—in order so as to be able to arrive at a conclusion, and thus the faking of precise progression actually becomes a progression toward the necessary statement, we are all mad. To restate roving as a progression *"a partibus ad totum,* or from the whole to the parts"—even if the world appears so chaotic that the order is artificially imposed—is to reform the chaos and so to prove that the things of the world are disordered but its structure is not permanently impaired; paradise can be regained.

The climax of the Preface that conduces to the book declares the recreative power of a scholarship that composes order out of the rude matter of confusion. Democritus Junior digresses from observation to make a paradise, a Utopia which is not a real world, but a vision of the mind. His "poetical commonwealth" has been admired amongst Renaissance Utopias for the practicality of its institutions and laws that allow for men's weaknesses and follies by setting bounds to them instead of fantastically eliminating them, providing not only hospitals and workhouses but rates of usury as well, and prescribing a monarchy rather than democratic rule since "Utopian parity is a kind of government to be wished for rather than effected" (p. 101). Yet because the Utopia appears to be an "improved version of England" and not an ideal society (Mueller, p. 34), we cannot conclude that it is a realistic rather than a poetical commonwealth.[10] For Democritus Junior insists that it is indeed poetical, a reformation in his mind of the existing shape of the world. It is the realization of precisely those "vain, absurd, and ridiculous wishes not to be hoped"; it is the scholar's reply to the wisdom of the satirist's blunt conclusion, "all must be as it is":

> *Because, therefore, it is a thing so difficult, impossible,* and far beyond Hercules' labours to be performed; let them be rude, stupid, ignorant, incult, . . . let them be barbarous as they are. . . . *I will yet,* to satisfy and please myself, *make an Utopia of mine own,* in which I will freely domineer, build wealth of mine own, in which I will freely domineer, build cities, make laws, statutes, as I list myself. And why may I not? . . . You know what liberty poets ever had, and besides, my predecessor Democritus was a politician, a recorder of Abdera, a law-maker, as some say; and why may not I presume so much as he did?   (Pp. 97-98; my italics)

The Utopia Democritus Junior shapes in his mind is the vision of what nobody can accomplish in the real world, yet the scholar—the craftsman, *artifex,* poet—can make of man by method and composition. It is therefore not only "part of the whole fictional work in which it appears" (Nochimson, p. 142), but the central part of that fiction, the declaration that what cannot be is, by the

10. J. Max Patrick, "Robert Burton's Utopianism," *PQ,* 26 (1948), 356.

power of the mind to construct out of the rude matter of humanity a time and place that do not exist. Not-being is given being, method and composition create an impossible creation.

The Utopia is thus Democritus Junior's useless construct which, like the Pharaohs' tomb, finds its justification in the making rather than in the completed form. Like the *Anatomy* (and as a microcosm of the *Anatomy*) it is eternally unfinished, its neat divisions and subdivisions—twelve or thirteen provinces with central cities and equidistant towns, navigable rivers and straight streets, public schools and colleges—all are confined within the straits that include the poetical commonwealth in the Preface (p. 107), yet the vision can always be adjusted, revised, reformed through the editions of the book. The Preface is an ill-defined unit containing at its heart the well-defined world of Nowhere (perhaps Australia, perhaps one of the Fortunate Isles) that is really in the world but is as really confined to Democritus Junior's—a fiction's, a nobody's—mind (the latitude is 45° north or south, the longitude known only to its creator [p. 98]).

The Utopia, then, is the digression in the Preface that determines the meaning of the Preface, for its presence reveals the place of prescription in an indeterminate, tangled world just as the digressions reveal the important facts of indetermination and indefinability to the re-formed world created by scholarship in the book. It is inverted digression, for it contains the means—method and composition—while the Preface outside it contains the matter—the melancholy world seen by and in Democritus Junior. Its presence in the Preface describes for us a relationship between logical construct and illogical truths that we will see reversed in the book, for the *Anatomy* imitates the Utopia while the digression and equivocation of the partitions imitate the Preface.[11] And in both cases the final meaning rests in the ambiguous, always potential relationship rather than in any actual predominance of either the original definition or the subsequent equivocation. Democritus Junior states through the poetical commonwealth what observation of the world itself denies, the effectiveness of pattern; the unreal world is made to exist as antithesis to the real world, as cure answering to the causes of ignorance, rudeness, oppression, riot, contention, poverty, swinelike wallowing (p. 97), as poetical equivocation to the true state of man.[12]

The Utopia, like the *Anatomy*, is constructed out of the stuff of books, and the laws that govern it come from man's universal attempts to order himself more perfectly. Democritus Junior takes the ideas of Aristotle, Plato, St. Paul, King Alfred, Thomas More, and many other historians, philosophers, governors, moralists, poets, and dreamers, like himself, of Utopias. He considers, disagrees with, accepts, and alters their laws for his own kingdom of the mind. And his Utopia becomes *onme meum, nihil meum,* a whole society designed by mankind out of the stuff of mankind's vision for itself. The shape the poetical commonwealth takes is the shape of an exact order that comprehends neither a dehumanized, mechanical man nor an impossibly angelic one. Equal territories and equidistant cities with

11. The Utopia as an "inverted digression" was first suggested to me by Professor Robert C. Jones.
12. Hurt, p. 253, cites the Utopia's introduction of the pattern of cause and cure seen in the *Anatomy*.

straight streets and fenced land will enclose a society of resident governors, busy workers, just judges, equally enforced laws. But the men will be human: "If it were possible, I would have such priests as should imitate Christ, charitable lawyers should love their neighbours as themselves, temperate and modest physicians, politicians contemn the world, philosophers should know themselves, noblemen live honestly, tradesmen leave lying and cozening, magistrates corruption, etc.; but this is impossible, I must get such as I may" (p. 102).

So the Utopia epitomizes the book in giving form back to a confused reality and yet epitomizes it in not pretending to be the actual form but the scholarly re-formation of the whole world of mankind. Democritus Junior as general visitor can make things be as they are not and can construct a thing that is not out of what is. But the ordering of the thing remains not so much a wish for England as a reality for the book, not contention or positive preaching, but statement of "fact" that is a projected fact of time and spirit rather than a fact of matter. When Democritus Junior says, "I will have no bogs, fens, marshes, vast woods, deserts, heaths, commons, but all enclosed. . . . I will not have a barren acre in all my territories, not so much as the tops of mountains: where nature fails, it shall be supplied by art: lakes and rivers shall not be left desolate" (p. 100), he is creating by the word, saying "Let this be," and so he is proving the power of art to restate Fortune's merry-go-round as progress. He is showing in the Preface what he does in the *Anatomy* when he encloses digression and equivocation within the formal order of the book; he prescribes a "world" of order so that he might reform man or civilize him by method and composition.

Democritus Junior's industry in creating the Utopia, as in creating the book, is "playing labour" which cures confusion by indicating the order to be reclaimed through constant work on the rude matter of the world; it is not an attempt to exclude from life the confusion— the nature, the *materia mundi*—which is mankind's existence. Democritus Junior has to return to his Preface: it will not let his Utopia take over and become the volume (p. 107) any more than the *Anatomy* will be able to exclude digression. The Utopia conduces to the *Anatomy* as much by declaring prescription and definition to be not finally supreme in life as it does by declaring these to be the basic composition and method of the book. If the Utopia could become the book, if the partitions could exist without their essential digression and equivocation, then the *Anatomy* would be a Pharaoh's tomb seen as a finished, pointless construct. It would be curious, but not a cure.

Democritus Junior turns, then, from the Preface which points out mankind's dotage "that so men might acknowledge their imperfections, and seek to reform what is amiss" (p. 120), to a book which sets out the single disease of man that can show him more about himself than any sermon or dogmatic argument, and which reforms his generally chaotic universe into a structured encyclopedia of things known:

> . . . yet I have a more serious intent at this time; and to omit all impertinent digressions, to say no more of such as are improperly melancholy, or metaphorically mad, lightly mad, or in disposition, as stupid, angry, drunken, silly, sottish, sullen, proud, vainglorious, ridiculous, beastly, peevish, obstinate, impudent, extravagant, dry, doting, dull, desperate, harebrain, etc., mad, frantic, foolish, heteroclites,

which no new hospital can hold, no physic help: my purpose and endeavour is, in the following discourse to anatomize this humour of melancholy, through all his parts and species, as it is an habit, or an ordinary disease, and that philosophically, medicinally, to show the causes, symptoms, and several cures of it, that it may be the better avoided. . . . Being then a disease so grievous, so common, I know not wherein to do a more general service, and spend my time better, than to prescribe means how to prevent and cure so universal a malady, an epidemical disease, that so often, so much, crucifies the body and mind.   (Pp. 120-121)

He turns to the book—"I will begin"—by allowing the book to turn back to the Preface. Impertinent digressions are omitted only by being made pertinent; the definite disease caused by melancholy humor equivocates and becomes the indefinite disease caused by lack of charity. The whole book speaks of the stupid, angry, drunken, silly, sottish, sullen, proud condition of man, perhaps not always in Democritus Junior's tone, but with the instrument he has established, the method and composition of a scholar-artist.

For the Preface collects all that mankind is and may be and conduces to our understanding that the true and the metaphorical are only equivocations, not opposites. And so it unites the logical constructs and illogical relationships of the three partitions by mediating between them in describing scholarship as art, not merely science: art which enables man to cure confusion with a wrought form. The Utopia is not a plan for a factual world, but a fact *per se*, a fact of the time and spirit of the *Anatomy of Melancholy*. And the Preface is not a plan, like the synoptic tables, for a book, but it is the book *per se*, the unifying vision of a man and of all men, of a time and spirit that defy definition and yet depend upon it as the means of progress. The Preface conduces to the book because its essence is in the spirit of Democritus Junior who is Democritus and Robert Burton and Nobody, the spirit of a man who looks forward and creates despite his recognition that mankind will keep on turning with Fortune's wheel and will always drift back from poetical impossibilities to the reality of melancholy and so will always need the cure of his book, the artifact which is made yet is always in the making.

CURE BY ART:

THE PROSODY OF THOUGHT

> Here was not the devouring silence of death or of the desert, rather a silence sustained by the music of nature and history, and scanned by the prosody of thought. In the air was a quiet tension, like the tension of truth; and this repose was only the equilibrium, at their centre, of all disputes and of all battles.
>
> —GEORGE SANTAYANA, *The Last Puritan*

Some years ago, one of Democritus Junior's admirers borrowed this description of Oxford to summarize his understanding of Burton's book and of the man who had conceived it.[13] He chose well, for the book of the Oxford scholar breaths the spirit of solitary reflection and conservatism even as it embodies all the tension that diversity of human knowledge energetically seeks to release. Because Santayana's description of the univer-

13. Henry William Taeusch, *Democritus Junior Anatomizes Melancholy* (Cleveland: The Rowfant Club, 1937), p. 32.

sity portrays not a college but a repository of human ideas, it may express as well the meaning or cure that is to be found in the structure of the *Anatomy of Melancholy*. Burton wrote the *Anatomy* to cure melancholy in himself and all men, "to prescribe means how to prevent and cure so universal a malady, an epidemical disease, that so often, so much, crucifies the body and mind" (Preface, 121). But melancholy, the book tells us in numerous ways, is more than the humor, and the *Anatomy* seeks not only to prescribe cure for disease, but to be cure for the melancholy that is life.

In seeking to cure melancholy, Burton searches for the cause and cure of this *rem substratum* of man not in the bodies of animals, but in books, for he is seeking to know about man, and that means understanding his spirit as well as knowing the mechanism of his body and mind. Constantly throughout the book, the anatomist speaks of what man is, only to qualify himself—"or at least, should be." That is the book: an expression of what the natural state of things should be but is not. And that is why in reading the book we must read its structure also, for the only definition in all of the *Anatomy* that is truly definite is the book itself; the only cure which satisfies the disease of the whole man is the reformation of his knowledge of himself into the shape of the book.

The *Anatomy* ends with a cure which indicates man's ultimate destination, heaven, as it began with his primordial definition, perfection. Yet its real cure for man as man is not eternal rest, not benediction. It is restlessness, for man is imperfect, and the "corollary and conclusion" of Burton's book speaks of what he should do now, in the world, to make himself what he should be, to keep himself, that is, from giving in to the melancholy that rules the world: "Only take this for a corollary and conclusion, as thou tenderest thine own welfare in this and all other melancholy, thy good health of body and mind, observe this short precept, give not way to solitariness and idleness. 'Be not solitary, be not idle' " (III.4.2.6;432). The proverb, we have seen, is Burton's chief weapon against melancholy, for it is distilled wisdom, and melancholy is concentrated folly. He uses the proverb as the final "dietary" cure for definite melancholy, turning the erudition of philosophers and the learning of medical men in the direction of the common-sense wisdom of commonplace life. He then turns proverb into litany when he has found the custom and form of men's laws not to be equal to the powerful force of passion, and by prayer—"good Lord, deliver us"— takes man's cheese-trencher wisdom and offers it to God, who can interpret the morals of man's stories in the light of His own commentary of mercy. The last proverb for mortal man as mortal man, that tendered for his "health of body and mind," is the advice not to be solitary or idle, which, the Preface has told us, means to involve oneself in mankind by work, and for Burton that means to involve himself in the attempt to express what man should be.

He has to make a book which is of this world yet not of it, for it has to find cure or wisdom where there is only disease or folly. He has to teach man civility where man insistently presents himself as uncivilized, brutish, not differing much from a dog, not showing himself to be Christian. But the remedy cannot truly be of the world, for that, Burton's book reaffirms, is impossible. Never, he has told us, will men be wholly rational;

never will their passions be controlled by reason. Bishops will never offer posts to deserving scholarly divines. Men will never be content with honest love bounded by the custom and form of law. Instead of helping man to be what he might be, Burton must take him as he is and do the impossible with him: he must make an Utopia not with the help of Christ-like priests, charitable lawyers, wise philosophers, honest tradesmen, but with men—"I must get such as I may." He must make a book which does not only anatomize what man is, but joins the articulation of his parts into a unified understanding of what he is not but should be. Somehow, the re-formation of man must take man out of the world even as it confirms his place in it; it must be "nothing by nobody."

Burton makes, then, an *Anatomy of Melancholy* out of the "rude matter" of man's knowledge of himself, giving an artificial form to human nature. His is not science, but "art or liberal science" which frees method from the necessity of exact correspondence to reality. He takes the reality of disorder and gives it the form of apparent order, and, in this, his book is not only a reflection of the "science and scientific thought" of the early seventeenth century, but an image as well of the art of that age.[14] The cure needed for men's souls is found in work, and the wisdom Burton gets by writing and we by reading his book is the understanding of order. He makes and remakes an artificial structure, the art of which is also artifice, for the disorder of the melancholy world is comprehended by and shaped to the

14. The phrase is the title of the chapter in which Douglas Bush treats Burton in *English Literature in the Earlier Seventeenth Century, 1600-1660*, 2nd ed., rev. (Oxford: Clarendon Press, 1962), pp. 272-309.

order of the book, so that life in all its variety is translated into art, impressed with a form it does not "really"
have. Reality is set down in partitions, sections, members, and subsections. Disease is made definite and indefinite. Causes, symptoms, prognostics, and cures are
defined by the rooms of the treatise even when learned
men cannot decide how, or even whether, to define
them. And so the wisdom that comes from being busy
to avoid melancholy is the conviction that in all the
disorder of the melancholy world there is order to be
found, retrieved, brought to light. The book, Burton
tells us (at first in the Conclusion, later in the Preface)
will seem as varied as a journey: "And if thou vouchsafe
to read this treatise, it shall seem no otherwise to thee
than the way to an ordinary traveller, sometimes fair,
sometimes foul; here champaign, there enclosed; barren
in one place, better soil in another: by woods, groves,
hills, dales, plains, etc. I shall lead thee . . . through
variety of objects, that which thou shalt like and surely
dislike" (Preface, 32). And so we do perceive it as infinitely varied, yet directed. As variety of scenery is
determined by the logic of a journey, the tragicomedy or
"mixed scene" of life is shaped by the craftsman into a
form which is the *Anatomy of Melancholy*.

In one of his essays, Leo Spitzer distinguished the
"poetic" from the "artistic" by definitions which might
aid in evaluating the art of Burton's book. Poetry, he
suggests, "is characterized by the vision it opens up
before us of a world radically different from our everyday and workaday world of ratiocination and practicality and by the relief it offers us from the daily burden
of our environment," while a work of art "is characterized by its self-sufficiency and organic perfection

which allow it to stand out as an independent whole."[15] The poetical, he contends, may be not artistic, not "beautiful," though the two may be conjoined. In these terms, I think we may look upon the *Anatomy of Melancholy* as an artistic if unpoetical work. The *Anatomy* is steeped in the most mundane matters of man's life, from his bodily functions to his worldly cares, from eating and exercise to jealousy and despair. The book does not let us get beyond this world except by offering the perception of God's mercy as cure for the world; it preaches last things in order to teach present things: "hope, ye unhappy ones; ye happy ones, fear." It works explicitly by ratiocination, allowing us to watch its author parsing out authorities, definitions, equivocations, into partitions and subsections: "yet, nevertheless, I will adventure." It digresses into the heady speculation of worlds beyond man, of infinite worlds, of mysteries of the divine nature, in order to progress back to the anatomy of man's disease, which is a way of finding things out and so a way of life. Yet if the *Anatomy* does not relieve us of this world but impresses us with it, nonetheless it is "beautiful" because it gives the stuff of the world the form of art. The structure of the *Anatomy* cannot embody perfection, for the world is imperfect, but it reflects the perfection which is inherent in life though now obscured.

Burton's book sets out to cure melancholy, and does so by being an ordered form for disorder, an answer to imperfection which contains imperfection but defines it

15. *"Explication de Texte* Applied to Three Great Middle English Poems," ch. xi in *Essays on English and American Literature,* ed. Anna Hatcher (Princeton University Press, 1962), pp. 218-219.

by art. Disease, Burton tells us, is the result of man's fall: it is everything that is wrong with the world. And cure, the *Anatomy* tells us, is the result of working: it is restating all questions, all questionable definition—even the ultimate human question, What is man?—in a form which is itself the answer, the postulate that distinct and differentiated ideas of man are to be joined in one by a process which combines all individuality into a common definition that is the consistently single and whole *Anatomy of Melancholy*. How does a man differ from a dog? Where are there Christians in the world? The book asks, and answers that man can be what he should be if he will expend himself in working. Being civilized, he will give order to disorder, wisdom to a foolish world; he will make out of chaos a pattern which orchestrates confusion and so gives form to matter without which matter cannot exist.

The book is given, besides the "Gothic" unity of the partitions, the "organic" unity present in the person of Democritus Junior. It is in him that facts, things known and things to be found out, become a treatise of mankind. It is in him that fiction, the make-believe world of irrational men, becomes a Utopia or vision of impossible rationality made actual. It is in him that man the rational animal and man the passionate animal become what man should be in the melancholy world, civilized. The reason of the scholar whose life is study and argumentation and the passions of the satirist who must see Folly and laugh or weep at its ubiquitous presence are joined in Democritus Junior, who is man the artist, working to compose himself and all men into a form of order. To read the book through the Preface, or to read the Preface in the book, is to see not an anatomy of melancholy, but

Democritus Junior's *Anatomy of Melancholy*, collected out of divers authors and made in the image of man working.

Thus the *Anatomy* is neither the partitions nor the Preface, but both. Rooms open into other rooms, definition is confused by redefinition, logical scheme is interrupted by pertinent digression or contradicted by an opposite logical scheme. The book reiterates, answers itself, but always contains itself. The artificial and organic unities coexist, allowing to the *Anatomy* only one final definition, a structure that states itself to be, and so proves itself. The *Anatomy of Melancholy* is cure for melancholy because it is "nothing," not real, but an artifact which is the antidote to everything that the world is. It is the chain linking and binding man's knowledge of himself into a form which can contain him because it subsumes his passion and his reason, his disease and its cure, his disorder and the image of his lost perfection. In the *Anatomy* man's nature and history are expressed in all their diversity and confusion, but expressed in a structure which comprehends them. The tension between the one structure of three equal partitions with their subdivisions and the other structure of Preface, First and Second Partitions, and Partition III reflects the "tension of truth" felt not as *"concordantia"* but as the "equilibrium . . . of all disputes and of all battles." Tangled like the world, the form is rhetorical though illogical proof that truth is not impaired because it is diverse and that order is not necessarily and finally lost because disorder is in the nature of things.

The pattern of the *Anatomy* is one of structures which equivocate but define all equivocation in a single word: melancholy. Like a shaped poem, the *Anatomy* puts thought into visible order, and its structure may be seen as the prosody which makes all of diverse human knowledge, all authority and speculation, fact and fiction, question and answer, into an artistic expression of truth. The book is finally a conceit, for it is science made into "art or liberal science," a structure of logic which will not be contained by logic, a treatise which digresses out of itself, turning rooms full of matters of fact into delightful fields full of love matters, but giving the fields the shape of rooms. It is a divine saying, "I will not be a divine, but a physician," and yet being neither, but a creating artist who is both and who imitates God in being both. It is art which says of life that art is life: "truly or metaphorically, 'tis all one." Through the *Anatomy* Burton shapes man—disordered, diseased, imperfect man—into a form of order which, like Herbert's "Altar," shows what it means by being. And like that poem, even when its author is not writing it, it is writing itself. Through its structure the book says, absolutely, that order in life is disordered but not impaired, for all disorder and all irrationality also exist comprehended by the form of art. The tangled chain of the *Anatomy* makes life itself, the history and nature of man, his time and spirit, scannable not by a metrical scheme but by the prosody of thought, the scholar's "composition and method" which is a design for submitting chaos to the control of artistic structure and a way of giving to folly the form of wisdom. The last proverb, the last wise and witty saying about the world, is the book Democritus Junior holds in his hand. The *Anatomy of Melancholy* is the exemplum of wisdom, the form that industry gives to man's knowledge and understanding of himself.

Index

Adams, Thomas, 14

Air Rectified: part of system made from authorities, 101

Anatomist as "cutter," 8-9, 12, 39

Anatomy, books of, 1

Anatomy of Melancholy: wholeness of, 5-8, 12, 202, 245, 272; editions, 6; changes in, 6-8, 28-29, 48, 137, 194-195, 218; changeless character of, 7, 8; as "cento," 8; structure as imposed order, 9, 36-39; opposing forms within structure, 9, 41; criticism of, 9-12, 217; chaotic tendencies of, 18; traditional methodology in, 19; as Gothic construct, 25, 27, 28, 33, 40, 209, 272; organic unity in, 40-41, 215; structure traditional, 45; as knowledge reached through question, 99; contains potential knowledge, 101; example of ordered knowledge, 121; book as final cure of melancholy, 141-142; committed to world ruled by God, 187; complaint that it could not be written in Latin, 227-228; constantly made and re-made, 252; pointless work or sustained industry in,

256ff.; never finally finished, 258; as cure of melancholy, 258, 267, 271-272; expresses state of what things should be, 267; conclusion of, 267-268; of but not of the world, 268; made out of "rude matter" of men's knowledge, 269; varied but directed view of world, 270; artistic work, 271; structure not perfect but reflects perfection, 271; consists of both Preface and partitions, 273; like shaped poem, 274; disordered but not impaired, 274. *See also* Apparatus, Conclusion of the Author to the Reader, Digressions, Love-melancholy, Partition III, Partitions I and II, Preface of Democritus Junior, Religious Melancholy

Aphorism, 109-110, 268; as directives for everyday life, 110; cure of love-melancholy, 158-159; cure of jealousy, 170; prayer as, 170-171; *Anatomy* as, 274

Apparatus, 122; as reader's guide, 21-22

poems, 3, 8, 30; abstractions of *Anatomy*'s contents, 32-33

Finlay, Daniel Henry, 5, 39, 45, 126, 138, 204
Fish, Stanley, 13, 12 n., 58-59 n.
Form: encyclopedic opposed to organic, 5

Hallwachs, Robert G., 48
Herbert George: the "Altar," 274
Hippocrates, 14, 236, 239
Humoral psychology, 48; subject of Partitions I and II, 46; relationship to digressions, 67-68; anatomy of medicine dependent on, 113; as "possible knowledge," 119; anatomy of drifts into equivocation in Partitions I and II, 210
Hurt, Ellen Louise, 214, 215, 262 n.
Hypocrisy: sister of atheism, 186. *See also* atheism

Idleness: warning against, 248, 256; view of as sustained industry or scholarship, 257
Illogical method, 4, 41; illuminates truth, 153
Indefinite melancholy, 42, 124, 125-126, 129, 131, 265; love as, 130; matter of story, 138; wanderings within treatise of, 148-149; rationalized into sections and subsections, 150

Jealousy, 165-171; equivalence to heroical melancholy, 150, 165; counterstatement to marriage, 166; equivocation of love, 166; "bastard kind" and structural equivalent of love-melancholy, 166; defined, 167; opposite of charity, 167; as recreation of marriage, 168;

symptoms and prognostics of, 168-169; cures for, 169-171; as folly, 169; counsels for, 169; inconclusive section on, 170-171; as center of discussions of love-melancholy and religious melancholy, 171
Jones, Robert C., 262 n.

King, James Roy, 11, 50, 206-207, 208
Knowledge, 18; need to question, 41; systematic questioning of, 49; digressions as discourse on, 52; as basis of new science, 52, 55; as hypothesis rather than Truth, 56, 67, 97-98; acceptance of misinformation perverts, 70; lack of self-knowledge perverts life, 77; bastardized in professions, 81; defect of as illness in society, 85-86, 88; Digression of the Air composed of questions about, 91; speculation potentially nonsensical, 95; Consolatory Digression as epitome of, 103; last three digressions concerned with, 114; purpose of Preface connected with, 245

Law: cure for love-melancholy, 160-161; twisted by jealousy, 168-169; cure for Love-melancholy, 173; divine turned into human parody, 175; need for to control atheism, 185; God as reference for, 185
Lievsay, John L., 49-50, 102-103
Logical order: Burton's artistic rather than scientific, 129
Love: indefinable, 130, 149; as equivocation, 130; subject of